greenville

greenville

Woven from the Past

An
Illustrated History
by
Nancy Vance Ashmore

Photo Research by
Judith Gatlin Bainbridge and Robert Warin Bainbridge

"Partners in Progress" by Jamie S. Pickrell

Introduction by A.V. Huff, Jr.

Produced in Cooperation with
the Greater Greenville Chamber of Commerce

Windsor Publications, Inc.
Northridge, California

Windsor Publications, Inc.—History Book Division

Publisher: John M. Phillips
Editorial Director: Teri Davis Greenberg
Design Director: Alexander D'Anca

Staff for *Greenville: Woven from the Past*
Editor: Jerry Mosher
Assistant Editors: Laura Cordova, Marilyn Horn
Director, Corporate Biographies: Karen Story
Assistant Director, Corporate Biographies: Phyllis Gray
Editor, Corporate Biographies: Judith Hunter
Production Editor, Corporate Biographies: Una FitzSimons
Layout Artist, Corporate Biographies: Mari Catherine Preimesberger
Sales Representative, Corporate Biographies: John Rosi
Editorial Assistants: Kathy M. Brown, Marcie Goldstein, Pamela Juneman, Pat Pittman
Proofreader: Susan J. Muhler
Layout and Design: Christina McKibbin

Library of Congress Cataloging in Publication Data

Ashmore, Nancy Vance, 1943-
   Greenville: woven from the past.

   "Produced in cooperation with the Greater Greenville
Chamber of Commerce."
   Bibliography: p. 272
   Includes index.
   1. Greenville (S.C.)—History. I. Greater Greenville
Chamber of Commerce (S.C.) II. Title.
F279.G79A75   1986   975.7'27   86-22483
ISBN 0-89781-193-3

Published 1986
Printed in the United States of America
First Edition

Frontispiece: *Greenville's textile industry did not develop until the late nineteenth century, but even in the county's earliest history women wove garments on hand looms for their family's use. Volunteers at the Roper Mountain Science Center's Pioneer Farm explain the complicated process which turned raw cotton into clothes and household goods for everyday use. Photo by Bob Bainbridge*

CONTENTS

Dedicated to my parents, who instilled in me their love for Greenville, and to the memory of Laura Ebaugh, who inspired the study of its history.

INTRODUCTION

Southerners have a continuing romance with place and time. For Greenvillians that place is part of the piedmont crescent that stretches north to Virginia and south and west to Alabama. The time includes three centuries beginning with Cherokee paths and hunting fields and reaches today's superhighways and glass and concrete office buildings. The figures that make up the story are not the stereotypical images of the Old South. There were few plantations and little of the deprivation of war. There are great landowners, to be sure, but many more yeomen farm families, town dwellers, business pioneers, mill workers, corporate families, and suburbanites.

Nancy Ashmore has skillfully woven the place, the time, and the people into a narrative in which she sees a pattern for progress. But she does not hesitate to tell us of some who were decent, God-fearing, hard-working folk, while others were scheming, grasping, and cruel. These pages are peopled with the hopelessly backward-looking and those ruthlessly committed to change. Many were a mixture of these qualities. Judy and Bob Bainbridge have assembled—and in some cases artfully created—a series of pictures that set us in particular places and recall specific people and their handiwork.

The year 1986 is the bicentennial of Greenville's creation as a county. We have had our share of parades and cakes and time capsules. It has been a time for pride and boosterism. In your hands is a more permanent result of that celebration. Perhaps it will bring a few moments of assessment and reflection. *Greenville: Woven from the Past* will confirm some myths of our past and challenge others. It is eminently worthy of your consideration.

A.V. Huff, Jr.
Professor of History
Furman University

The Poinsett Bridge, spanning Little Gap Creek in northern Greenville County, was completed in 1820, the last of the three bridges on the old state road which connected Greenville with Asheville. Joel Poinsett, for whom it is named, was a Greenville summer resident and Commissioner of Roads. Photo by Bob Bainbridge. Courtesy, Greenville Central Area Partnership, Inc.

ACKNOWLEDGMENTS

AUTHOR'S ACKNOWLEDGMENTS

No writer works alone. Without the assistance and encouragement of numerous loving and learned individuals this new look at Greenville's history would never have been born. A.V. Huff, historian and friend, provided invaluable guidance and direction on every step of the project from research to manuscript review; without his strong support the task could not have been accomplished. My teammates, Judy and Bob Bainbridge, made work a joy with their incomparable spirit and enthusiasm. And I am grateful for an understanding boss, Walter B. Edgar, who always offered encouragement and never seemed to notice when other duties were moved to a back burner. Without the typing and good-natured assistance of Tibby Dozier there would literally be no manuscript.

Able staff members at the Greenville County Public Library, especially Steve Richardson and Patton Bryson, made my visits there both painless and profitable. Staff assistance at the South Caroliniana Library, the State Development Board, and the South Carolina Archives made research in Columbia much easier. In addition, Louise Bailey, Bill Bryson, Dr. Glenwood Clayton, Foster Farley, J.W. Grady III, and John C. Roberson made clear some fine points in hard-to-decipher references. From the Greenville Chamber of Commerce special help came from Jamie Pickrell, Carolyn Darnell, and Bill Miller.

The following transplanted Greenvillians, now living in Columbia, willingly shared their personal and family memorabilia on Greenville: James Dunlap, Tinie Freeman, Snooks and Jules Haley, and William D. Workman, Jr. Others who freely shared their Greenvilliana are: Durant Ashmore, Ollie Childress, Edward Frierson, Jo Hinson, Mary W. Hughey, Helen and Bob Martin, Ann T. Poole, E. D. Sloan, Jr., and James H. Woodside, Sr. Thomas Hooper offered great assistance in locating reliable resources on the black community.

To those who blazed the trail in searching out and analyzing Greenville's history I am most grateful. Without their groundwork, I would have been lost. Numerous authors of books and articles—particularly Albert N. Sanders—have inspired the goal of excellence and accuracy, setting high standards for this author. Their articles in the *Proceedings and Papers of the Greenville County Historical Society* provided important views of various aspects of Greenville's past. They provided the parts of the puzzle for me to piece together.

Last, and foremost, I offer heartfelt thanks to my parents, Billy and Robert T. Ashmore, for their unique insight and suggestions on content, eagle-eye proofreading, and unfailing moral support throughout the research and writing. Indeed, this volume is the tangible result of many Carolinians' contributions and the pride they feel for Greenville.

Nancy Vance Ashmore

Rising from a spring just north of Travelers Rest and winding its narrow, rocky way through the middle of the village, the Reedy River and its falls provided waterpower for early grist and textile mills, as well as for farms and small plantations. *Photo by David Jenkins*

Page 10-11: *S.C. Berry's mill, built around 1900, originally featured a cotton gin and grist mill powered by a wooden water wheel. According to tradition, the grist mill (foreground) was built on the foundations of John Weaver's early cotton factory on Beaverdam Creek. The mill demonstrated that even small streams could generate adequate power for industrial enterprises. Photo by Bob Bainbridge*

PHOTO RESEARCHERS' ACKNOWLEDGMENTS

Identifying, selecting, gathering, and printing the photographs, maps, and documents that would best illustrate 200 years of Greenville history was at first an overwhelming task and finally a real joy because of the cooperation and interest of librarians and archivists, collectors and local citizens.

Our first and greatest debt is to photographer Blake Praytor and his associate, John Conway, who printed most of the illustrations used in *Greenville: Woven from the Past.* Working from torn snapshots, blurred manuscripts, and oversized paintings, they produced duplicates far better than most originals.

Steve Richardson at the Greenville County Library and Dr. Glenwood Clayton, Furman University's archivist, shared their knowledge, identified new sources for illustrations, and allowed us total access to their collections. Allen Stokes at the South Caroliniana Library, David Moltke-Hansen at the South Carolina Historical Society, and Roger Stroup at the South Carolina Museum were also most helpful.

The Greenvillians who shared their collections, family albums, cherished paintings, and favorite photographs made photographic research an opportunity to learn much about this county as well as make new friends. We are grateful to Oscar Landing, Gene Eckford, Roy McBee Smith, John Baker Cleveland, Earline Gilreath White, Henry B. McKoy, Mr. and Mrs. Alester G. Furman III, Mrs. Fred Ellis, Ron Copsy, Joe Jordan, Richard Sawyer, Ben Geer Keys, and Mrs. J.D. Ashmore. E.D. Sloan, Jr., particularly shared our enthusiasm and provided needed criticism.

We especially appreciate the guidance and encouragement of Windsor editor Jerry Mosher.

Judith and Robert Bainbridge

Although Greenville was Cherokee country until 1777, in all probability the area was not used for permanent settlement by the tribe, as Oconee County was. The Caesar's Head area was a battle retreat, however, and early campers at Camp Greenville carried away boxes of pottery fragments and arrowheads; along the Reedy River were hunting camps used by the native Americans as they pursued wild game in the area. Courtesy, South Caroliniana Library

CHAPTER ONE

FROM PEARIS TO PLEASANTBURG (1768-1806)

Hazy blue mountains, sparkling water, and a pleasing climate have drawn settlers to northwestern South Carolina for more than 200 years. The Cherokee Indians had long known the value of the land and cherished it as valuable hunting territory. Herds of buffalo, elk, and deer roamed the dense forests and cane brakes while pristine streams bursting with power and beauty flowed nearby.

The Cherokee, who lived in lower towns along the Savannah, Seneca, and Keowee rivers, traveled and hunted throughout the unspoiled piedmont, including the area that eventually became Greenville County. The Upper Warriors Trail (now part of South Carolina Route 11—the Cherokee Foothills Scenic Highway) was used by Cherokee braves as they moved eastward to fight the Catawba Indians in the Spartanburg area. Remnants of their presence—stone

Above: *This old spring house, on the Austin place by Gilder's Creek on the eastern edge of the county, was for many years the water source for Greenville's first white settlers. The Nathaniel Austin family settled in Greenville in 1761; Austin's daughter was killed by the Cherokees whose territory they invaded. Photo by Bob Bainbridge*

Right: *Among the early settlers of Greenville County were the Scotch-Irish Peden clan, who founded Fairview Presbyterian Church in 1786. The second oldest congregation in the county (only Lebanon United Methodist is older, dating from 1785) erected their second sanctuary, shown here in an etching, in 1857. Courtesy, South Caroliniana Library*

Opposite page: *The earliest settlers of Greenville made their way down the Great Wagon Road from Philadelphia through the Valley of Virginia to the Carolina piedmont. Because Greenville County was a part of Cherokee Territory until 1777, only the most intrepid and independent made their way into the foothills before the Revolution. From Rouse,* The Great Wagon Road, *McGraw-Hill, 1973*

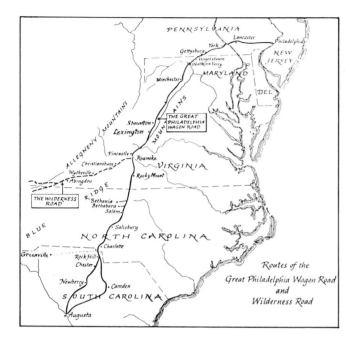

Routes of the
Great Philadelphia Wagon Road
and
Wilderness Road

hatchets, white flint arrowheads, and pieces of pottery—were found along the Reedy River and throughout the county as late as 1900. The Cherokee respected this land and its fruits, treating it as a paradise.

White men came into this piedmont Eden very gradually. Only after a 1755 agreement between the British and Cherokee were white settlers allowed anywhere in the region. But there were boundaries, very definite ones. Part of the eastern boundary of the Cherokee Nation was the vertical line which now divides Greenville and Spartanburg counties. Greenville was firmly within the Cherokee stronghold, and only the bravest of the brave dared penetrate that invisible line.

Perhaps the challenge was too great for Richard Pearis, who made his way from Virginia to settle on the banks of the Reedy River in 1768. He crossed that line, making a permanent and prosperous home some thirteen miles within the Indian territory. Pearis was a swashbuckling frontiersman and an amiable fortune hunter with an excellent British military record in the French and Indian War. He was an Indian trader

with a Cherokee "side wife" and a half-breed son, relationships which account for his acceptance in the Indian world. As an experienced backwoodsman with intelligence and courage, his friendship was valued by other white settlers. He possessed an uncommon ability to succeed in both worlds.

Pearis apparently recognized the potential of the Reedy River and its rushing falls, for there he built his grist mill and trading post, the first of many industries to flourish on that waterway. He began amassing adjacent lands into an estate called "Great Plains." Pearis' method of land acquisition is open to conjecture, but it appears that he pulled off a real estate deal as only he could do, bypassing both Cherokee and English regulations. In December 1773, three Cherokee chiefs deeded 150,000 acres to George Pearis, Richard's half-Cherokee son. Four months later George exercised his option as the son of an Englishman to become a naturalized English citizen. Under British law, George then deeded a sizable portion of his holdings to his father. (Sources differ on the exact size; amounts from 50,000 to 100,000 acres have been suggested.) The expanse of this vast Pearis paradise extended from the south fork of the Saluda River to the Indian path on the North Carolina line, over to the Tyger and Enoree rivers and back to the Saluda on the south. The area covered approximately ten square miles and included all of the present-day city of Greenville and Paris Mountain.

Other hardy Scotch-Irish settlers followed Pearis' lead, coming primarily along the Great Wagon Road from Pennsylvania, Virginia, and North Carolina. Several may have been acquaintances of Pearis in Virginia: the Hites, who settled on the Enoree River; the Austins near present-day Simpsonville; the Hamptons near Greer; and the "Red" Earles and the Princes on the Pacolet River. These pioneer families were plain,

ELIAS EARLE

Plantation owner, congressman, road builder, ironmaster—Colonel Elias Earle was one of the two most important residents (the other was Lemuel Alston) of the Greenville District at the beginning of the nineteenth century.

Born in 1762 on a Virginia plantation that he inherited when he was seven years old, Earle moved to South Carolina when he was twenty-five to join two older half-brothers who had already immigrated from Virginia to the frontier lands. John, who settled in the North Carolina mountains just north of the boundary between the two states, had built Earle's Fort, which served as a refuge from the Indians during the Revolution. Bayliss had settled in Landrum, in Spartanburg County, during the 1760s and was an attorney. Elias immediately began to buy property in the Greenville area, beginning with 500 acres along the Saluda River in 1787. In all, he purchased 4,476 acres in the county between 1787 and 1816, including more than 700 acres along Richland Creek, a branch of the Reedy River about two miles away from the center of the village of Greenville. It was near there on the Rutherford Road that he built his gracious home, "The Poplars," where he was living by 1796. At this "seat of hospitality" he entertained many visitors to the upcountry and became deeply involved in politics.

Among his holdings were two plantations, "White Horse" and "Reasonover" (the county's lon-gest road may have been named for the former) in Greenville, as well as thousands of acres in other upcountry districts. Colo-nel Elias Earle was a major landowner, but he was more than just a plantation owner. Beginning in 1794 he partici-pated actively in public service, serving as a state legislator (1794-1798), as a state senator (1798-1804), and as a U.S. con-gressman (1805-1807, 1811-1815, 1817-1821). While he was in Congress he served as first commissioner of Indian Affairs, a member of the commission to open the Saluda River to navi-gation, and as the initiator of the Great Wagon Road across the western mountains from Tennessee to South Carolina.

The availability of iron ore in the upcountry interested Earle from his early days in Green-ville. Not only did he develop iron works and a gun manu-factory on his Saluda River plantation, but he negotiated (although unsuccessfully) with Cherokees in Tennessee to set up iron works at the mouth of Chickamauga Creek in Indian Territory. Earle claimed ex-penses of $985 against the fed-eral government "for damages sustained by him in the Chero-kee County while detained there by the Indians" in 1814. His interests in iron and in manufacturing may have led him to move from his Green-ville Village plantation to "Centerville" in the Pendleton District in 1811. He sold his property to Henry Middleton of Charleston as the site for Mid-dleton's resort home, "White-

Elias Earle settled in the Green-ville District in 1787, and was liv-ing at "The Poplars" by 1796. He sat for this portrait around 1805. From The Earles of Evergreen, *1984. Courtesy, Margaret Earle Blanks Collection, Greenville County Library*

hall," the oldest house within Greenville's city limits.

One legend has it that Lemuel Alston, who owned 11,000 acres around the Reedy River in the center of the city, refused to sell his holdings to Earle be-cause he had defeated Alston in the congressional campaign of 1810 and instead, with the help of Revolutionary War hero Billy Young, sold the land to Vardry McBee.

At any rate, Earle moved to

land along "Twenty-Six Mile Creek" and began to develop a major manufacturing enterprise. He had a "cotton machine," tanyard and stable (where he may have kept his famous Arabian stallion, Black Sultan, a gift of the Bey of Tunis to the government of the United States), iron works, saw and grist mills, a gun factory, distillery, general store, clock works, and post office. In 1821 he began to undertake the making of silk after growing mulberry trees and importing silk worms.

In 1815 he received a government contract for 10,000 "stands" of arms (including the flintlock musket, bayonet, and ramrod) and imported thirty-two machinists from Harpers Ferry, Virginia, for his factory. Because he returned to Congress, however, he turned his contract over to Adam Carruth, who manufactured the muskets on the banks of the Reedy River. Not content with the land along Twenty-Six Mile Creek, Earle, visualizing a great river port at the confluence of the Tugaloo and Seneca rivers, purchased hundreds of acres of the town of "Andersonville," which he hoped would become a central trading center of the upcountry. The coming of the railroads doomed Andersonville and twentieth-century floods washed away remains of the houses; all of Earle's thousands of acres have disappeared under the waters of Lake Hartwell.

Earle died in 1823 after a long and painful illness, but his family name remains important in Greenville County, and this early entrepreneur left an indelible imprint on the region's early history.

Judith Gatlin Bainbridge

---

practical, and Presbyterian, working hard to create a new life in a beautiful but rugged wilderness. Many of these folk were among the last driven from Ireland to America as textile refugees when problems beset the wool and linen industries there. As historian A.V. Huff has observed, this was certainly not the last time textile manufacturers came to Greenville searching for a new home.

As the Revolution approached, both Patriots and Loyalists sought out Richard Pearis. Characteristically, he withheld overt allegiance to either side as long as possible but was considered an ally to the Patriots in the early days. In fact, the Patriots officially designated him as the escort for Cherokee representatives to the Provincial Congress in Charles Towne in September 1775. They had been invited for a pep talk by fiery Patriot leader William Henry Drayton and were entrusted to Pearis' care. It was soon learned that the Cherokee had never received a large supply of ammunition, which the Council of Safety had allocated to them as a bribe/peace offering. The gift had been hijacked en route by Patrick Cunningham

and other Tories who took it to the Ninety-Six area. Pearis was asked by the Patriots to explain the situation to the Indians and ease their dissatisfaction. Instead, Pearis used the occasion to switch sides, aligning himself with the king's men. Perhaps this chameleon shift was a move he had planned before the ammunition fiasco; perhaps it was to seek a higher military rank with the Loyalists; perhaps it was a gesture of thanks to the royal government which had condoned his real estate maneuver on the Reedy River. Whatever his reasons, Pearis remained an ardent Tory for the rest of the Revolution.

In pursuit of the gunpowder promised to the Cherokee, Tories and Patriots clashed briefly and inconclusively in November 1775 on the battlefield in Ninety-Six, the first blood shed in South Carolina during the war. Richard Pearis was present at the skirmish and served as a Loyalist witness to the truce agreement, much to the chagrin of his former Patriot friends. Pearis returned to his home on the Reedy only to be captured there two months later along with other Tories. Colonel Richard Richardson reported

A colonial craftsman carves a pitchfork at Greenville's Roper Mountain Pioneer Farm. The region's abundant forests led settlers to build log cabins and frame structures; later bricks from the red clay soil became the preferred materials. Photo by Bob Bainbridge

gleefully to the Provincial Congress the taking of several prisoners "of the first magnitude," one of whom was turncoat Richard Pearis. Imprisoned in Charles Towne for some nine months, Pearis dared complain to the Congress about jail conditions and later appealed for compensation in property loss. The Congress turned him a deaf ear.

Meanwhile, on the Reedy River sentiment toward Pearis and his family was less than warm. Indian raids and revenge-minded Patriots conspired to wipe out Pearis' holdings in the summer of 1776. Backwoodsmen led by Colonel John Thomas destroyed his Reedy River establishment, taking his cattle and possessions, burning his home and mill, and driving out his family. When released from prison, Pearis continued fighting with British forces, maintaining his reputation for flamboyance and courage. Following the British takeover of Charles Towne he moved for a while into British East Florida and then on to Nassau, where he lived out his days with part of his family in near affluence on a royal pension.

Pearis was compensated monetarily by the British for the confiscation of his piedmont land, but never again did he see the beautiful hills and streams of his "Great Plains." His name lives on, with altered spelling, in the name of the prominent 1,000-foot Paris Mountain and a small hamlet at the mountain's base. His pioneer spirit survived in those who followed him to the banks of the Reedy River and persisted in building a town.

No major military encounters took place in the Indian territory during the Revolution. However, there was one maneuver that occurred just inside the territory (now lower Greenville County, three miles south of Simpsonville) which proved a particularly sweet victory for revenge-minded Patriots. Led by die-hard Patrick Cunningham, some 200 Tories, including a son of Richard Pearis, were camped at the Great Cane Brake on the Reedy River in mid-December 1775. Learning this, Colonel William Thomson set out on December 21 with a band of 1,300 Patriots on a fast-paced overnight march into Cherokee territory. At daybreak on the 22nd they made a surprise attack on the Cane Brake camp, nearly surrounding the sleeping Tories before sentries sounded the alarm. Confusion and fighting ensued. Unfortunately, Cunningham proved too slippery for his attackers. He jumped from his bed, stopping neither to saddle his horse nor to don his pants, and rode off shouting for everyone "to shift for himself!"

Cunningham's greatly outnumbered men were completely routed; only six were killed but 130 were taken prisoner, including young Pearis. Also captured was the long-missing cargo of ammunition for the Cherokee which had originally enflamed the backcountry. An uncharacteristically heavy two-foot snow fell on the returning Patriots, prompting them to refer to this victorious venture as the "Snow Campaign."

Spirits ran high in the upcountry, and there was no lack of colorful characters and intriguing wartime stories. Chief among local personalities was a young girl named Laodicea Langston, known to her friends as "Dicey." Fact and fiction merge regarding the exploits of this unusual heroine; according to legend, she risked her life numerous times for the Patriot cause. As an enthusiastic fourteen-year-old, Dicey set out in the night to find and warn her brother and his Patriot allies that a band of outlaw Tories, the "Bloody Scouts," were on the way. En route, crossing the swollen Tyger River, she was nearly swept away. She arrived at their camp, bedraggled and nearly drowned, to deliver her news to a camp of tired and hungry men. According to one story, Dicey stayed long enough to cook a hoecake for the boys. Then she sped home, arriving before dawn and before her family missed her.

The forewarned Patriots abandoned their hiding place; when the Tories arrived they found only an empty camp.

Some believe that complaining Tories came to Dicey's father, saying he was responsible for his daughter's actions. It is said that Dicey stepped between her father and one accusing Tory who was threatening to shoot him. "Kill me first!" she cried. Overwhelmed by her courage, the accuser fled the Langston home. Other stories abound concerning her eavesdropping, message bearing, and double agent activities. Dicey lived her adult life near present-day Travelers Rest, where a marker was erected in 1933, commemorating her as a "Heroine of the American Revolution. To her daring and courage, many Patriots owe their lives."

Another youthful Patriot was Captain William Young, who brought such torment to backcountry Loyalists that he was known as "Five T," or "That Terror to the Tories." He was one of General Francis Marion's men, a fine hide-and-seek fighter who was only twenty-three years old when the Revolution ended. About 1819 he built a large sturdy home with granite stones, perhaps brought from Caesar's Head. The "Rock House" still stands about halfway between Reedy Falls and present-day Travelers Rest, a lasting reminder of the contributions made by its builder.

On the other side of the political coin were two "Bloody Bills" who wreaked havoc, fear, and confusion all over upper South Carolina. Both were so-called Tories. One was "Bloody Bill" Cunningham, scout and murderer. The other was "Bloody Bill" Bates, thief and outlaw. Sometimes they worked as a team; more often they operated separately. Their escapades were seemingly meaningless and brutal; neither was to be trusted.

"Bloody Bill" Cunningham was the black sheep of the otherwise honorable Cunning-

Above: *Captain Billy Young, a Revolutionary War Patriot who served in the Snow Campaign, built his "Rock House" on the Buncombe Road about 1819. The house later served as a stagecoach stop and then, abandoned for many years, was considered a haunted house by local children. In the early 1960s it was restored by Mr. and Mrs. Harry J. Haynesworth. Photo by Bob Bainbridge*

Left: *The unknown "limner" who painted this miniature of a respectable gentleman in 1776 probably did not know that his subject was known in the upstate as "Bloody Bill" Cunningham, a savage Tory who descended on defenseless Patriots. His granddaughter, Ann Pamela Cunningham, repaired family honor through her efforts to preserve Mt. Vernon. Courtesy, Greenville Museum of Art*

ham family, all of whom were strong Tory supporters. He led a band of outlaws known as the "Bloody Scouts," which operated chiefly in the Carolinas and Georgia. Richard Pearis knew him—his daughter, Sarah, and son, Richard, Jr., had married into the Cunningham family—and may have joined him in some savage anti-Patriot backcountry raids late in the war. Cunningham's lust for blood continued long after the war ended.

Many say "Bloody Bill" Bates concentrated on the Greer-Gowensville area, in what is now upper Greenville County. He had a band of ruthless outlaws recruited from the Glassy and Hogback mountain areas who helped him terrorize isolated settlers. One story tells of the time he led his group against James Wood's fort near the Indian boundary line where poorly equipped

Glassy Mountain, with its 1,000-foot cliff and sheer rock face, has been a visible landmark in northern Greenville County since its description by a passing traveler in 1805. The surrounding community retains a rural character with scattered farms and churches and some ongoing logging activity. Photo by Bob Bainbridge

At a General Assembly begun and holden at Charleston on the third day of January in the year of our Lord, one thousand seven hundred and Eighty five and in the ninth Year of the Independence of the United States of America. and from thence continued by divers adjournments to the Twenty second day of March 1786

An Ordinance for establishing a County and County Courts in the new Ceded Lands on the North side of Saluda river

Whereas the Inhabitants of the new Ceded Lands on the North side of Saluda river, below the Indian line have experienced many inconveniences by being annexed to some of the Counties heretofore established. Be it Ordained by the Honorable the Senate and House of Representatives now met and sitting in General Assembly and by the authority of the same. that a County shall be established in the new Ceded Lands by the name of Greeneville, and shall be bounded by Saluda river and the fork thereof; the old Indian boundary and the North Carolina line. and shall be entitled to County Courts to be held on the third monday in February. May. August. and November, which Courts shall hold, exercise and enjoy the several powers and jurisdiction which are by law vested in the said County Courts heretofore established.

In the Senate House the Twenty second day of March in the year of our Lord one thousand seven hundred and Eighty six and in the Tenth year of the Independence of the United States of America.

John Lloyd President of the Senate.

John Faucheraud Grimké Speaker of the House of Representatives

Above: *"A county shall be established on the new Ceded Lands by the name of Greeneville," proclaims the state charter, signed on March 22, 1786. The charter gave legal recognition to the settlers who had, for more than twenty years, been drifting into the Carolina backcountry. Courtesy, South Carolina Department of Archives and History*

Right: *Decorative horse-headed hitching posts stand in front of the Block House in Tryon, North Carolina, just yards from the South Carolina border. Fortified against Indian attacks, it was a refuge for eighteenth-century settlers fleeing from attacking Cherokees, and a headquarters for armed militia. Photo by Bob Bainbridge*

Patriots had gathered for safety. They quickly surrendered when Bates promised protection. However, he broke his word and killed all but one of his captives. Wood pursued the raiders into the mountains and managed to capture most of them, but Bates escaped.

Bates received his comeuppance in time. After the war, he was arrested for stealing a horse and jailed, finally, in Greenville. The son of one of Bates' former victims got word of his whereabouts, gathered some lynch-minded friends, and marched on the jail, where they unceremoniously shot and killed him. Some believe Bates was buried on the grounds of what was later the Victorian City Hall and that his ghost long haunted those turrets.

Even though the Cherokee had been generally peaceful, upcountry dwellers were never entirely free of the threat of Indian raids. Those fears were realized in 1776 when Cherokee swarmed many northern white settlements following the British attack on Charles Towne. That summer a Cherokee party attacked the Anthony Hampton family, which lived along the South Tyger River near the Cherokee-British line. Anthony, his wife, one son (Preston), and one infant grandson were murdered and their farm burned. One son, Edward, escaped the massacre, but was killed in cold blood by "Bloody Bill" Cunningham and his band in 1781. Another Hampton son was out of state at the time of the massacre; his name was Wade. Wade Hampton later distinguished himself in the Revolution, and the well-known Hampton family has made many contributions to South Carolina history since the family line's narrow escape in 1776.

Militia under General Andrew Williamson retaliated against such Indian attacks by sweeping through Cherokee territory, devastating their land and bringing submission. The following spring, meeting at De Witt's Corner, the Cherokee ceded most of their re-maining land in South Carolina to the state government. The May 20, 1777, treaty extended the state's western boundary to the Savannah River, thus opening the northwestern corner for legal settlement. From this chunk of virgin piedmont acreage were later carved the counties of Greenville, Pickens, Oconee, and Anderson.

Following the Revolution the new state legislature took steps to open up the former Indian lands. In May 1784 a land office was opened to sell land in the soon-to-be-Greenville area. On the first day, one of the state commissioners, Colonel Thomas Brandon of Union, bought 640 acres on the Reedy River; Richard Pearis' old domain was finding new ownership. Two years later, on March 22, 1786, the South Carolina General Assembly officially created a county "by the name of Greeneville," making it the twenty-second county of the state.

There are no records regarding the reason for the selection of the county's name, and differing views have been expressed. Traditionally, the most commonly accepted theory has been that the area's lush green forestation dictated the name. However, recent re-examination of the original 1786 act and other early documents reveals that the county's name was first spelled "Greeneville." While this is not conclusive proof, the presence of the middle "e" strongly suggests that the name was probably intended to honor Nathanael Greene, commanding general of the southern army during the later stages of the Revolutionary War.

The wedge-shaped county was laid out with the mountainous North Carolina state line forming its northern boundary; the old Indian boundary standing as the dividing line with Spartanburg and Laurens on the east; and the Saluda River on the west, tapering until it crossed the former Cherokee line, separating Greenville from Pickens County. The boundaries have been virtually

The Carolinian Florist.

In which,
Upwards of one thousand plants are mentioned: and the places of growth, and times of flowering of many of them, are ascertained.—

By

John Drayton.

Author of Letters written during a Tour through the Northern & Eastern States of America; Of a View of South Carolina, as respects her Natural and Civil Concerns: and Member of the Royal Society of Sciences of Gottingen in Hanover.

1807

In 1798 naturalist John Drayton traveled through the mountains of the upcountry, where he identified Greenville's own yellow honeysuckle for the first time. His Carolinian Florist was one of the earliest botanical studies of the state's plants and flowers. Courtesy, South Caroliniana Library

Greenville was, in all probability, named in honor of Revolutionary War general Nathanael Greene, the hero of the southern campaign in 1780-1781. General Greene, a Rhode Islander, replaced Horatio Gates after the Battle of Camden and managed to harry Cornwallis and his troops through the Carolina upcountry. His success led directly to the victory at Yorktown. Courtesy, Chamber of Commerce, Town of Ninety-Six, S.C.

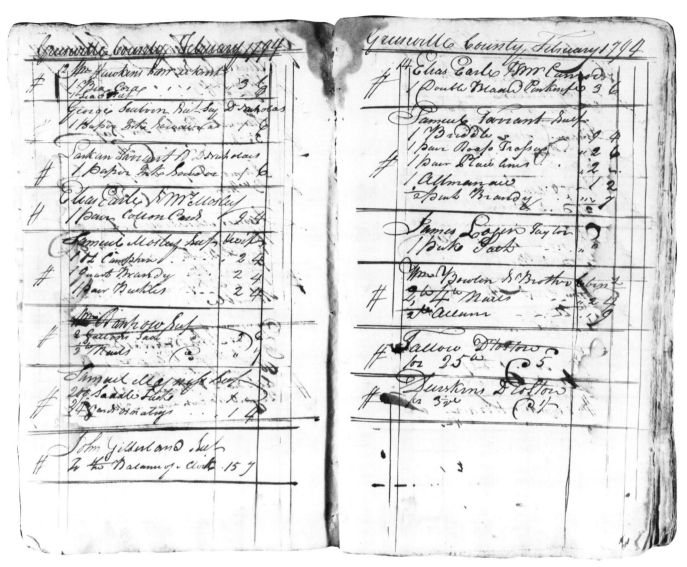

Alexander McBeth's daybook, marked "Greeneville County, February 1794," records purchases as varied as Elias Earle's double-bladed penknife, a bridle, half pint of whiskey, four penny nails, a quart of brandy, and trousers. Truly a "general store," McBeth's was the gathering place for the summer residents who lived in the Tanglewood area west of Greenville. Courtesy, Greenville County Library

unchanged ever since. The new county stretched to a length of forty-eight miles and a width which varied from seventeen to twenty-three miles, covering a total area of approximately 789 square miles. The northern portion is quite rugged and mountainous, while the lower reaches are rolling farmlands. The county seat, established at Reedy Falls, is almost in the center of the county and its two-tiered terrain.

The area's beauty drew noted botanists of the period who found much to study. William Bartram had visited in 1776, and later wrote enthusiastically in his *Travels* of the "... fragrant strawberry fields, masses

LEMUEL J. ALSTON

As a young man Lemuel James Alston moved to the South Carolina upcountry where he became a gentleman of wealth and influence, holding political and military posts, and founding the first town within Greenville County, "Pleasantburg." Alston was born in northeastern North Carolina in 1760, the son of Sarah and Solomon Alston, Jr. After the American Revolution he emigrated to South Carolina where he studied law and was admitted to the bar.

About 1786 Alston began a chain of land acquisitions when he was granted 3,820 acres in Ninety-Six District. In May 1788 he purchased from Thomas Brandon some 400 acres of prime land on the Reedy River for 217 pounds and 10 shillings. This spot, originally settled by Richard Pearis twenty years earlier, is where Alston chose to make his home. He continued adding to his holdings until his Greenville County acreage totaled 11,028.

Alston built an imposing house, "Prospect Hill," which one visitor described as the most beautiful house he had seen in the state. The elegant hilltop mansion was approached through an impressive avenue lined with sycamore trees, a formal oasis in an otherwise rustic area. (The house stood for well over a century at Westfield Street and McBee Avenue, later the site of Greenville High School and Greenville Junior High School.)

As something of the lord of the area, Alston offered a portion of his land in 1797 to be laid out as a village for the county courthouse and jail and for homes and businesses. He drew a plat for the picturesque eight-square block village, located just above the beautiful falls of the Reedy River, and dubbed it "Pleasantburg." He had great faith in the future of his little town.

Alston began his career of public service in 1788 when he was chosen by the north side of Saluda District as a delegate to the state convention for ratification of the U.S. Constitution; he voted in favor of adopting the document. The next year he became the official empowered to qualify persons to administer estates in Greenville. In 1795 he was commissioner to approve the securities offered by the sheriff of Washington District. In the military, Alston served as lieutenant colonel of the Fifteenth Regiment, Fourth Brigade of the South Carolina militia (1794-1795 and 1799-1801).

Alston's oratorical skills served him well in the political arena where he held both state and federal offices. He represented Greenville District in the South Carolina House of Representatives in 1789-1790, and in the state Senate in 1794-1795, and again from 1812 to 1815. For the Congressional seat, which represented Greenville and Pendleton districts, Alston see-sawed with another noted Greenvillian, Elias Earle.

Yankee observer Edward Hooker visited the area in September 1806 during the heat of the Congressional race in which Alston and a Dr. Hunter were challenging incumbent Earle. Hooker noted in his diary that Alston "was exerting all his energies to get a seat in Congress." Alston threw a barbecue for the voters in the Twelve Mile Creek area and attended a nearby church on Sunday, which excited the mountaineers who seemed to favor his candidacy. Hooker observed the glad-handing skills of all three candidates and found that Alston was "perfect master of the art." Hooker commended his oratorical powers but found him a bit superficial in other areas. He recorded the comment of one townsman who said that Alston's prominently displayed family Bible was not bought until he became a candidate for Congress "and was then got for the purpose of making good impressions on such as might call in." In Hooker's opinion, Representative Earle "loved the people more than any of them." The voters chose Alston, however, and reelected him for a second term in 1808. But the political tables turned again in 1810 when Alston lost his bid for reelection to Earle, a defeat which caused him a great deal of bitterness.

Although Alston returned to the state Senate and was still a prominent citizen, he became increasingly dissatisfied with his situation and infatuated with the lure of new lands opening in the West. By 1815 Alston decided to abandon his village of "Pleasantburg," then

generally known as Greenville Courthouse. He sold his Greenville land and home to Vardry McBee and moved to Clarke County, Alabama, settling near Grove Hill on property he called "Alston Place." There he presided as judge of the Orphan's Court and the County Court from November 1816 to May 1821.

Alston was twice wed. He married Elisabeth Williams, daughter of Joseph John Williams and Elisabeth Alston of North Carolina. They had six sons and two daughters, but only one of the children, William Williams, survived his father. Following the death of his wife, Alston married the widow of his first wife's half-brother, Elisabeth Norfleet Hunter Williams. They had no children. Lemuel James Alston died at "Alston Place" in 1836.

Nancy Vance Ashmore

Lemuel Alston's "Prospect Hill," built around 1799, became Greenville's first hotel in 1815 when Alston sold his property to Vardry McBee. It was razed in 1920. Courtesy, South Carolina Historical Society

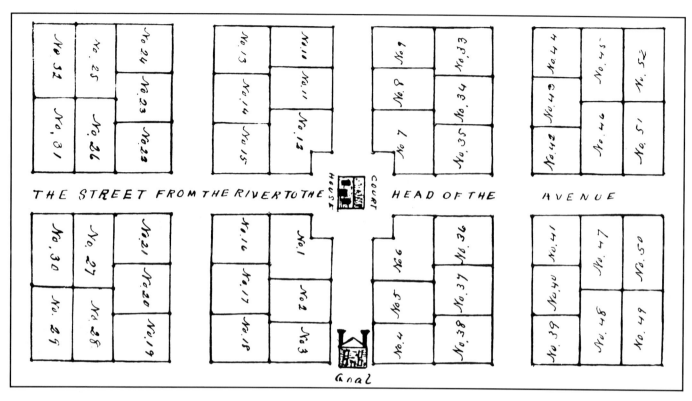

The predominance of the gaol and courthouse in Lemuel Alston's original 1797 plat of Pleasantburg reveals the need for law enforcement in the early, lawless frontier community. A legislative act of 1785 provided that county courts should be established in the upcountry and that justices should erect a courthouse and gaol, together with a pillory, whipping post, and stocks. Courtesy, Greenville County Library

of azaleas, rhododendron, Carolina mallow, peach and plum orchards, ginseng and larkspur" which he found. Indeed, nature had been kind. In 1798 naturalist John Drayton—later governor—closely examined the flora on Paris Mountain and discovered on its southern slope a variety of yellow honeysuckle "not yet noticed in any botanical book respecting this state." This indigenous plant, yellow Carolinian woodbine (*Lonicera flava Sims*), can be claimed as Greenville's own flower.

The county was still sparsley populated. According to the census of 1790, some 5,888 whites and 615 blacks lived in Greenville County. Landowners were widely spaced, making social and trading contacts somewhat difficult. One popular gathering place was Alexander McBeth's General Store, which began operation in the early 1790s near the intersection of the White Horse Road and Island Ford Road in an area known as Tanglewood. Customers came from far and near, for it was one of the first stores in the northwestern part of the state. A look at its daybook for 1794 shows sales of varied stock: deerskins, punch bowls, coffee, spices, frying pans, rum, almanacs, playing cards, teapots, gloves, paper, pins, and "negro shoes." By far the most popular item was whiskey, which sold for seven and a half cents per half pint. Apparently, friendly Indians who still inhabited the region also shopped in the compact, one-room store and barroom. McBeth no doubt obtained his wares from wagons on the road to Augusta which brought goods from Charleston and Philadelphia. Thus, seeds of trade and communication in the area had begun, even three years before the village and county seat were laid out.

Interest in organization and permanence was generated by land baron Lemuel J. Alston, who moved to the county in the mid-1780s and began buying packets of land that eventually amounted to 11,028 acres. Among his holdings were the treasured banks of the Reedy River and Falls, which had passed from Pearis to Brandon, and now to Alston. In 1797 he offered a portion of his land, including the falls area, as the site for the county's official courthouse village. He agreed to have it surveyed and laid out as a planned town, and his offer was accepted. Alston thus founded the county's first village, which he called "Pleasantburg." Twentieth-century historian Mary C. Simms Oliphant has written of the site's beauty, the vegetation along the Reedy River, and the pure mist of the falls, concluding that "no more idyllic spot could have been chosen for the location of the courthouse town."

A plat was drawn for the embryonic village, and streets were marked off. The plat called for a main street two blocks wide extending four blocks up from the river's bank. The courthouse was to be in a square, dead center in the middle of the village with the gaol one block to the south. At block five

was a broad avenue at right angles to Main Street which led through two rows of sycamore trees to the landscaped grounds of "Prospect Hill," Alston's mansion that overlooked his village. The town was pleasant—hence its name—but raw and unembellished. The early buildings represented first-class frontier architecture; the first courthouse was a two-storied log structure, and the gaol a handsome three-storied one.

The earliest recorded observations of the village were made in 1806 by Edward Hooker, a Connecticut native and tutor at South Carolina College in Columbia. He visited the Lemuel Alston family at "Prospect Hill" and wrote in his diary impressions of their elegant home and the village at its feet. He found Pleasantburg to be "quite pretty and rural, the streets covered with green grass and handsome trees growing here and there ... the place is thought by many to be as healthy as any part of the United States." However, there was not yet much business; "only two or three shops and some other little buildings." He reported only one attorney, and one traveling clergyman who preached periodically at the courthouse. With the exception of Alston's manor house, he noted "a want of good houses."

Although the village was appropriately named by its donor, the term "Pleasantburg" never caught on in popular usage. Only a few of the earliest deeds use that name. Other documents and most of the area's residents referred to "Greenville Court House" or "Greenville District," a term used after the county was abolished and reorganized by the South Carolina General Assembly in 1799. It was not until 1831 that the budding village was officially incorporated by the General Assembly as "Greenville," but as Oliphant observed, "by 1806 the name Pleasantburg seems to have been relegated to the past."

The Record Building, erected in 1824, was for many years Greenville's most distinguished architectural landmark. Designed by Robert Mills, a South Carolinian who was one of the nation's first professional architects, the fireproof building with its circular stairs was razed in 1924. Courtesy, Gene Eckford

CHAPTER TWO

A VILLAGE BLOSSOMS
(1806-1850)

The town was raw and poor at the turn of the century, composed chiefly of small farmers and passing drovers eking out a living; but great changes were made in the decades that followed, transforming the village into an amazingly sophisticated upcountry retreat. This growth was due largely to farsighted leadership, especially that of Vardry McBee and Benjamin F. Perry. While it was Lemuel Alston who literally created the village and served it well for some twenty years, it was McBee who pulled the loose threads of the settlement together into a progressive pattern for expansion.

In 1815 Alston sold all of his land to McBee and moved west to Clarke County, Alabama. The mantle of ownership and leadership fell to McBee, who filled the role with aplomb, although he continued to live in North Carolina

First headmaster of the Greenville Female Academy, William Bullein Johnson had a distinguished career as both an educator and minister. He taught at Greenville's first school for young women from 1823 until 1829, developing a well-rounded curriculum. Courtesy, South Carolina Baptist Collection, Furman University

until 1836. Even as an absentee landlord, however, he exerted positive influence on the attitudes, economy, and general development of the courthouse town. A constructive thinker who foresaw the potential of the county's climate and waterpower, McBee made numerous contributions to Greenville and attracted others to come to the area to expand its horizons.

Indeed, McBee became something of a "Godfather" by donating land for the first four churches and two academies. In 1819 he deeded thirty acres to Jeremiah Cleveland, William Toney, William Young, John Blassingame, Spartan Goodlett, and Baylis Earle as trustees for the establishment of the Greenville Female Academy and Greenville Male Academy. A public subscription of $4,500 financed the two schools. These institutions soon attracted talented students who came for schooling but often remained in town, making long-range contributions to the area. Among these first budding scholars was Benjamin Perry, from the hills of Oconee County, who came to read the *Iliad* and pursue mathematics and natural philosophy under the Reverend Mr. Hodges. Perry became the upcountry's political leader and thinker in the years that followed.

Early churches had been established around the county by Methodists, Presbyterians, and Baptists, the groups which have long dominated Greenville's religious scene. Lebanon Methodist (1785), Fairview Presbyterian (1786), and Reedy River Baptist (1787) predate the establishment of the village. However, it was on McBee-donated land that the town established its first four churches. In 1820 a handful of enthusiastic lowcountry Episcopalians who summered in Greenville organized St. James Mission, predecessor to Christ Church, making it the oldest church in town. The Baptist Church came next, in 1826, with an initial congregation of nine females and one male. This

Left: *Founded in 1820 as the St. James Mission, Christ Episcopal Church is the oldest congregation in the city of Greenville and its church, consecrated in 1853, the oldest church structure. It is the only sanctuary remaining on what was once Greenville's "church" street. Photo by Joe Jordan*

Below left: *Ebenezer United Methodist Church, built in the 1850s, is a major landmark of the Batesville-Pelham community in eastern Greenville County. Probably founded by Rev. Thomas Hutchings, the congregation erected this structure on land donated by William Bates in 1845. Photo by Bob Bainbridge*

Below right: *Elaborate gates as well as simple stone markers commemorate Greenville pioneers. Chains and this decorative wrought iron gate guard the tomb of Mr. and Mrs. H.R. Hammett, parents of textile mill owner Henry Hammett, in the old cemetery at Ebenezer Methodist Church in the Batesville-Pelham community. Photo by Bob Bainbridge*

VARDRY MCBEE

Vardry McBee, a self-made man who amassed quite a fortune in his life, was guided by the need to serve the community and his fellow man. After buying Lemuel Alston's extensive Greenville properties in 1815 (for the price of $27,500), McBee was an active, generous leader in the area until his death in 1864. His wide-ranging interests in agriculture, business, industry, transportation, and education made him the foundation for the young town's stability and diversity.

In 1804 McBee married Jane Alexander, daughter of Colonel Elias Alexander of Rutherford County, North Carolina. They were the parents of nine children: Joseph Gallishaw, Melinda Penelope, Silas Leroy, Luther Martin, Patsy A., Hannah Echols, Vardry Alexander, William Pinkney, and Alexander. The large family lived in Lincolnton, N.C., before finally moving to Greenville in 1836.

Personally and professionally McBee was respected and admired. While he was still alive, McBee was honored by a tribute published in *De Bow's Review* in September 1852. In nineteenth-century prose, the verbal portrait describes "What may be called a Model Man of Enterprise for the South and the Country." The article concludes:

Mr. McBee has never used his wealth as an usurer, or broker. He has always employed it in the support of honest and industrious mechanics, and others laboring for a livelihood. In-

stead of hoarding up his money, and lending it out at interest or investing it in a bank stock, he has employed it in the improvement of the country, and in the support of the poor and needy. To mechanics for their labor alone, he has paid in the course of his life near two hundred dollars. How many hundreds and thousands have been furnished with bread! At this time there are several hundred poor persons supported by him for their labor, in his factories and mills, or in some other employment under him.

In morality, and all the proprieties of life, Mr. McBee has no superior. His habits are all strictly temperate and methodical. He is a man of great industry and activity of life. He retires to bed early, and rises before daylight every morning. He breakfasts very early, and then employs himself in riding and superintending his business till dinner. Having been crippled whilst a young man, by being thrown from his horse, he is not able to walk any distance. He consequently lives mostly in his saddle during the day. Although now nearly seventy-seven years old, he rides fifty miles a day, and feels no inconvenience from it! He enjoys fine health, though his constitution has always been delicate. There is the same uniformity and regularity in his dress that there is in his habits and manners. His dress is a drab coat and light vest and pantaloons. In person, Mr. McBee is small, with a mild and pleasing expression of face. In his manners, he is kind

The "Father of Greenville," Vardry McBee purchased more than 11,000 acres from Lemuel Alston in 1815. He changed the face of the county, establishing mills along the Reedy River and donating land for the city's first four churches and for the academies. He sat for this portrait by William Scarborough about 1850. Courtesy, Roy McBee Smith

and gentle, with the simplicity of a child. Seldom is he excited by any thing, but there is in him a sleeping passion, which is sometimes roused.

In 1847 Mr. McBee made a visit to the northern states, for the purpose of obtaining information in regard to Rail-roads. He had been appointed a delegate to the Rail-road convention in Columbia, and went on from there after the adjournment of the Convention.

Whilst at the north, he was induced to subscribe ($10,000) Ten Thousand Dollars to the Seaboard and Roanoke Rail-road. In order to encourage the Charleston, Louisville and Cincinnati Rail-road, he had taken fifteen or twenty thousand dollars in that road. He took twelve thousand dollars of stock in the Greenville and Columbia Rail-road, and afterwards increased it to fifty thousand dollars . . . It may with great truth be said of Mr. McBee, that very few men who have made their fortunes have appropriated so much of them to public purposes, and to the support of honest industry, to the improvement of their country in her agriculture, manufactures, schools, houses, and public buildings, rail-roads, etc.

It may with equal truth be said, that Mr. McBee never engaged in an enterprise that did not succeed. As a saddler he commenced his fortune, had a high reputation for his work, and laid the foundation of that immense estate which he now owns! As a merchant, with numerous branches of his mercantile business at Lincolnton, Spartanburg, Greenville, and elsewhere, during some fifty years, he has been everywhere successful! As an extensive manufacturer of cotton and woolen cloths and paper, he has been equally successful. All this success he has seemingly accomplished without an effort on his part. When he subscribed largely to the Charleston Railroad, every one thought his stock would be of little or no

value. But it now pays him seven percent. The state of South Carolina issued some years ago a six percent stock which Mr. McBee, as President of the Rail-road, endeavored to induce the company to take for certain purposes. They declined and he took several thousand dollars of it himself. This stock was soon worth a premium of ten percent! There are some men whose judgement seems unerring, and who have an intuitive notion of success. Vardry McBee is one of that class, and like all truly great men, is without pride, ostentation, or pretensions. Such men are generally successful, whilst their opposites are almost invariably wanting in success.

Nancy Vance Ashmore

About 1840, Vardry McBee and his millwright, John Adams, constructed this dam on the Reedy River at Conestee to power a pulp-wood and cotton mill. At the same site, the Conestee Cotton Mill was built about 1898. Photo by Bob Bainbridge

graphically illustrates Henry McKoy's contention that it was the "founding mothers" who are truly responsible for the birth of Greenville's churches. The Methodists organized a congregation in 1834 which became Buncombe Street Church, and the Presbyterians in 1848 laid the groundwork for First Presbyterian.

McBee's personal and paternalistic interest in the village continued through the years. One family story illustrates the extent of his magnanimous spirit. When it was necessary to widen some of the streets in the growing village, McBee became concerned for the townsfolk who would lose dearly bought land from their lots. It is said he mounted his horse and rode around the soon-to-be-widened streets announcing, "As much as the village takes away from you to widen the street, go back on my land the same distance so that you will continue to

have what you bought."

The seeds of a textile domain were planted in those early days, but so were those of diversity. McBee contributed to both. He built two flour mills at the falls, on the site of Richard Pearis' original trading post. South of town, near present-day Conestee, he constructed a cotton factory, a woolen mill, and a paper mill, also on the banks of the Reedy. He maintained a chain of stores in both Carolinas through which he marketed these and other locally made products. The paper mill supplied newsprint for newspapers in Greenville, Spartanburg, and Charlotte.

The industries of the day are readily visible on Robert Mills' 1825 *Atlas* map of the district. Almost every stream had falls on which were located grist mills such as Edwards Mill and Peden Mills. On the Enoree River was McCool's Cotton Factory and a

Above: *William Bates built his home, on the hill above Rocky Creek and his mill, in 1835. A native of Rhode Island, he designed his home on the New England model with double doors and porches. The house had fallen into ruins before Mr. and Mrs. David Ward restored it in 1981. Photo by Bob Bainbridge*

Opposite page: *The Gilreath wheat and corn mill was built in the early 1800s by a local contractor, Mr. Alewine, for its original owner, Joel Bruce. The mill is one mile from the old P.D. Gilreath place on Shoal Creek, and is easily accessible on Highway 101 north of Greer. It was operated for many years by Buford Bryant and his four sons. Photo by Bob Bainbridge*

little south was Benson's Iron Works. The Reverend Thomas Hutchings had a textile mill which came to be known as Lester's Mill. Sheribal F. Arnold began Berry's Mill, and John Weaver opened a mill at Thompson's Beaverdam. In the early 1830s William Bates, a native of Rhode Island, erected a mill on the Enoree which began to manufacture both yarn and cloth. This Batesville Mill grew in significance and later was taken over by the Confederate government.

The roots of economic diversity ran deep. Adam Carruth had a musket factory about 1816. Jeremiah Cleveland, who began with a small store on lots #37 and #38 in Pleasantburg, pyramided his business into a large mercantile endeavor. Josiah Kilgore maintained investments in both cotton production and mill ownership. The thriving Greenville Carriage Factory, built at the falls by Ebenezer Gower and Thomas Cox, made use of

Left: *The upcountry's "salubrious climate" began to draw summer visitors to Greenville in the 1820s, leading to the building of the Mansion House Hotel in 1824. Until it was demolished 100 years later to make way for the even larger Poinsett Hotel, the Mansion House maintained a reputation as being one of the finest "hostelries" in the South. Courtesy, Greenville County Library*

Opposite page, top: *Adam Carruth's musket factory on the Reedy River manufactured 2,250 guns, using the river's power to blow his forges from 1815 until 1821. Congressman Elias Earle helped Carruth obtain an army contract, and the state, anxious to promote local manufacturing, subsidized the operation. This lockplate clearly shows an 1818 date of production. Courtesy, South Carolina Museum*

In the shadow of Greenville's new downtown skyline, the 1832 Kilgore-Lewis house, once located on Buncombe Road, now serves as the headquarters of the Greenville Council of Garden Clubs. Built by Josiah Kilgore, a mill owner and early developer, the Greek Revival home has been meticulously restored and relocated to property where Waddy Thompson's garden once stood. Photo by Bob Bainbridge. Courtesy, Greenville Central Area Partnership, Inc.

South Carolina's greatest architect, Robert Mills became the state's chief architect and engineer in 1819 after studying with James Hoban and working with Thomas Jefferson. He was interested in improving trade and transportation in South Carolina, and may have designed the Poinsett Bridge. His Statistics *and* Atlas *were both informative guides and encouragements to future development.*

waterpower while adding still more variety to the economic climate.

In the 1820s Main Street began to shed some of its early frontier look and take on a little style. Its first sophisticated building was a graceful, two-story brick structure with semicircular stairs in front, believed to have been designed by noted architect Robert Mills. The "Old Record Building," as it is called, replaced the original log courthouse and stood as a classic landmark on Main Street for a full century (1824-1924).

Just across the street was the Mansion House, a grand hotel which drew visitors with its magnetic appeal. To accommodate the growing number of summer residents who sought out Greenville's healthful climate, William Toney constructed the twenty-three-room "home away from home" in 1824. Beautiful and elegant, it quickly became the place to see and be seen. It was the first building in town to have many luxuries such as marble tile and a cut glass chandelier; it even had a rope elevator to take baggage to the third floor. The Mansion House maintained an excellent reputation throughout the nineteenth century, and considering its close proximity to the Record Building, it was no doubt the scene of many political discussions. John C. Calhoun made it his headquarters when he was in Greenville, preferring room 92.

Of course there are no photographs of this period, but a traveling physician-artist, Joshua Tucker, painted a lovely landscape of the village in the mid-1820s. His "Southeast View of Greenville, S.C." focuses on the anchors of Main Street—the Record Building and the Mansion House—while including neighboring lots, houses, and gardens. The only visible means of transportation is a two-wheeled cart and horse. It is a peaceful, pastoral scene, perhaps belying the vigor of the village's inhabitants.

Architect and trained observer, Robert Mills traveled south across the mountains of the piedmont on the newly opened state road in 1824, noting every detail of life and landscape in Greenville District. His observations are carefully recorded in *Statistics of South Carolina,* published in 1826. He hailed the grand range of beautiful mountains in the upper reaches of the district as "an ornament to our state." We had done well, he said, to wrest them from North Carolina when the state line was determined at the thirty-fifth degree of north latitude. Mills gave a vivid description of Caesar's Head and the Dismal Valley area which "lie in the northwest nook of the district, formed by the Saluda River and the Blue mountains." He noted two other mountain peaks on the opposite side of the district, near the Spartanburg line, whose names reveal their appearance: Hogback and Glassy mountains.

Mills related his approach to Greenville thus: "The mountains and hills melt away in the distance like the waves of the sea so perpetual are the undulations of the country. Directly south rises Paris Mountain, conspicuously behind which lies the village of Greenville." The town was a pleasing one situated on a plane above the falls of the Reedy River which he described as a "beautiful cascade, over an immense body of rocks." Noting the village's location and weather, Mills called Greenville's climate "one of the most delightful in the world." Many still agree with his assessment.

Mills reported that the census of 1820 had enumerated a population of 14,530 in Greenville District; he found the village itself to have "about 500" residents. Whereas other parts of the state were plagued with out-migrations of farmers leaving cotton-exhausted land, Mills accurately noted that "few or no emigrations now take place" from Greenville. While some cotton was grown, it was by no means the chief agricul-

"Thank God For Water"—*the prayer inscribed on the keystone of the spring of the Waddy Thompson house, now the site of the Kilgore-Lewis house*—*fervently acknowledges the early settlers' reliance on springs and streams. Now the centerpiece of the Greenville Garden Club's terraced gardens, the old stone spring was once an important resource for city dwellers. Photo by Bob Bainbridge*

tural crop. Most farmers grew wheat, small grains, tobacco, and corn, working hard for a fair yield. Indeed, Mills noted that the productiveness of the soil was related "in proportion to the industry bestowed by the cultivator."

According to Mills, corn sold for thirty-five cents a bushel; wheat for seventy-five and a half cents; and cotton for twelve cents per pound. A traveler interested in boarding in the area would need to budget three to six dollars per week in the village or sixty to eighty dollars annually in the district. He commented on the excellent academies and other private schools available for the youth who could afford them, and on the newly created free schools for the "children of the poor." Mills reported that during the preceding year some $1,039 of state funds had been spent to educate 166 children. This was a meager beginning for a public school system destined to become the largest in the state.

Pure and powerful water has always been important to Greenvillians. In fact, the falls of the Reedy River are the town's *raison d'etre,* a source of industrial power and beauty. Mills said Greenville was "finely watered" with its abundance of streams and creeks. The purity of drinking water was an early important issue for local leaders, as is evidenced by the actions of the Commission of the Streets and Markets in 1827. When the commissioners learned that Gaol Spring and Rock Spring had fallen into an "un-wholesome State," they declared it "their indispensable duty, as conservators of the health of the citizens . . . to adopt measures to assure the purity of their waters . . ." Immediately they appropriated twenty-five dollars for Gaol Spring and two dollars for Rock Spring to be applied toward the "clearing out, fencing in and improving of said Springs . . ." Furthermore, they made an official note that they viewed the well on Main Street above David Henning's land "as of great public utility and do take it under . . . cognizance, and will when necessary,

Above: *From the mid-nineteenth century until the mid-twentieth century, travelers rested at the Anderson-Montgomery House on the old Buncombe Road. The house operated as an inn on the stagecoach route to North Carolina and Tennessee for many years before it was purchased by Robert Wright Anderson in 1873. It was later enlarged and renamed the Spring Park Inn. Photo by Bob Bainbridge*

Opposite page: *The rather dilapidated bridge shown in this 1950 photo is a segment of the old Jones Gap Road in upper Greenville County. The road itself, long since replaced by a modern highway from Travelers Rest to Caesar's Head, perpetuates the name of Solomon Jones, a pioneer road builder in the area. It is said that Jones followed the route chosen by one of his pigs, whose instincts led him along the most gradual slope of the mountain. Photo by W.D. Workman, Jr.*

if in funds, contribute to its improvement also."

The state road passing through Greenville District joined the area with mountainmen in North Carolina, Tennessee, and Kentucky, and also with lowcountry aristocrats in Charleston and the coastal regions. Both groups were attracted to the upcountry village and made their mark on its development. The White Horse, Buncombe, and Augusta roads opened village contacts with inland regions to the south and west. Drovers of horses, mules, cattle, hogs, and turkeys needed a rest stop after traversing the difficult Blue Ridge Mountains on their way to lowland markets. Many stopped north of the village in a place which thus came to be known as Travelers Rest. Others pressed on to Greenville to rest up for a few days before moving out. They added a colorful di-

Above: *"Whitehall," probably the oldest home in the city of Greenville, was built in 1813 by Governor Henry Middleton of Charleston as his upcountry retreat. Typical of the resort homes of lowcountry planters, the house was designed on the Charleston model, although the verandas were added later. Courtesy, Oscar Landing*

Opposite page: *Once clearly an impressive mansion, this dilapidated old house on Alice Street near the Woodside community may have been the summer home of South Carolina governor Joseph Alston and his wife, Theodosia Burr Alston, the daughter of Aaron Burr. Photo by Bob Bainbridge*

mension to life on Main Street. Meanwhile, lowcountry families seeking relief from malaria and heat were making the laborious trek on the often rutted state road to the mountain city on the Reedy River. They brought with them china, craftsmanship, and culture. Divergent influences were beginning to meld—not clash—in the antebellum village.

The 1820s and 1830s found Greenville increasingly popular as a resort for the wealthy elite. Some spent their summers in hotels—the Mansion House, Greenville Hotel, or Chick Springs (built in 1840)—while others constructed permanent homes. Former Governor Henry Middleton purchased land from pioneer settler Elias Earle and built "Whitehall" as his summer home in 1813; it still stands as the oldest house within the city. (Side piazzas added later create a lasting reminder of Charleston's architecture and influence.) Governor Joseph Alston and

his wife Theodosia maintained a family farm in the district. Joel R. Poinsett, designer of the Gothic stone bridge on the state road, built his summer home, "Tanglewood," west of town. Politician Thomas Lowndes constructed "Lowndes Hill" just south of the village. With this influx of refined and cultured part-time residents came a widening of horizons for all associated with the village. New levels of culture—poetry, theatre, concerts, debates, jockey clubs—were introduced and retained.

A local middle class of professionals identified increasingly with the educated summer residents. Benjamin Perry, Baylis Earle, Tandy Walker, William Choice, William G. Gantt, Henry Townes, and Waddy Thompson enjoyed the stimulation of social contact with the summer folk. Among the regular visitors were such South Carolina political leaders as Joel R. Poinsett, Robert Y. Hayne, David Huger, John Belton O'Neal, and their families. There was a fluid, multifaceted spirit that made the piedmont town unusual. As Greenville historian Albert Sanders noted, "this welding of the middle class and the summer visitors made Greenville a pleasant place to live from 1820 to 1850."

As ideas were discussed, tolerance grew in Greenville. This was especially apparent when nullification became a heated issue in the 1820s. Lowcountry cotton planters who opposed the federal government's ever-increasing protective tariffs were particularly galled by the high tariff of 1828, the "Tariff of Abominations." Vice President

JOEL ROBERTS POINSETT

Greenville County's most distinguished summer visitor in the antebellum years was certainly Joel Roberts Poinsett, whose name is remembered in a highway, a hotel, a private dining club, and a mill village as well as in the Christmas flower which he discovered, yet whose achievements are almost unknown.

The only son of a wealthy Charleston Huguenot doctor, Poinsett, born in 1779, was a brilliant but physically weak child who was exceptionally well educated, first in England, later at an excellent Connecticut school, and again in England, where his interests were in languages (he knew French, Spanish, German, some Russian, Latin, and Greek by the time he was seventeen) and military tactics. He studied medicine at the University of Edinburgh, where the climate was too cold, but where his interests in science, especially botany, were encouraged; he studied military engineering briefly in England; and he returned to Charleston to read law, but found that study uninteresting.

Travel seemed to help his health (he lost the use of a lung as a young boy), and beginning in 1801 he began ten years of travel which took him to Finland, the Ukraine, Persia, and Portugal, among many other countries. In 1812, at the beginning of the war with England, President James Madison appointed him his special envoy to Chile and Argentina. There Poinsett worked to make friends

Statesman Joel Roberts Poinsett, a summer resident in the county, supervised the building of the old state road which opened Greenville to lowcountry visitors and increased trade. Courtesy, Greenville County Library

for America and was considered by the British to be "the most suspicious character" that the United States had in South America.

When he returned home, he immediately undertook a 2,000-mile tour of the American West, concluding his tour by exploring the Carolina mountains on his way home to Charleston, thus giving him a sense of the needs and possibilities of the up-country.

Small and physically unprepossessing, Poinsett was, by 1816, one of the most sophisticated and knowledgeable of Americans. He was probably more widely traveled than any American of his time and he had developed strong political ties in Washington. He chose, however, to serve his state for the next few years, first as state legislator and then as head of the South Carolina Board of Public Works (1817-1820) where he was responsible for public improvements—roads, bridges, and ports. In that position he supervised the building of the state road from Charleston to the mountains, which opened Greenville to lowcountry visitors and rapidly increased trade. He may have designed the arched stone bridges in Greenville County which still exist, and he certainly was responsible in 1820 for building a stone spring by the side of the highway which refreshed travelers on their way to the

mountains. That small marble fountain is now located next to the Poinsett Hotel on Greenville's Main Street.

In 1820 he was elected to represent South Carolina in the United States Congress; there he became President Madison's special advocate for soil conservation and, in the years that followed, became closely associated with the Unionist side in the nullification controversy which wracked the nation between 1825 and 1835. The nullifiers, led by John C. Calhoun, were strong in South Carolina, but Poinsett accepted a secret commission from President Andrew Jackson to lead the Unionist opposition, and is said to have stockpiled arms and ammunition in case of an armed revolt.

In the late 1820s Poinsett was appointed minister extraordinary and plenipotentiary to Mexico, and it was there that he was first shown the beautiful flower which he later domesticated in South Carolina. He worked hard to avoid a war with Mexico and was deeply interested in the country's archaeological remains and natural beauties. He returned to Charleston in 1833, when he married a widow who had a rice plantation, "the White House," in Georgetown, and a summer home, "Casa Blanca," in the Tanglewood section west of Greenville off the White Horse Road. There he spent every

summer until his death in 1851. In 1837 he was named secretary of war by President Martin Van Buren.

Poinsett was thoroughly involved in Greenville life. He became a close friend of Benjamin Perry, and shared his views with other town leaders. Much of his fortune had vanished in his years of travel, and he worked hard to make a modest country retreat into a comfortable summer home. He joined the county agricultural society (he served as a cattle judge for the state agricultural show in Greenville in 1844, awarding first place for milk cows to Vardry McBee), was a member of the vestry of Christ Church and even designed plans for the church's sanctuary, and became deeply concerned about the growth of the upstate. At the same time he promoted plans in Washington for a national museum for the promotion of arts and sciences which eventually became the Smithsonian Institution.

Joel R. Poinsett died in Stateburg, South Carolina, in 1851, during a trip from Georgetown to Greenville. He is buried there in the churchyard of Holy Cross Episcopal Church, with only a simple marker above his grave. But his name is remembered in Greenville even if his achievements as a diplomat have been forgotten.

Judith Gatlin Bainbridge

John C. Calhoun penned a retort—The South Carolina Exposition and Protest—which proclaimed the right of South Carolina and other states to nullify such "unconstitutional" acts. However, unlike their coastal counterparts, Greenvillians were generally opposed to such ideas of nullifying federal authority and possibly dissolving the Union. They held strongly to the staunch federal views of Poinsett and Perry. Yet, leaders on both sides of the issue summered in Greenville as social equals, and, for the most part, all went well.

Newspapers and literary efforts emerged as significant voices of various segments of the community. A visiting Yankee musician-dramatist-poet, John Hill Hewitt, established the first local newspaper, *The Greenville Republican,* in 1826. The first issue, dated July 12, reported the patriotic observation of Independence Day and reprinted

Above: *In addition to his summer home, "Tanglewood," Joel Poinsett also purchased a cabin near Gap Creek, where his bridge still stands. This rustic mountain farm gave Poinsett a retreat from the social obligation of entertaining summer visitors. Local historian Laura Ebaugh, who photographed the cabin in the 1950s, dated it to 1794. Courtesy, Greenville County Library*

Opposite page: *The graceful gothic arch of the Poinsett Bridge is now almost hidden by the lush vegetation of Little Gap Creek in northern Greenville County. Probably designed by architect Robert Mills, the bridge was completed in 1820. Courtesy, Ted Ramsaur*

First described by John Drayton in his 1798 publication The Carolinian Florist, *the yellow honeysuckle is Greenville's own flower, still growing in the rocky woods, bluffs, and hillsides of "Paris's Mountain in the Greenville District." Its scientific name,* Lanicera flava Sims, *honors botanist John Sims, who further described it in 1810. Photo by Leland Rodgers*

Above: *In 1825 state engineer Robert Mills described Caesar's Head, Greenville County's highest point, as a "mass of granite, rising from the vale, through which a rapid river winds its turbulent way...the ledges of stone, rising almost perpendicular, and at length, [hang] over at top, so that they seem to totter to their fall." Courtesy, Pat Crawford*

Left: *Greenville summer visitor Joel Poinsett discovered Mexico's beautiful, winter-blooming wildflower when he served as ambassador to the country in the late 1820s. He naturalized the poinsettia when he returned, and it is now the traditional symbol of the Christmas season. Photo by Leland Rodgers*

Opposite page, top: *Traveling physician-artist Joshua Tucker painted this "Southeast View of Greenville, S.C." in 1825. Rising above the budding village's houses and gardens are the two newly constructed anchors of Main Street: the Mansion House (left) and the Record Building. Courtesy, Abby Aldrich Rockefeller Folk Art Center, Williamsburg, Virginia. Gift of Arthur A. Shurcliff*

Opposite page, bottom: *Addison Richards' tinted lithograph of the Reedy River Falls appeared in* Orion *magazine in 1844, after Vardry McBee had built his grist and wheat mills on the river. The wooded riverbanks attracted families and courting couples in the nineteenth century; today their beauty is once more being realized. Courtesy, Henry B. McKoy*

Despite its location in Pickens County, Table Rock has exerted a strong influence on Greenville. Indian legend identified the huge rock as the dinner table of a giant chieftain. A hotel opened there in 1848, just after this engraving was made by Addison Richards for Orion *magazine, and provided a magnificent attraction for tourists. The land in the foreground was acquired by the Greenville Water System in 1924 and now provides 28.5 million gallons of water daily to Greenville. Courtesy, Henry B. McKoy*

Opposite page: *Christ Episcopal Church, consecrated in 1853, was built on land donated by Vardry McBee, who is buried in its churchyard. Photo by David Jenkins*

McBee Chapel in Conestee, built by millwright John Adams to serve Vardry McBee's workers at the Reedy River Mill, is one of only three remaining octagonal churches in the nation. The church building may be the oldest one in the county. Photo by David Jenkins

Built about 1838 by George Dyer, Falls Cottage was used as a tailor shop and residence before the Civil War. Later it was a cobbler shop, a school, and in the twentieth century, a gas station. It is now the home of the Metropolitan Arts Council. Photo by David Jenkins

Hewitt's poem, "Jubilee Song," which had been composed especially for the fiftieth celebration of American independence. The weekly paper was well received and provided an outlet for other budding writers in the area. Although Hewitt liked Greenville and admired its beauty—he said it was "embedded amid the Saluda mountains, like a pearl surrounded by emeralds"—he was something of a drifter who moved on after a few months. Obed Hart Wells and Benjamin Perry took over his *Republican* as editors and publishers and continued producing it for a few years.

The *Greenville Mountaineer,* founded under Perry's editorship in 1829, became politically influential in the antebellum period. A strong Union-loving opponent to nullification, Perry both led and reflected the rural upcountry attitudes of free thinking and independence. He was a well-educated lawyer, politician, and journalist. While both sides of current issues were given news coverage, his editorial space went to Unionist views. Unanimity of opinion did not exist, however, and a rival paper, the *Southern Sentinel,* was established in 1832 during the heat of the nullification controversy. Its editor, Turner Bynum, made bitter attacks on Perry, who challenged Bynum to a duel—and won. Years later Perry mused that this tragedy was "the most painful event of my life."

While Greenvillians may not have made headlines in the literary world, professor Alfred Reid concluded that "more activity has appeared in Greenville than is commonly known." Fledgling literary achievement and awareness began in the 1820s and continued for a half-century, bolstered by a circulating library, the Polemic Society, literary societies, bookstores, lyceums, and of course, the newspapers. The village played its own part in the national Romantic period. There was a playful, happy air astir, sometimes reflected in the lines of poetry published in

Attorney, editor, writer, governor—Benjamin F. Perry may have been the strongest intellectual voice in antebellum Greenville, and he certainly was the most forceful political presence from the time of the Civil War until his death in 1886. A devoted Unionist, he finally acquiesced to secession and supported the Southern side during the conflict. After a brief tenure as Reconstruction governor, he retired to his mansion, "Sans Souci." From Perry, Letters to his Wife, *1890. Courtesy, Mrs. Fred Ellis*

JOHN HILL HEWITT

Greenville was "a pretty District town, embedded in the Saluda Mountains like a pearl surrounded by emeralds," wrote John Hill Hewitt when the twenty-three-year-old music master arrived here in the summer of 1824. The son of America's first composer, James Hewitt, the young man had spent four years at West Point, where he had studied music under the band conductor. Failing to graduate because of low grades, he had joined a musical theatre group touring the South, and in Columbia met Elizabeth Macklin, a charming young woman who was finishing her education at the well-established Greenville Female Academy. The Macklin family were summer residents of the upstate resort community, and Hewitt decided to pursue romance and a career in the village.

He became almost immediately an important figure in the small town. Appointed a professor of music at the Female Academy by Headmaster William Johnson, he also began to study law with Judge Baylis Earle. Under the sponsorship of Elizabeth's father, who did not know that the young musician was secretly pursuing his daughter's favor, and with the encouragement of Judge Earle, Hewitt decided to begin the town's first newspaper. After purchasing a press and type, in 1825 he started the Greenville *Republican,* under the management of a master printer and with the help of an apprentice, a Negro "devil," and himself as editor.

Benjamin Perry was also reading law in Judge Earle's office, and the two young men agreed in their opposition to nullification, the major political issue of the day, although Hewitt was more interested in literature than in politics. He filled the pages of his paper with elaborate love poems and patriotic odes as well as with reports of balls and entertainments in which the list of distinguished

All Quiet Along the Potomac Tonight *stands as one of the finest songs of the Civil War era. The poem's origin is unclear, but it is certain that John Hill Hewitt set it to music. Courtesy, Special Collections Department, Robert W. Woodruff Library, Emory University*

guests invariably included his own name.

"The romantic little town" of Greenville, as Hewitt refers to it in a rambling unpublished diary, seems to have inspired both his poetic genius and his emotional attachment to Miss Macklin. In 1825 he published "The Minstrel's Return From the Wars," a ballad which immediately gained popular attention, but one which his brother, a music publisher, did not copyright, so he received no financial advantage from it. "The Minstrel's Return," however, did begin Hewitt's long career as a balladeer. He also wooed Elizabeth Macklin, tutoring her on the piano and taking her for long walks along the Reedy River's falls.

In the pages of the *Republican* Hewitt praised the progress of the growing village, encouraging the town fathers to think about the future of their country town. They seem to have believed his predictions, for in 1826 the prices of town lots increased dramatically. As newspaper editor, Hewitt had become an important personality and his attentions to Elizabeth Macklin grew warmer. But all was not well. Hewitt was a New Yorker, although he had been appointed to West Point by John C. Calhoun, and evidently his political ideas about Unionism began to creep into the pages of his paper. And more ominously, a second suitor sought Miss Elizabeth's hand.

His problems came to a head on July 4, 1826, the fiftieth an-

niversary of the Declaration of Independence. A special edition of the *Republican* complete with Hewitt's own "Jubilee Song" was published and the editor had arranged for an impressive ceremony in Court Square to mark the celebration. When he arrived early in the morning to make final arrangements, however, he found a stuffed effigy of himself hanging from the courthouse beams with a poem pinned to its chest:

I am the curly headed poet
A man of wit but cannot share it
I'm every inch for liberty
And want to set the nigger free.

Being parodied as an abolitionist was devastating, but even more slanderous were the rumors that Elizabeth's other suitor began circulating: Hewitt, he said, was a mulatto. Elizabeth turned cold; her father instructed him that he was no longer welcome in their home. The young editor fought back: he asked his mother to certify that he was her child and Calhoun to state that he had appointed him to the Military Academy. With documents in hand, he challenged the rumormonger to a duel, but settled instead for a letter of abject apology. But the damage had been done.

The incident made him unhappy in Greenville, and the town's first literary figure left at the end of 1826, never again to return. His later career, however, is interesting. He settled eventually in Baltimore, where

he became editor of a popular magazine. There he entered a poetry contest, defeated Edgar Allan Poe for first prize, and thus began a life-long enmity with the poet that led to a street fight in Washington, D.C. Music, however, was his first love, and there is a tradition that he sold ten of his songs to Stephen Foster, including "Old Folks at Home." He wrote four cantatas, four operas including "Rip Van Winkle," and a volume of miscellaneous poems.

By 1860, he had become a thorough southerner, fleeing from Baltimore to Richmond at the outbreak of the Civil War. The sixty-year-old former West Point cadet offered his services to Jefferson Davis, who made him a drillmaster to new recruits. During the war he wrote a number of sentimental ballads which became popular with Confederate troops, including "The Mountain Bugle," "Take Me Home," "All Quiet Along the Potomac," "Rock Me to Sleep, Mother," "Where the Sweet Magnolia Grows," and "Take Me Home to the Sunny South," which led him to be called "The Bard of the Stars and Bars."

Admittedly a minor figure in young America's literary and musical life, John Hill Hewitt, who lived until 1890, was nevertheless a prolific writer and relatively talented musician who began his long career in Greenville.

Judith Gatlin Bainbridge

praise of nearby landmarks or recited by lovers who strolled near the roaring falls of the Reedy.

The personal libraries of Representative Waddy Thompson and Benjamin Perry are indicative not only of their own tastes but of a community that nurtured such cultured men as leaders. Although they stood at opposite ends of the political spectrum on the nullification issue, both Thompson and Perry were avid readers who accumulated extensive libraries. It is said that Thompson's collection reached 3,500 volumes. When he built a new home on Paris Mountain in 1852, the library was housed in a separate building, and it attracted visitors from afar. Thompson, who had succeeded Poinsett as minister to Mexico, maintained a healthy portrait gallery and a collection of Mexican curios along with his library.

Perry's library was his avocation and chief extravagance. He frequently bought books at auctions in Columbia and Charleston and ordered others from Philadelphia. He once boasted that his library was "the best out of Charleston," and others agreed that his rare collection of law books was valuable indeed. Two large library rooms were featured in his retirement home, "Sans Souci," to house one of the state's best-selected libraries. In addition, Perry contributed to future libraries through his own voluminous writings and correspondence, which are now considered important resources for historians of the period.

Music, dance, and drama also found a home in the hearts of village residents. Both local and traveling talent were seen in concerts and plays usually held during the resort season. In 1838 the Garcia and Nelson families gave a concert at the Mansion House which was held over for several weeks by popular demand. Music courses were taught at the Female Academy; Nelson's Thespians performed for a few years in the late 1830s.

Formal balls became an important part of the social scene, especially at the Mansion House, which was known for its glittering ballroom.

Greenville was assuming its own personality, developing a unique character that set it apart from other towns. As historian Albert Sanders has pointed out, it has never been just another southern town. In the antebellum days it was both a trading center for the hinterlands and a resort for the rich. It was a holdout from the tide of South Carolina nullification and disunion sentiment, remaining strongly Unionist until after 1850. It was basically agricultural but had underpinnings of textile manufacturing and other industries. The people were a blend of all types and sorts, creating an interesting plaid complexion on the courthouse steps. In Sanders' words, "the town square [was] filled with farmers, rough drovers, genteel planter families, wagoners, and local business and professional people—a unique blend of frontier and aristocrat with a healthy leavening of in-between groups."

Opposite page: *Waddy Thompson came to Greenville in 1826 to practice law, and was almost immediately elected to represent the county in the state legislature. There he preached nullification, opposing the tariff law of 1824 which had angered so many southerners. He boycotted eastern and western products, declaring that he would live on snowbirds rather than eat western pork and make the judicial circuit on foot rather than ride a western horse. Thompson later served in Congress and as an ambassador to Mexico. This circa 1840 portrait was painted by William Scarborough. Courtesy, South Carolina Museum*

Benjamin Perry built his mansard-roofed mansion, "Sans Souci," in 1870. Here he mellowed from the fiery Unionist spokesman of the 1830s and 1840s to an elder statesman who supported Wade Hampton and spoke for moderation. After his death the elaborate home, complete with extensive library, became a finishing school for young ladies and later the first home of the Greenville Country Club. Courtesy, Mrs. Fred Ellis

Furman University's Italianate bell tower, the symbol of the college from the time it was built as part of "Old Main" in 1853 until it was razed in the 1960s, announced Confederate victories during the Civil War as well as "Purple Hurricane" conquests on the football field in later years. Photo by W.D. Workman, Jr.

CHAPTER THREE

SOUTHERN TO THE CORE (1850-1877)

With mid-century came a revving of southern motors. The pace of life quickened, bringing Greenville closer links with other South Carolina towns, the challenge of new leadership, and a widening gap between various social and political groups. The tone of life in Greenville began to shift. As historian Albert Sanders observed, the "easy unity of previous decades" gave way to some divisiveness. Nationally, the decade of the 1850s was a period of heated political debates and polarized opinions; the Greenville electorate was not excepted from these sentiments. The power of the press and more rapid rail connections with Columbia and Charleston assured the piedmont's eventual unity with the rest of the state.

In 1851 Furman University ended its migratory history by moving to Greenville, where it has made an indelible imprint ever since. Vardry McBee had long

Above: *James Clement Furman preached secession from the Baptist pulpits of Greenville County from the time that he and the university named for his father came to the city in 1851. Conservative even for his time, dedicated to his church and his university, he declared in the difficult Reconstruction years that he had nailed his "colors to the mast" and would go down with the ship if Furman failed. Courtesy, Furman University*

Opposite page: *By the 1920s the Greenville Woman's College was almost complete. The Ramsay Fine Arts Building is still under construction in this aerial view, but the four connected classroom and dormitory buildings are finished. To the rear is the college dairy barn; beyond it, farmland bordering Buncombe Road, all that was left of the original thirty-three acres deeded to the Greenville Academies in 1820 by Vardry McBee. Courtesy, Furman University*

made overtures to attract the Baptist institution, which had begun in Edgefield and later moved to High Hills of the Santee and then to Winnsboro. A campus, which occupied McBee land, was established on the southwest bank of the Reedy River where it remained for the next century. The Richard Furman Classroom Building, known more fondly as "Old Main," was completed in 1854. An example of Italianate architecture, the building's most obvious feature was a tall, square bell tower which quickly became the easy-to-recognize symbol of the school. The first president was James C. Furman—intelligent, conservative, persuasive, and secessionist. He quickly challenged—and eventually overturned—Perry's Unionist leadership in the area.

The education of women was not overlooked. On the site of the original academies, the South Carolina Baptist Convention opened the Greenville Female College in 1855. Through the years its name has been altered to Greenville Woman's College (1914) and the Woman's College of Furman University (1933), before it fully merged with Furman in 1938. Throughout, it has provided quality education for young women and exerted strong cultural influence on the community.

At the end of the decade came another infusion of Baptist teachings with the opening of the Southern Baptist Theological Seminary in 1859. A young, energetic, and scholarly faculty was soon visible and audible in the community. It was led by the "Big Four"—James Petigru Boyce, John Albert Broadus, Basil Manly, Jr., and William Williams—who set the intellectual tone of Greenville for the next eighteen years. Carefree summer residents and sober Baptist divines did not always agree.

Horizons were literally widened in 1852 with the advent of the first railroad. It was a momentous event when the Columbia and

Greenville Railroad reached its western terminus on Augusta Street, the culmination of another McBee dream. The depot was known as College Place. A new era of speedy travel and communication, of guaranteed industrial success, of closer commercial ties with Columbia and Charleston (rather than Augusta and Savannah), and of downright excitement had been inaugurated.

Everyone came to see the train—the young and the old, the curious and the bewildered. One onlooker described the happy first day in these words:

Greenville now begins her iron age of existence. She is wedded to Columbia by bands of iron, and the strange-looking engine, the 'Abbeyville' announces its coming with a shrill whistle arousing the West End, [calling] together an enthusiastic crowd to cheer the welcome.

Most Greenvillians appeared content with their lives and surroundings, or at least they did not give in to twinges of "western fe-

ver," which hit many of their lowcountry cousins in epidemic proportions. Droves of South Carolinians had abandoned cotton-poor land and moved westward to Georgia, Alabama, and other states in the lower South, but the trend had not been popular or necessary in economically stable Greenville. However, there was one notable exception.

Welborn Barton, a physician in Tigerville, had as a young man gone with a friend to Texas, where he remained for about a year. Homesickness brought him back to his home county and to his sweetheart, but he never quite forgot the lure of those wide open spaces. Dr. Barton lived and practiced medicine in the piedmont foothills for a few years, but he dreamed of life on the range. He often discussed it with friends and family, who gradually became more interested in moving there. Finally, in 1854, 100 families and wagons from the Tigerville area gathered and started out with Barton as their pilot. The wagon train was slow, but safe; there were no accidents on the three-

This early daguerreotype (1850) shows Basil Manly, Jr., at twenty-five. He came to Greenville with the Baptist Seminary after serving as president of a small Alabama college, and helped set a serious intellectual tone for the small town. During the Civil War he edited hymnals and Sunday School tracts and made Greenville a kind of publishing headquarters for religious materials. Courtesy, Furman University

month trek. Blacks, families, and young and old were part of the hardy group that settled in Williamson County, Texas, leaving their Carolina home behind. These folk did not carve "GTT" into Tigerville trees, but well they might, for they had "Gone to Texas."

Another popular hunger was fed with the Butler Guards, Greenville's first volunteer military company. They made a colorful spectacle parading at almost every holiday and public gathering, along with the Furman University Riflemen. While the Butler Guards were officially neutral on political issues, several of its officers were active in the secession movement as it progressed. The very presence of the guards may have engendered a martial spirit and a desire for conformity among the spectators.

The secession tide was building in Greenville, as reflected in and led by the press. Rival newspapers bandied opposing economic and political views. The *Mountaineer* had acquired a secessionist editor in the late 1840s, forcing Ben Perry to establish a new Unionist organ, the *Southern Patriot,* which he combined with his former paper in 1855 to form the *Patriot and Mountaineer.* About the same time William Price began editing the *Southern Enterprise,* which exerted a strong pro-slavery and secessionist influence.

As historian James W. Gettys, Jr., has pointed out, public opinion in Greenville was completely transformed in a thirty-year period, from staunch Unionism to secessionism. The persistence of secessionist propagandists and time made a winning combination. In the upcountry, secession would not have succeeded in 1840 or 1850, but by 1860 a new generation of adults, who had grown up on such talk, were in control. Gettys observed: "What had been an extremist position in the 1830s, a moderate position in the 1850s, was by 1860 accepted

JAMES P. BOYCE

Greenville took on a new, more somber, and intellectual tone when Furman University moved to the upstate village in 1851. Although the school was relatively small, its faculty consisted of a half-dozen well-educated men who were, by 1860, the community's leaders. James Petigru Boyce is an example of this new leadership.

Born in 1827, the son of the president of the Bank of Charleston, as a child Boyce was a practical joker, an avid reader, and a negligent student. Exceedingly unathletic, the "barrel-shaped" young man spent his days reading novels on the piazza of his George Street home rather than studying. His irritated father finally removed him from the Charleston High School and put him to work for six months as a clerk in a dry goods store. The experience proved salutary; when he was allowed to enter the College of Charleston in 1843 he became a more industrious student, although one of his professors remarked "Boyce will be a great man if he does not become a devil."

After his sophomore year at the college, Boyce continued his education at Brown University. The jovial South Carolinian became increasingly serious about both religion (he had had a conversion experience which led him to join the Baptist church) and about studying at Brown, where he did brilliant work in philosophy. His father wished him to become a lawyer after his graduation in 1848, but he decided to study theology and

Theologian James Petigru Boyce was one of Greenville's leaders from 1855 to 1877. From Broadus, James Boyce, *1888. Courtesy, Furman University Library*

become a minister. Three years later, after completing Princeton Theological Seminary, he accepted a call to pastor the Baptist Church in Columbia. In 1854 his father died, leaving the twenty-seven-year-old minister the executor of an extremely large estate.

Boyce was offered a professorship in systematic theology at Furman University in 1855. He was wealthy, well educated, and dedicated to the proposition that the South needed a Baptist seminary. When Boyce moved to Greenville, he purchased an estate on the outskirts of town running from Christ Church to the creek at Cleveland Park, and from East North Street to the Reedy River. He taught at Furman,

raised funds for the seminary, and gardened diligently. He drove his two-horse buggy throughout South Carolina to raise a $100,000 endowment for the seminary, and on his acres grew flowers and vegetables with enthusiasm. He was most successful: by 1858 he had raised enough money to open the doors of the Southern Baptist Seminary, located in the old First Baptist Church on McBee and Church streets, and he produced 50,935 pounds of rutabaga turnips on his "Boyce Lawn" farmland.

Like many of his friends, Boyce was violently in favor of slavery and equally violent in his support of the Union. In December 1860, he ran, with Benjamin Perry, on the anti-secession ticket to represent Greenville at the South Carolina Secession Convention, but they were soundly defeated by Furman president James C. Furman and other secessionists. Although Boyce favored slavery (he called himself an "ultra pro-slavery man"), he felt that the South had sinned in the treatment of slaves: "The Negroes have not been cared for in their marital and religious relations as they should be; and I fear that God is going to sweep it [slavery] away." But as a Unionist he loved both his state and his country and he could not support the movement to secede.

As a man of means who was well-schooled in financial matters, he believed that "The war will be decided by money and the winning side the side that best manages its revenues." He refused to convert the seminary's antebellum securities into Confederate investments, and he stockpiled food and supplies for his close friends in the early days of the war because he foresaw its length and the perils of future inflation.

After serving briefly in 1861 as a chaplain to a local regiment, Boyce returned to Greenville to manage his estate, to serve in the state legislature, and eventually to become acting provost-marshal of Columbia at the conclusion of the war. He said that he was the last Confederate soldier to leave Columbia as Sherman's troops marched into the city.

At the conclusion of the hostilities, Boyce's home was looted and a Union soldier held a pistol to the scholar's head and demanded the hiding place of his wife's diamonds and the family silver. He coolly said that his brother had loaded his valuables on his wagon the previous day and had taken everything to safety. While his personal belongings were safe, by 1866 much of Boyce's fortune had vanished.

In the years after the war, he borrowed money to pay faculty salaries at the seminary, which had reopened with seven students in the fall of 1865. He struggled valiantly to keep the seminary going while the entire region suffered the pangs of poverty. His commitment to his seminary was complete: he even turned down an offer to become the president of the South Carolina Railroad Company (at the magnificent salary of $10,000 a year) in order to stay in Greenville with the seminary.

But it could not survive in South Carolina. After great struggle Boyce decided that the only way it could continue would be to have a larger base of supporters and a far larger endowment than could be raised in South Carolina. With great sorrow, he decided that the Southern Baptist Seminary must move from Greenville to Louisville, Kentucky. In 1877, that move was completed and James Boyce went with his beloved seminary to a new state and a new home.

Judith Gatlin Bainbridge

by the vast majority of the Greenville electorate." The election of Lincoln simply triggered an emotional reflex action.

One vocal moderate who was swept into the secessionist camp in 1860 was John DuRant Ashmore, who represented Greenville, Pickens, and Anderson counties in Congress from March 1859 to December 1860. Speaking on the floor of the U.S. House of Representatives, he defended slavery as a Constitutional right, one which should not draw the ire of northern accusers. He described his constituents as:

a people domestic in their habits, quiet in their deportment, raised to habits of toil and industry, and who daily labor by the side of the slaves whom they have raised, and whom they treat more as companions—as they are—than as the miserable, downtrodden, servile creatures your fruitful imaginations have depicted them.

Continuing his oratory, Congressman Ashmore declared if public anti-southern sentiment did not soon abate, he would return home, sound the alarm, and with his own hands "kindle the beacon-fires from hill-side and mountaintop" that his people might rally to the defense of their rights. "My voice shall not be silent," he said, "but ... my cry shall be 'to arms! to arms! to arms!'" In effect, Ashmore did exactly as promised.

Former Unionists began defecting to the secessionist side in the mid-1850s. Even Vardry McBee and C.J. Elford, a former Perry protege, joined the strong disunion tide by 1860 and sided with James C. Furman, A.B. Crook, George F. Townes, Perry E. Duncan, and William Price. By the end of October, Greenville—the former Unionist stronghold—had organized its company of Minute Men. With more than gentle persuasion coming from Ashmore, former Representative James L. Orr, and

Above: *John Durant Ashmore represented Greenville in the U.S. House of Representatives from March 1859 until December 1860, when he withdrew on the day South Carolina voted for secession. Born in Greenville District in 1819, Ashmore had been a clerk, teacher, lawyer, and farmer before entering the South Carolina legislature in 1848. He was in charge of the defense of Greenville during the Civil War. Courtesy, Dr. J.D. Ashmore*

Opposite page: *Near downtown Greenville, granite was quarried with hand drills and slave labor for a number of years before the Civil War. Now beautified as a city park, the old stone quarry has been landscaped with quiet pools and footpaths, but the stone face at the falls still reveals prominent vertical drill marks from the quarrying process. Photo by Bob Bainbridge*

President Furman, the move for secession following Lincoln's November election was a foregone conclusion.

In December the charismatic James Furman rallied secessionists and led a five-man delegation to the state convention that passed the Ordinance of Secession. Other members of Furman's Greenville delegation who signed the Ordinance were William Hans Campbell, Perry Emory Duncan, William King Easley, and James Perry Harrison. The die was cast; there was no turning back.

When he heard the news, Ben Perry swallowed the bitter pill and acquiesced to secession, as did Robert E. Lee in Virginia. In what Professor Alfred Reid has called "perhaps the most famous remark ever uttered by a Greenvillian," Perry gave vent to his fears and his loyalty. He declared: "I have been trying for the last thirty years to save the State from the horrors of disunion. They are now all going to the devil, and I will go with them."

Perry was as good as his word. He joined the Confederate militia, helping to organize upcountry troops. Many of his war-era letters reflect his anger at other politicians who had urged secession but retired to their comfortable homes to wait out the fighting.

Greenville enthusiastically mustered men

and materiel for the Southern effort, although it remained geographically removed from the fighting front. All totaled some 2,500 men volunteered as Confederate soldiers, with the Butler Guards the first unit to go. There was something of a "me first" attitude among the young men as they clamored to be a part of the excitement. Writing years later, veteran W.T. Shumate reminisced proudly about being the county's number one soldier. He wrote:

The Butler Guards of Greenville was the first company of all the soldiers to be mustered into the Confederate Army. We had troops ahead of the Butlers, but they were state troops. I accepted the position of fifth corporal so it would place me in the front rank, at the head of the company. Therefore, I was the first one to march out as a Confederate.

A total of six volunteer companies were raised: the McCullough Lions, the Craft Mountain Rangers, the Furman Guards, the Tyger Volunteers, the Carolina Mountaineers, and, of course, the Butler Guards. Greenville was the only county in the state to organize a regiment composed solely of home-county residents, the Sixteenth South

Above: *Almost sixty years after they were mustered out, Confederate veterans gathered for a 1922 reunion in McPherson Park. Many were members of Greenville's Sixteenth South Carolina regiment; others had served with the Furman Rifles, Butler Guards, or the Hampton Legion, which escorted Jefferson Davis in his flight south after Appomattox. In later years, reunions bound survivors with memories of the lost cause. Courtesy, Henry Parr*

Left: *Colonel Thomas C. Gower went off to fight the Yankees at the very beginning of the Civil War, leaving his carriage factory in the hands of his daughter and a slave. After a year, however, he was given leave to return to Greenville to produce caissons for Confederate guns and ambulances for wounded soldiers. Courtesy, Thomas C. Gower*

Carolina. A martial spirit filled the air and created solidarity and support in the community.

Chief among the supporters were the women who remained at home. Not only did they take over household and business management for the first time, they also devoted countless hours to the war cause, organizing into a highly effective unit called the Greenville Ladies' Association in Aid of the Volunteers of the Confederate Army. They met weekly from July 19, 1861, to May 1, 1865, to, in their words, "relieve the sick and wounded among the soldiers by forwarding to them linen, underclothing, cordials, bed ticks, socks ... and to make winter clothing for the volunteers in the Confederate Army." In addition, the women established and maintained a Soldier's Rest hospital, first on the campus of the Female College and later at the corner of Main and Washington streets, to care for sick and wounded soldiers who were often dropped off or left stranded by the less-than-efficient railroad. This project assumed gargantuan amounts of time, energy, and money. Fundraising socials were held, and personal resources were pooled, but mutual support and *esprit de corps* were the backbone of these iron magnolias.

Members of the Ladies' Association not only did good work, they also kept excellent records. In 1937 the thorough minutes of their meetings were selected for publication for what they reveal about Greenville and the entire South at that time. The Greenville Ladies' Association is considered an outstanding microcosm of the work of all Southern women during the Civil War.

Everyday life took on a new spartan tone of isolation and deprivation. The economy was almost exclusively geared to the war effort. Railroads were cut off from civilian use; communications and mail delivery were mostly accidental. For long periods there were no open stores and no currency. All mills in the area primarily produced war goods, and the Batesville Mill was completely taken over by the Confederate government. A local factory, the State Military Works, produced rifles. The Gower, Cox and Gower Coach Factory, the largest carriage factory south of the Potomac River, sold its entire output to the Army, which eventually owed the company $140,000. Just before the end of the war half of that debt was paid, but it was in Confederate currency, which soon proved to be worthless. Although the balance of the account was never paid, the factory was able to weather the economic setback.

Greenville may have been caught up in wartime spirit, but it was far removed from the battlefields. It was considered a haven for families from Charleston and other coastal areas threatened by Union forces. Many refugees came to the "Mountain City" to wait out the war. They brought with them servants, silver, jewelry, furniture, family treasures—virtually anything that was portable. In late 1864 Cornelius Burckmyer wrote to his wife, "The town is full of refugees from Charleston ... These fill the place pretty full and there is not much room to spare." The state bank in Charleston sent $35,000 in specie to Hamlin Beattie, which he hid in his store for safekeeping.

One of the best known of the Charleston refugees was Caroline Howard Gilman, who came to Greenville in March 1862 with

Greenville's role as a kind of publishing center of religious periodicals continued after the Civil War, as this page from "Kind Words for the Sunday School Children" indicates. Minutes of the South Carolina Baptist Convention for the war years show a continuing demand for hymnbooks and inspirational materials which Basil Manly and John Broadus tried to meet. Courtesy, Southern Baptist Collection, Furman University

KIND WORDS.

FOR THE SUNDAY SCHOOL CHILDREN

Published by the Sunday School Board of the Southern Baptist Convention.

VOLUME I] GREENVILLE, S. C., SEPTEMBER, 1866. [NUMBER 9

THE WAYWARD SON.

Only look at his ragged clothes! How weak, and thin, and hungry he seems to be! He was a very bad boy and ran away from home, because he thought he would be happier in wicked company. After a while his money was all gone, his wicked companions turned him off, he could not get any new clothes, and nobody would give him anything to eat. He slept with the pigs, and was glad to eat the trash which was thrown to the pigs.

Then he thought of the good home he had left, and of the kind father he had offended, and oh! he was so sorry! You see him in the picture when he has got almost home. Don't he look ashamed and guilty? Do you see the old house on the hill? Do you see his old father coming down the path with his arms open? He is going to put his arms around him, and kiss him, and take him home into the house, and give him new clothes and a plenty to eat. What a good father! I hope he is going to be a good, loving, obedient son after this.

If you want to know more about this beautiful story, get your Testament and turn to the 15th chapter of Luke; and there you will find it. Ask your father to explain it all to you. B.

THE POPLAR TROUGH.

About sixty years ago, a man lived in the edge of a forest, whose father had raised him very tenderly, and loved him very trustfully, and finally given all his property to this son, as his wife and his other children were all dead, and he intended to stay with his beloved son as long as he lived.

But the old man lived too long. He became blind, and lame, and foolish. He lost the sight of his eyes, and he lost the good use of his hands, and alas! he lost the love of his son. His hands became so feeble and trembling, that he would drop the spoon or the cup while he was trying to drink.

He broke so many cups and plates, and made so much grease on the carpet, that the son's wife used to scold, and said, "He is good for nothing, and in the way: he does nothing but break crockery, and make grease." And so the old man's life was very unhappy.

One day the man saw his old father drop a plate and break it. He burst out into angry scolding, and said, "I will stand it no longer—I will make you a trough. You are as dirty as a pig, and you shall eat like the pigs." Poor old father!

So he started out to the woods with his ax on his shoulder. His little son, about six years old, followed him. He soon found a poplar tree, cut it down, and began to hew out a block for the trough. After a little he was tired, and stopped to rest.

"Pa, what are you going to do with that tree? Are you going to burn it?"

"No, I am not going to burn it."

"Are you going to make rails out of it?"

"No, I am not going to make rails out of it."

"Well, Pa, what are you going to do with it?"

"I am going to make a trough."

"What for, Pa?"

"For your grandfather to eat out of."

"For grandpa?" And then the little fellow stopped to think. After a while he added, "Yes, that will be so nice; and I'll make you a trough too, Pa, when you get old and blind."

The man let go his ax, and he began to think. His little boy had unconsciously touched him in the only tender place. He sat down and began to remember all his father's love to him when a little boy. He wept. He went back and told his wife what had happened.

From that hour the good old man was kindly cared for, his wants supplied, his mistakes overlooked, his weakness provided against by constant attention, till he died.

Do you ever feel worried with the care your parents or aged relatives need? Remember how they cared for you once; and how you may need kindness from your children.

daughters, grandchildren, and household belongings and remained until November 1865. Her extensive correspondence gives an excellent view of Greenville at the time. She took an active part in all aspects of local life and society, joining the Ladies' Association and becoming its directress by June 1863.

Literary activity of a Baptist nature not only continued during the war but actually increased. With Furman Seminary closed for the duration of the war, its leaders were freed for chaplain duties and writing. Basil Manly and John A. Broadus wrote religious tracts to encourage Confederate soldiers in honor and courage. These were published in Raleigh, North Carolina, but the effort and organization came out of Greenville. Manly and Broadus also headed the Sunday School Board of the Southern Baptist Convention, organized in 1863 in Greenville. C.J. Elford served as its printer, and the Elford Press stayed busy publishing tracts, hymnals, and catechisms for soldiers and other Southerners who were cut off from Northern printing houses. Elford compiled and printed *The Confederate Sunday School Hymn Book,* which was soon sold out. A second edition was run, but most of its copies were burned in Columbia before being distributed. Other titles from this publishing house included: *The Little Sunday School Hymn Book,* edited by Broadus and Manly; *Elford's Primer for Little Boys and Girls*; and *The Southern Almanac for the Year of Our Lord 1865, Being ... the Fifth of the Independence of the Confederate States.* Thus Greenville became something of a center of religious literary activity for the Confederacy.

It is interesting to note that both Manly and Broadus continued their literary and scholarly activity long after the Seminary left Greenville in 1877. Their names are part of the foundation of Baptist publications; in fact, the first syllable of the names Broadus and Manly were combined permanently in

Broadman Press.

Not everyone was a patriotic Confederate, however. Some men resisted the draft that was dictated from Richmond, and others deserted after a brief taste of regimented military life. The mountainous portions of upper Greenville County, especially the area called Dark Corner, provided ideal hiding places for these evaders. They banded together, even built refuges fortified against capture, and preyed on local property owners. The situation became so extreme in 1863 that Major John DuRant Ashmore (the former congressman) requested from the Confederate army a cannon to destroy one of their blockhouses in Dark Corner. Authorities often used bloodhounds to pursue deserters into the mountains. But, as one old mountaineer explained, "The dawgs would run ahead yelping, and the boys would take a crack or two at 'em with a rifle, and that would be the end of the dawgs."

Indeed, mountaineer independence dies hard. Solomon Jones, the Unionist patriarch of the mountains known for his road building skills, illustrates the point. More than sixty years old but alert and outspoken in his dislike for the rebel government and his patriotism to the United States, Jones was persecuted during the war. He was forced from his house and hid for weeks in the forest, where family and friends would leave him food. Finally he was caught and thrown into the Greenville jail with common crooks. Benjamin Perry, a like-minded spirit and lawyer, had Jones freed and declared, "If Jones deserves prison I deserve it, for he has done no more than I."

As observer John William De Forest pointed out, Perry nevertheless charged and collected $100 from his client. Still, there were few other men in the South who would have had the will or the fearlessness to perform that service at any price.

ELIZABETH PERRY

Close examination of the life of Elizabeth McCall Perry provides an excellent view of the world of a southern middle class lady. As the wife of a public figure—Benjamin Franklin Perry—the mother of a large family, and the mistress of a successful household, she fits the public image of a helpful but unassuming mate. However, her strong interest in political issues, her ambition for her husband's career, and her involvement in community affairs mark her as an individual worthy of note in her own right.

Much of the voluminous correspondence between Elizabeth and Benjamin Perry has been preserved, revealing the strength of her character and influence. In many ways she was the power behind the throne.

Elizabeth Frances McCall began life in Charleston where she was born on October 28, 1818, the daughter of Hext and Susan B. Hayne McCall. The family was an aristocratic one; her uncle was Robert Y. Hayne, who later gained political fame as a nullification spokesman. Her father died when she was quite young, leaving Mrs. McCall with the responsibility of rearing and educating several children. During her seventeenth summer, while vacationing in Greenville with her family, Elizabeth met her future husband. The McCalls summered at the Mansion House, which was the year-round boarding home for Benjamin F. Perry, a promising young lawyer and editor.

Their courtship was a whirl-

wind one. They were introduced and Benjamin was immediately smitten with the young girl's beauty and intellect. She later admitted that her affection for him grew more gradually. They took long walks by the falls and undoubtedly talked of many subjects. By the fall of 1836 Benjamin wrote in his journal: "My love is as pure as the object of it—and never was human nature more artless, more innocent than it is in Miss Elizabeth." They became engaged—with Mrs. McCall's blessing—and were married the

William G. Brown painted this portrait of Elizabeth Perry in 1853. From Letters Acknowledging Receipt of Gov. B.F. Perry's "Letters to His Wife," April 27, 1891

following spring, on April 27, 1837. Elizabeth—or "Lizzy," as her husband came to call her—was eighteen years old; the groom was thirty-one.

The newlyweds' first home was a two-story wooden house on Main Street, in the block between Court and Broad streets. There they lived for thirty-five years, adding on and making adaptations as the family grew. The Perry marriage was a long and happy one, based on romantic love, mutual respect, and trust which never dimmed. "It would be impossible to write of them separately," one observer noted. Perhaps their marriage was no more devoted than that of many other couples, but their frequent, loving letters gave tangible documentation of the strength of their relationship.

Although her formal schooling ended at age fourteen, Elizabeth was no intellectual slacker. Early in their marriage, Perry often read to his wife from his extensive library. She developed a fondness for reading and writing which became increasingly important in her life. She was well versed on political and social issues of the day and did not hesitate to offer her views to her husband, even when they differed from his. For instance, in her letters to her absent legislator-husband, Elizabeth urged him not to introduce the unpopular idea of a state penitentiary and she tried to curb his enthusiasm for the Mexican War. She was assertive and outspoken with her husband and prodded him to further his political career by seeking higher office.

Once when Representative Perry chose not to run for re-election to the South Carolina House of Representatives, Elizabeth wrote to him, "the two reasons you give for wishing to leave, namely love of home and finding Legislation hard, I cannot admit of, the first is effeminate, the second selfish." While he seemed content with hearth and home, her ambition burned brightly. She was not satisfied with his being only a "plodding Greenville attorney."

Although both had opposed secession in the early days, they acquiesced to the Ordinance of Secession and supported the Confederacy during the war years. Elizabeth was loyal to the cause as a member of the Greenville Ladies' Association in Aid of the Volunteers. In addition, she served as secretary and treasurer of the "Ladies Hampton Legion Association." She believed her husband was near-perfect and admired his courage and patriotism, comparing him to "David, who dared oppose Goliath." After his death, when assembling his papers for publication, she concluded, "He had never an equal and never will have in South Carolina."

Elizabeth bore seven children; in the bustling household, she kept the children in line, directed the servants, gained a reputation for her gingerbread and pound cake, entertained as a charming hostess, found time for reading and correspondence, and created an "atmosphere of love and contentment." All was not bliss, however; there were sorrows and disappointments. Elizabeth suffered at least four miscarriages and delivered two stillborn children. In addition, she lost three of her children to tuberculosis. But the family stood together as a solid unit.

Elizabeth Perry's days were exceptionally busy. She was involved in the lives of her friends and family and in the activities of Christ Church (Episcopal). Following her husband's death, Elizabeth spent the remaining five years of her life at "Sans Souci," their Victorian retirement home outside the city, making her own literary contributions. She republished some of his works, wrote a "Sketch of the Life of Governor B. F. Perry," and published volumes of his correspondence and their exchange of letters.

Elizabeth McCall Perry died September 24, 1891. She was buried in Christ Episcopal churchyard between her beloved husband and her three children who had preceded her. In the words of the Greenville *News,* "A Good Woman [had] Gone to Her Reward."

Nancy Vance Ashmore

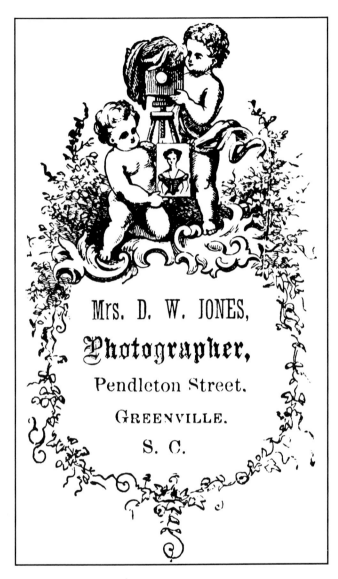

Mrs. D. W. JONES,

Photographer,

Pendleton Street.

GREENVILLE.

S. C.

Mrs. D.W. Jones invited patrons to her new studio on Pendleton Street at its opening in 1869. This early Greenville businesswoman advertised the spaciousness and privacy of her rooms, and photographs of the day indicate that she did a good business. Photography was evidently a career open to women; in the 1890s Chicora College offered course work in "the Kodak camera" as an appropriate study for girls. Courtesy, Blake Praytor

Greenville did experience one military invasion in the closing days of the war. After Lee's surrender in April 1865, Jefferson Davis retreated southward from Virginia with Union troops in pursuit. One of these detachments, led by General George Stoneman, swept through upper South Carolina and gave Greenville a firsthand view of a military raid. Their occupation of the town was brief, lasting only one day (May 2) and met no resistance. Even some levity was produced. Caroline Howard Gilman's house of refugee females requested a guard from the Union soldiers, which they promptly received. Albert, one of the Gilman servants, was asked to "take the gentleman's horse." But Albert replied, "I ain't goin' to touch no Yankee horse. Let him hitch him his self."

Greenvillians were generally treated with courtesy by the troops. There was only one death—a drunk who threatened a raider— and one house was set on fire though it did not burn. However, there was a great deal of looting and scouring for valuables. Homes and warehouses were searched for arms and horses, empty shops were pillaged, and treasures sent from the lowcountry for safekeeping were ferreted out, including the $35,000 belonging to the Charleston Bank. The Ladies' Association was wiped out when their storerooms and the Soldier's Rest Hospital were plundered. "Everything was rifled," Gilman wrote in her account. "Books, costly plates, wines, pictures, bed linens thrown in the streets to be picked up by any passerby. All the afternoon we saw white and black, laden with goods, passing by the house."

The storm of Stoneman's raid soon passed, and a certain calm returned, but life was never exactly as it had been before the war. A garrison of federal troops occupied the former Soldier's Rest Hospital on Main Street. Refugee families began returning to their lowcountry homes and repairing their war-torn property. Gradually, many freed

HARDWARE.

JAS. T. WILLIAMS & CO.

MAIN ST.,   GREENVILLE, S. C.

WHOLESALE AND RETAIL DEALERS IN

Guns, Cutlery, Hardware, Mechanics' Tools, Builders'
Hardware, Manufacturers' Supplies, Machinery,
Saws, Fencing, Pumps, Mowers, Reapers,

Binders, Grain Drills, Horse Rakes, Plows, Cultivators,
Force Pumps, Separators, Farm Engines,
Cotton Gins, etc., etc.

In the Latest Improved Agricultural Implements

WE COMPETE WITH MANUFACTURERS.

Above: *Subsistence farming had dominated Greenville's economy in the antebellum era, and it was
only after the introduction of phosphate fertilizer
that full-scale cotton growing became commercially
important. Hardware stores offering every "improved
agricultural implement" bloomed along Main Street
in the postwar years, inviting farmers to inspect the
newest inventions to make their work easier. From
An Illustrated Guide to South Carolina, 1884. Courtesy, Greenville County Library*

Opposite page: *For more than fifty-seven years Miss
Eliza Powell "kept a school" associated with Christ
Church, and for sixty-five years she taught in the
church's Sunday School. Her strength, integrity, and
moral values made "Miss Eliza's" school one of the
most popular in Greenville during the postbellum
era. Courtesy, Greenville Museum of Art*

slaves began to leave their former owners.
Businesses began to shift gears and resume
civilian production. A new era of reconstruction was on the way.

Greenville's Benjamin Perry was appointed
by President Andrew Johnson as provisional
governor of South Carolina, a post he held
from June to December 1865. He was an appropriate political peacemaker, pouring oil
on the troubled waters of postwar confusion
and bitterness. During his brief, tranquil administration, a great deal was accomplished:
a new state constitution was adopted, members of the General Assembly were elected,
civil officers on all levels were restored, and
a new full-term governor was elected. True
to his forward-looking nature, Perry advocated giving the franchise to qualified blacks,
but to no avail. Twentieth-century historian
Allan Nevins has called Perry's view of racial equality "A remarkable attitude for any
Southerner in 1865!"

A keen observer came to Greenville in the
fall of 1866 and remained for fifteen months
as the head of the occupying federal troops
and the Freedman's Bureau. Major John
William De Forest, formerly a professional
writer known for his objectivity, intelligence,
and impatience with stereotypes, gave pierc-
ing and fair-minded insight into everyday
life in Greenville just after war's end. The
officer whom he replaced told him he was
getting the best station in the state. The
people, he said, were "orderly, respectful to
the national authorities, disposed to treat
the Negroes considerately, and, in short,
praiseworthily 'reconstructed.'" With this
positive introduction, De Forest assumed his
post in "the little borough of Greenville,"
which he grew to like in the following months.

De Forest praised the scenery and the
picturesque countryside where he enjoyed
long, solitary walks. The climate pleased
him greatly, as did the Mansion House,
where he boarded for the duration of his

stay in Greenville. He called it "one of the best country hotels then in the South" and compared it quite favorably in quality and expense to similar facilities in New York. As he left the Mansion House and began one of his daily walks up Main Street, De Forest described the scene before him as follows:

... There were some sights worthy of a glance, and perhaps of a smile, in the eight or ten brief streets of the village. There were the two or three leisurely gentlemen who "did the heavy standing round," one in front of his favorite grocery and another at his pet corner. There were those wonderful acrobats, the cows, who climbed into market wagons after ears of corn and bunches of fodder. There were occasional soldiers—

staggering, noisy, quarrelsome, and slovenly, if they had been lately paid off; otherwise, quiet even to demureness, buttoned from waist to chin, and brushed as clean as dandies. Women of the low-down breed, in the coarsest and dirtiest of homespun clothing, and smoking pipes with reed stems and clay bowls straddled by with so mannish a gait that one doubted whether they could be hipped in the feminine model. The young ladies of the respectable class were remarkably tall, fully and finely formed, with good complexions, and of a high average in regard to beauty. The men were of corresponding stature, but in general disproportionately slender, and haggard from overuse of tobacco. At least half of the villagers and nearly all of the country people wore gray or butternut homespun; even Governor Perry, the great man of the place, had his homespun suit and occasionally attended court in it.

De Forest found the worst social feature to be poverty, which was no respecter of race or social status. He was frequently besieged by poor whites and poor blacks for handouts. A May 1867 certified list of destitute citizens in Greenville District totaled 1,311 whites and 978 blacks. That month De Forest had bushels of corn from the federal government to distribute for relief of the destitute. He commented on the desperate economic status of the 400 widows of Confederate soldiers and the countless orphans with no visible means of income. Many old Negroes, he observed, were living on their bankrupted former masters.

De Forest did not feel unwelcome in Greenville; he felt no hatred of northerners directed at him. Despite being a Yankee, a military officer, and a Freedman's Bureau agent, he was invited to breakfasts, teas, dinners, and picnics, much to the credit of both host and guest. He wrote, "It is my belief that if I had set my heart upon it, I

JOHN WILLIAM DE FOREST

John William De Forest, the Union officer who served as head of the Freedman's Bureau in Greenville in 1866-1867, was uniquely qualified to render an impartial and realistic view of life in Reconstruction South Carolina.

A skilled professional writer who had grown up in Connecticut and had traveled extensively in Europe and the Middle East, De Forest had written before the Civil War a history of Connecticut Indians, two travel books about France and Syria, and a fictionalized account of the Salem witchcraft trials. A keen observer who was consistently objective about his subjects, De Forest had completed *Miss Ravenel's Conversion from Secession to Loyalty,* based on his own experiences in the Union army, late in 1865. His army experience, as a captain of the 12th Connecticut regiment, had led him into battle in Florida, Louisiana, and, under Sheridan, in the Valley of the Shenandoah. Invalided out of his regiment because of a wound received in the Mississippi Valley campaign, he had returned to his home in Connecticut to write, but he continued to serve in the Veterans Reserve Corps following the end of the war. Never an abolitionist, he was committed to saving the Union.

But he was more than just a Yankee soldier and published writer. In 1855 he had met Harriet Silliman Shepard, a classics scholar and the daughter of Charles Shepard, an internationally known geologist who served as both a professor of chemistry and natural history at Amherst College and as professor of chemistry at the Medical College of South Carolina. Shepard later became a founder of the state's phospate industry. When the Shepards traveled to Charleston for the winter term, De Forest, who was courting Harriet, accompanied them. He married her the following year, and for most of the next two years they made their home in South Carolina. In fact, they were in Charleston in 1861 and sailed north on the last steamer to leave before the fall of Fort Sumter. Thus De Forest was already acquainted with the manners and traditions of southern society when he arrived in Greenville in October 1866, even if he was not particularly sympathetic to what he called "civlarous southrons."

His position in Greenville was not enviable, although his accommodations at the Mansion House were clearly superior. Except for mere civilities, he was not accepted by local leaders. How objectionable he was he acknowledges: "To my native infamy as a Yankee I added the turpitude of being a United States Military officer and the misdemeanor of being a sub-assistant commissioner of the Freedman's Bureau."

There can be little doubt that he performed his duties faithfully, for his biographer says that he was offered a first lieutenancy in a black regiment of the regular army. He wished to return home to resume his

Author John William De Forest headed the Freedman's Bureau in Greenville during the early days of Reconstruction. From Cirker, Dictionary of American Portraits, *1967. Courtesy, Meserve Collection*

literary labors, however, so he refused the offer and was finally mustered out of the army in January 1868.

The literary labors were those of recording his impressions of life at the Greenville Freedman's Bureau. Five months after his departure he published an article titled "Drawing Bureau Rations" in *Harper's Monthly,* and within a year had finished eight others about aspects of Reconstruction for major magazines. Because of the objectivity, they were popular with neither northerners nor southerners. At the same time he collected his personal record of the war into a manuscript which he titled *A Volunteer's Adventures.* Both book-length manuscripts mouldered in the Yale University library for many years, for neither was published until the 1940s when

they were rediscovered. His articles about his Greenville experiences were published as *A Union Officer during Reconstruction.*

De Forest's reputation in American literature rests primarily on his novel, *Miss Ravenel's Conversion,* which traces the changing attitudes of a young Charleston woman who marries a Connecticut volunteer just before the Civil War. Drawing heavily on his personal experiences, De Forest wrote a remarkably realistic and ironic novel unique not only in its first-hand knowledge of warfare and battle, but also in its rendering of New Orleans during the time of "Beast" Butler, and in its unusual sexual frankness. (The more titillating conversations are, however, written in French.) The influence of W.M. Thackeray's *Vanity Fair* is ob-

vious throughout its pages. The only major Civil War novel to have been written during the war years, *Miss Ravenel's Conversion* is now considered one of the major landmarks in the development of American realism.

In the years following the war, when De Forest returned to Connecticut, he continued to write, often scathing political satires like *Honest John Vane* (1875) which found few readers in America's Gilded Age. He died in 1906, almost unknown to a generation of readers who preferred to read with rose-colored glasses and a kind of sugar coating. For Greenvillians, however, his record of fifteen months in the city's history remains an extraordinarily important historic document.

Judith Gatlin Bainbridge

could have made a footing in Greenville society." However, his chief would not allow the officers to be on familiar terms with the citizens they oversaw.

Perhaps the most appealing part of life in Greenville for De Forest was the Literary Club, which had weekly lectures and a library, both of which he frequented. In general he noted a considerable "bookish, if not literary" element among the leisure people. Musicians, minstrel shows, circuses, drama companies, and other cultural groups often visited the village. These influences, coupled with the scholarly faculties at Furman and the Female College, led De Forest to label Greenville as "the Athens of the upcountry."

Blacks composed approximately one-third of the district's population at this time. (The 1860 census reported 14,631 whites,

7,261 blacks.) With few legal restrictions to hamper their progress, black businessmen and artisans began to carve out a place for themselves in the community. Material progress began to come their way. However, the hurdles of poverty and a lack of education kept many boxed in as laborers and domestics. Emancipation brought freedom, but it did not bring utopia.

As for the relationships between the races, De Forest made the following assessment:

Honesty bids me declare that, in my opinion, no more advantage was taken of the freedmen than a similarly ignorant class would be subjected to in any other region where poverty should be pinching and the danger of starvation is imminent. So far as my observation goes, the Southerner was

Above: *James Rosemond was a literate slave who preached to congregations both black and white before and during the Civil War. At the conclusion of the conflict he organized John Wesley Methodist Church and sixteen others in upstate South Carolina. Courtesy, Greenville Urban League*

Opposite page: *In 1873* Harper's Weekly *reporter Edward King attended Greenville's first agricultural fair, where he sketched the crowd which gathered to watch a horse race. Area schools were dismissed for the event, which also featured stock judging and prizes for the largest vegetables and most elegant needlework. King praised the climate, scenery, and "reconstructed" attitudes of Greenville residents in his book,* The Great South. *From King,* The Great South, *1874*

not hostile toward the Negro as a Negro, but only as a possible officeholder, as a juror, as a voter, as a political and social equal. He might cuff him, as he would his dog, into what he calls "his place"; but he was not vindicative toward him for being free, and he was willing to give him a chance in life.

De Forest went on to say that the black was neither vicious nor irrational, as some reactionary journals claimed. However, in his opinion, he was "very ignorant, somewhat improvident, not yet aware of the necessity of persistent industry, and is in short a grown-up child."

Perhaps the most determined assistance for freedmen came from within their own ranks. Charles Hopkins, a former slave himself, founded the Negro Elementary School in 1866, with the help of two assistants, Lewis Rivers and Cecil Coleman. During that summer they taught spelling and reading to some sixty black students, initially using a deserted hotel room as a classroom. When the hotel reclaimed the room, Hopkins appealed to the community for support in establishing a more permanent facility. Through his enthusiasm and reliable nature, he raised a subscription of $260, no mean feat considering the impoverished nature of most Greenville citizens at that time. He purchased an old storehouse which had belonged to the former state arsenal works, leased a lot on Laurens Street, and gathered a group of freedmen to dismantle the building, move it across town and reassemble it on its new location. The deed was done but the debt was great. Costs ran over budget to twice the amount raised in the subscription. Times were tough; Rivers and Coleman had to abandon ship after several months with no income. But Hopkins was persistent and finally successful. Late in the year the New York Missionary School financed two white

Silver Hill Methodist Episcopal Church was the first black congregation organized in Greenville after the Civil War. Its first building was erected at Choice and Cleveland streets on land reputedly donated by Alexander McBee. In 1900 the church, now John Wesley United Methodist, moved to its current location (pictured here) at Court and Spring streets. It was extensively renovated in 1980-1981 with financial assistance from the City of Greenville. Photo by Bob Bainbridge

Mattoon Presbyterian Church at 415 Hampton Avenue was built in 1887 to house a black congregation organized by B.F. McDowell in 1878. The church was named for the Reverend S.M. Mattoon and was a continuing part of the movement to establish separate black churches in the postwar years. Photo by Bob Bainbridge

teachers who joined Hopkins and taught the upper classes of geography, arithmetic, English grammar, and writing. Textbooks were supplied by a leading New York publisher. By late 1867 two more white teachers had joined the staff and enrollment had reached 300 students.

Another school which grew into Sterling Institute (later High School) was established through the generosity of a Boston family. This school was an important institution in the black community for more than a century.

The religious community was another area of growing independence for blacks. Freedmen withdrew from white churches they had formerly attended and established their own congregations and leaders. Black Methodists, led by the Reverend J.R. Rosemond, founded John Wesley Methodist Episcopal Church in 1866. Springfield Baptist Church, organized by the Reverend Gabriel Poole in 1868, drew some eighty-five members from First Baptist Church. Both Rosemond and Poole were outstanding community leaders for many years after the war, positive Christian influences who were respected by whites as well as blacks. Other denominations gradually took hold: Mattoon Presbyterian Church (1878), established by B.F. McDowell; Allen Temple-African Methodist Episcopal (1879), by W.D. Hambert; and Leon Baptist Church (1882), by the Reverend J.A. Pinsen.

Political participation by blacks was limited to a small inner circle conspicuously led by Wilson Cook. De Forest called the North Carolina immigrant "the most notable colored man in his district." An intelligent businessman with savvy and strong character, Cook was active in politics in the late 1860s and early 1870s. He served as a delegate to the 1867 Constitutional Convention in Charleston and in 1868 was elected to the South Carolina House of Representatives.

Cook's political career waned after the election of 1876, but he remained a large property holder and an important community figure.

Greenville began economic postwar recovery with relative ease. In 1869 it was officially designated a city by the General Assembly, leaving village mentality behind. Hamlin Beattie founded the National Bank of Greenville in 1872. The same year the Greenville Cotton Oil Company was established to capitalize on cotton production. With the coming of a second railroad, the Atlanta and Charlotte line (later Richmond and Danville and Southern Railroad), new doors of trade were opened. The completion of this railroad in 1874, with its depot on West Washington Street, was due largely to the efforts of General William King Easley.

These early postwar years found the modern textile industry getting a firm toehold in the community. The presence of a willing labor force and a plentiful water supply encouraged northern entrepreneurs as well as local businessmen to invest in the expansion of cotton mills. Conditions were ripe. In 1873 a group of New England investors joined young Vardry McBee in establishing Vardry Mill on old Pearis land at Reedy Falls. This grew into Camperdown Mill by 1875, the first textile plant to operate within the city limits. The next venture was a purely local and highly auspicious one. Colonel Henry P. Hammett, native son and part owner of Batesville Mill, led a group in financing the Piedmont Manufacturing Company, which opened on the Saluda River with 5,000 spindles and 112 looms. Historian Felicia Furman Dryden sees the establishment of this mill as "the turning point for the textile industry in Greenville County." Its success convinced other local banks, lawyers, and merchants who had little experience in manufacturing to build more mills in the county. It inspired local investment

Above: *Excess in everything, including plants, was a hallmark of successful businessmen who flourished with the textile trade. Built on Augusta Street about 1868 for William Wilkins by builder James Cagle, this home was the city's social center for many years. Peacocks strutted on the gracious lawns as Greenvillians of wealth gathered beneath the crystal chandeliers. Today the Wilkins house is the Jones Mortuary. Courtesy, Oscar Landing*

Left: *Wade Hampton III, a direct descendant of the Hampton family which had been massacred by the Cherokees in 1776, won the governorship for the Democrats in 1876. A political moderate who had been a Confederate cavalry general under Jeb Stuart, Hampton and his "Red Shirts" were supported by Benjamin Perry and by most voters—both black and white—in the upcountry. From Wellman,* Giant in Gray, *1949*

and therefore assured further economic expansion.

The election of 1876, a landmark event in South Carolina political history, affected Greenville as it did the rest of the state. General Wade Hampton III ran for governor on the Democratic ticket against carpetbag Republican incumbent Daniel Chamberlain. Hampton advocated moderation, nonviolence, and fairness to blacks. Encouraged by former Governor Benjamin Perry, Greenville actively supported Hampton's candidacy. An enthusiastic "Hampton Day" rally was held in the city on September 5. A holiday spirit was evident as an afternoon crowd of 5,000 gathered to watch a parade of 1,500 mounted men escort Hampton through the streets. That evening a "brilliant, noisy, memorable" meeting was held at which a large number of black men were present.

When election day came in November, Hampton carried Greenville County by a 2,446-vote majority, but the results were less clear in other parts of the state. Because of fraud on both sides, the election was contested. Both parties claimed victory and installed their officials, each set of rivals claiming to have been duly elected. Federal troops, sent to Greenville on October 17 to assure election day calm, remained for several months. Confusion reigned across the state. Finally, the South Carolina Supreme Court upheld Hampton's election and he officially became governor in April 1877.

Meanwhile, similar confusion prevailed in the disputed 1876 presidential election. When it was resolved, with Rutherford B. Hayes becoming president, the new Republican administration withdrew occupying troops from the South. The last army troops departed Greenville on April 19, 1877. With no military forces to back up his gubernatorial claim, Chamberlain and the radical claimants withdrew their efforts to control the state government. Wade Hampton was

Running on Wade Hampton's Democratic reform ticket, Greenvillian Hugh Smith Thompson was elected state superintendent of education in 1876. Working to establish "separate but equal" schools for both white and black children, Thompson was responsible for setting up the state's system of free public education. He served as governor from 1882 to 1886, when he became assistant secretary of the U.S. Treasury. From An Illustrated Guide to South Carolina, *1884. Courtesy, Greenville County Library*

clearly the winner.

With the victory of Hampton's Democratic ticket, several Greenvillians were swept into important state offices: Joseph Earle was elected attorney general and Hugh Smith Thompson became state superintendent of education. On the local level Perry D. Gilreath was elected sheriff, a position he held with distinction for the remainder of the century.

The days of Reconstruction were over. Greenville was on its feet with a sound economy, wise leaders, and a future full of promise.

The delivery team for Finlay's Grocery Store takes a rest during a quiet moment on North Main Street in 1902. Signs of progress are evident everywhere as commercial buildings press in upon the remaining residences, streetcar tracks are installed, new granite curbs and gutters trim the edges of the dirt street, and electrical poles line the thoroughfare. Courtesy, Gene Eckford/The Coxe Collection

CHAPTER FOUR

A SLEEPING GIANT
(1877-1905)

The closing quarter of the nine-teenth century was not a glamorous time, but it found Greenville growing in strength and stability, building muscles that it would flex with the dawning of the twentieth century. Just as hibernating bears and sleeping giants do not reveal their true potential, Greenville had not yet tested its full powers. An even, slumbering tenor permeated the 1877-1905 era, despite the growth and progress quietly taking place.

The population increased rapidly. The greatest surge came between 1870 and 1880 when the total county population jumped from 22,262 to 37,494; included in that total were blacks, whose numbers more than doubled from 7,141 to 14,511. The increases abated somewhat, but population continued to grow. By 1900 the city claimed 11,857 people, the county 53,487. Business, transporta-

tion, industry, and colleges were attracting more and more people to the Greenville area.

In an 1882 address Benjamin Perry advised Carolinians to educate the masses, work hard, industrialize, and seek northern money to develop southern resources. His hometown took him seriously, acting out this "New South" philosophy in the following years. Literature and the arts took a back seat; industry and economic advance became tin gods. As historian Albert Sanders explained, "Defeat, poverty, frustration, the wearying sense of being eternally on the defensive stifled the creative spirit, and Greenville yielded to the demands of a materialistic era."

With the departure of the Baptist seminary and its faculty (1877) and the death of Benjamin Perry (1886), there was room for new local leadership. The void was soon filled by a group of mill and economic promoters including Captain Ellison Adger Smyth, Daniel Augustus Tompkins, Francis J. Pelzer, and Lewis W. Parker. Economic influence became tantamount to leadership in the community. A new war was being waged against the North, this one purely economic. The textile industry was the battlefield; spindles and bobbins were the weapons; effective leadership and investments were crucial. In this postbellum mood, Greenville submerged itself in the textile movement.

New mills sprung up like mushrooms. In 1880 Pelham Mills was incorporated near old Batesville Mill. Two years later Ellison Adger Smyth and Francis J. Pelzer opened Pelzer Mills with 10,000 spindles. The second plant in town was Huguenot Mill, which began operations in 1882 near its predecessor, Camperdown. Lewis W. Parker came from Abbeville to practice law but instead became president of Parker Cotton Mill Company, with a capital of fifteen million

dollars. With his innovative leadership, the mill soon controlled one million spindles, more than any other company in the nation. Lanneau Manufacturing Company was built in 1894 but was later destroyed by fire. 1895 was a record year with American Spinning Company, Mills Manufacturing Company, F.W. Poe Manufacturing Company, and Victor Cotton Mill (in Greer) all getting off the ground. Five years later came Monaghan Mills, Brandon Mills, and Franklin Mill (in Greer). The Woodside Brothers organized Woodside Mill in 1902; the next year McGee Manufacturing Company was established. The ball was rolling and textiles—ownership, manufacturing, and influence—would dominate Greenville for years to come.

As early as 1882 Greenville County employed more "hands"—as workers were called—in cotton mills than any other county in the state (1,250, including children). Nationally, South Carolina ranked third, be-

Left: *Founded in the 1880s, the Huguenot Cotton Mill was the last textile manufacturing plant built in downtown Greenville at the Reedy River. After more than twenty years of successful operation, it was unable to compete with the huge new mills built outside the city limits, and it closed suddenly in 1907, to be replaced by an apparel factory owned by philanthropist Fred Symmes. The building still stands on Broad Street. Courtesy, Greenville County Library*

Below: *From the English midlands to New England to the Carolina piedmont, the textile industry was a migrant one, consistent only in its search for waterpower and cheap labor. Greenville County's earliest "cotton factories" were founded by northerners Thomas Hutchings and William Bates. After the Civil War, Henry Hammett chartered his Piedmont Mill in 1873 with local capital but with the same need for waterpower and child labor. Courtesy, Joe Jordan*

Right: *One of the finest remaining turn-of-the-century commercial buildings in downtown Greenville, the Huguenot Mill Office was for many years the office of Nuckassee Manufacturing Company president Fred Symmes. Donated to the Greenville County Historic Preservation Commission in 1979 by Morris Weisz, the building was restored in 1980 and now houses the Greenville Central Area Partnership, Inc. Photo by Bob Bainbridge*

Below: *The Greenville Board of Trade boosted Greenville, "the pearl of the Piedmont," in a 1901 publication which invited diversification but pointed with pride to its active cotton mills. While it is no longer "untrammelled by Labor Laws," many of the same inducements—climate, abundant water, and good transportation—are used today to attract northern industry to the county. Courtesy, Greenville County Library*

Whirr of Many Wheels.

Textile Interests.

ALL conditions conspire to make Greenville a cotton mill center. We have unrivalled water powers, cheap fuel, abundant and contented native labor, which is untrammelled by Labor Laws or Unions, cheap mill sites and mild climate, with low freight rates and rapid service guaranteed by the competition of three leading railroads. The growth of the cotton manufacturing movement is seen in the following statement of mills which contribute directly to Greenville's prosperity:

MILLS	Capital Stock	Looms	Spindles	No. Ops.	Estb.	Cap'ln. per Spn'l
Victor Manufacturing Company,	$350 000	700	27 000	325	1896	$13.10
Mills Manufacturing Company,	371.000	734	27,000	500	1895	13.74
Monaghan Mills,	450,000	700	25,000	300	1901	17.93
Brandon Mills,	220,000	320	15,200	150	1901	13.81
Reedy River Factory,	178.375	372	12,360	275	1840	14.43
Huguenot Mills,	75 000	305	6.000	250	1883	12 50
F. W. Poe Manufacturing Company,	500,000	1,455	53,760	900	1895	9.62
Carolina Mills;	50.000		5,600	80	1901	8 92
American Spinning Company,	350,000	328	21.652	500	1895	16.69
Piedmont Manufacturing Company,	800.000	2,000	64,000	1,500	1873	12.48
Pelzer Manufacturing Company,	1,000,000	3,200	120,000	2,800	1883	8.33
*Pelham Manufacturing Company,	300,000		11,000	300	1882	27.27
Batesville Factory,	65,000		2.600	65		25.00
Franklin Mills,	65,000		5,000	100	1900	13.00
Fountain Inn Mills,	50,000		7,500	65	1893	6 66
Fork Shoals,	33,200		2,848	50	1900	11.65
	$4 857,575	10,114	406,520	8,180		

As will be seen ten mills have been built since 1895, adding to the amount already invested $2,539,200 capital stock in the county.

*Pelham has also 100 knitting machines for hosiery.

hind Massachusetts and North Carolina; within the state, Greenville was in the textile vanguard. Most employees were poor and white, refugees from the nearby farms and mountains. In 1905 recruiters from many mills went into the mountains of western North Carolina and Georgia seeking workers and promising a better life. A "great migration" of families resulted, providing a ready labor force to run the mills. Pay was low, illiteracy was high. Jobs were often boring and tedious, but they were steady and secure. Paternalistic management provided housing and virtually all other necessities in mill villages which surrounded the plant. A

Paternalistic mill owners financed schools, churches, and even recreation centers to attract workers from nearby mountain communities. Some of these Woodside School children, pictured circa 1915, would later enter Parker High School; many more would become mill hands like their parents. Courtesy, South Carolina Historical Society

ELLISON ADGER SMYTH

The "Dean of Southern Cotton Manufacturers," Ellison Adger Smyth was born in Charleston in 1847 of a substantial family which traced its roots from Irish textile mill owners. Educated in private schools in Charleston and for a year at the Citadel before joining the Confederate army in 1864 when he was sixteen, Smyth exemplifies of the lowcountry commercial men who became the manufacturing leaders of the upstate after the Civil War.

Gaining his title, "The Captain," from his leadership of a Rifle Company formed to keep order in Charleston during the early days of Reconstruction, Smyth was made a partner in his family's wholesale firm, J.E. Adger & Co., in 1869. That business went bankrupt, however, and Smyth, who had never been inside a textile mill, decided to embark on a new venture with a long-time friend, F.J. Pelzer. Together they established the Pelzer Mill on the banks of the Saluda River with 10,000 spindles and a capital investment of $400,000. A potent force in the New South's surging industrial growth, Smyth, who served as president and treasurer of Pelzer for forty-three years, worked diligently to bring new inventions and improved living conditions to the mills and mill villages he established.

The "Captain" brought to Pelzer the first incandescent lights ever installed in a mill, the first electric drives, and ordered the first Draper looms for the mill which opened in 1881.

Ellison Adger Smyth, pictured circa 1930, was considered the "Dean of Southern Cotton Manufacturers." Courtesy, Greenville County Library

Three additional mills were built at Pelzer, and by the mid-1890s the number of spindles had increased to 136,000 and stock was valued at one million dollars. Recruiting workers for his mills from the Appalachian foothills and the mountain country, he added training programs to teach employees to use the sophisticated new machinery, and provided schools, churches, a library, social hall, YMCA, roller skating rink, and a military company. Smyth did not believe in company stores, but he did set up banks so that employees would be encouraged to save their money. In 1923, when he sold Pelzer for nine million dollars, he left a mill village with a population of

5,000 people.

Smyth made his home in Greenville for forty years while he ran and organized mills throughout the upstate. At the invitation of residents, he began the Belton Mill in 1899 and organized the Bank of Belton, which he headed until 1920. In Greenville he organized the Chicora Savings Bank and purchased a 75 percent interest in the Greenville *News,* which he owned for seventeen years, and from which he received no salary or dividends, preferring instead to improve the facilities of the newspaper. In addition to Belton, he organized or reorganized cotton mills in Greenwood, Anderson, and Ninety-Six, as well as the Dunean Mill in Greenville.

By the time he was sixty, Captain Smyth in effect controlled the textile industry of the upstate: he was a director of half a dozen banks and thirty-six corporations, including the Brandon Mill, Woodruff Mills, Saxon Mills, Victor Manufacturing, Union Bleachery, Alice Manufacturing, and Ninety-Six, Dunean, and Conestee mills. At the conclusion of World War I, *Commerce and Finance Magazine* called him "one of the few remaining links between the Old and the New South."

A paternalist who was against child labor, in favor of compulsory schooling, and an avid reader, Smyth sold his holdings in South Carolina in the mid-1920s and planned to retire to his summer home, "Connemara," (later the home of Carl Sandburg) in Flat Rock, North

Carolina. That retirement was short-lived, for he almost immediately established Balfour Mills in Henderson County, and in November 1930, when the banking system collapsed in western North Carolina, began the State Trust Company in order to provide banking facilities for the depression-hit region. He was still working full-time in his Balfour Mills office at eighty-eight. He had created a textile fortune and had been responsible, nearly single-handedly, for the rebirth of upstate South Carolina. He left behind him a textile dynasty: two sons-in-law and four grandsons were deeply involved in cotton manufacturing. His great-grandsons, Ellison S. McKissick, Jr. and Foster McKissick, are Greenville business leaders today.

Judith Gatlin Bainbridge

new social class of mill workers or "lint heads" had been created. Their labor fueled the flourishing Greenville economy but they were not considered on a social par with the bankers, merchants, and professionals who prospered most from their presence.

Batesville Mill continued to make history with its new leadership. In 1890 Mary Putnam Gridley became the first female mill president in South Carolina, and possibly the first in the nation, when she inherited the Batesville establishment from her father, George Putnam. She ran the business successfully for twenty-two years, signing all correspondence "M.P. Gridley." She said it was no one's business whether she was a man or a woman. Gridley was interested in the community, remaining active for many years in cultural and civic affairs after she retired from Batesville.

Greenville's downtown area took on more life and activity during the 1880s and 1890s. Established hotels and livery stables were joined by a new opera house and city hall. The initiation of telephone service and home mail delivery made 1882 an auspicious year for city dwellers. A decade later a rambling red brick Victorian post office was built on the corner of Main and Broad streets. Designed by Joseph Lawrence, the distinctive building quickly became the city's architectural landmark. Later it became City Hall, before its demolition, amid great controversy, in the 1970s.

However, one important city benefit was missing: a public water supply. Two businessmen, Mssrs. Ferguson and Miller, installed a pipeline in 1887 from a spring on Spring Street to a wooden tank on the roof of their general merchandise store at the corner of Main and Washington. The apparatus supplied water for their store and a few neighboring merchants, but only briefly. The tank and the building soon burned and the effort collapsed. However, the merchants

This striking photograph shows the 1973 demolition of the old City Hall with the new one behind it. The destruction of the Victorian Romanesque structure, built in 1892, stirred controversy between preservationists and city officials. Photo by Joe Jordan

Page 95: *Mary Putnam Gridley (center) and her sisters posed in 1905 for this domestic family scene. One of the very few female textile mill presidents, M.P. Gridley, as she signed herself, also started the Thursday Club, the oldest women's study group in the city, and worked hard to establish a tuberculosis hospital. Courtesy, John Baker Cleveland*

had liked their taste of running water and sought a more abundant supply. Albion A. Gates (entrepreneur and manager of the Mansion House) went to Philadelphia, where he persuaded the American Pipe Manufacturing Company to visit Greenville and design a water system. They came and built the Paris Mountain Water Company, which had dams and reservoirs on Paris Mountain, and pressure, filter, and steam pumps on Richland Creek. The sweet, abundant water that had attracted early settlers to the area was now readily available. The water was so pure that no sterilization was applied until 1917. It has long been one of Greenville's primary attractions.

Maintaining law and order was no easy task in those days of economic change and shifting mores. Enlightened and effective law enforcement officers were hard to find, but Greenville was blessed with one—Perry D. Gilreath, who served as sheriff for a record twenty-four years (1876-1900). He was a quiet, almost gentle man with unquestioned courage that stood him well in every danger. So seldom was he armed, Gilreath became known as "the sheriff who never carried a gun." Instead, he used common sense, fairness, and a reputation for keeping his word as his weapons.

Sheriff Gilreath enforced all laws, protected all prisoners. He even withstood the wrath of lynch mobs, appealing to their sense of reason and logic. The story is told of one such incident in the 1880s when Gilreath and his one-deputy staff (his son, J.D. Gilreath) faced an angry mob who wanted to steal from the jail a black prisoner named Andrews accused of murder in the Simpsonville area. Stalling for time, Gilreath talked to the crowd in front of the jail while deputy J.D. slipped the prisoner out the back door and hid him in the courthouse overnight.

The mob was not satisfied, however; they

Some Greenvillians may still remember when City Hall stood on the northeast corner of Laurens Street and McBee Avenue, with its fire station and police department adjoining. The pride of the city in the 1880s, by 1910 the building had been overshadowed by the Victorian splendor of the Federal Post Office, yet it continued to be used until the 1930s before it became a victim of progress. From An Illustrated Guide to South Carolina, *1884. Courtesy, Greenville County Library*

Above: *"High Sheriff" of Greenville County from 1876 to 1900, P.D. Gilreath was a successful farmer who had grown up on a plantation on the Tyger River. Elected on the same Democratic ticket that swept Wade Hampton into the governor's office, Sheriff Gilreath stood for law and order but never carried a gun. From John H. Gilreath,* P.D. Gilreath, High Sheriff, *1968. Courtesy, Earline Gilreath White*

Left: *While Greenville's 1892 City Hall was destroyed in 1973, the building's elaborately carved finial still holds a place of honor behind the First National Bank Building at Elford Street across from Springwood Cemetery. Its decorated terra cotta top may remind some of a fire hydrant, but others treasure its placement as a reminder of what used to be. Photo by Bob Bainbridge*

returned later that night demanding their man. According to a Greenville *News* account, Gilreath calmly addressed the group in these words: "Men, I cannot tell who you are with those hoods on, but I'll tell you this, I am going to see that Andrews is hung after due process of law and if you want to attend the hanging, come up here and give me your name and you will be invited to the hanging." There were no takers in the crowd. One spokesman replied for all, "We know Perry Gilreath never made a promise he did not keep, so let's go home."

Eventually, the suspect was convicted of the crime and sentenced to be hung. Sheriff Gilreath flung open the trap door himself. Justice was done within the law; mob control had been averted. But few lawmen of the day took so courageous or dangerous a stand as did Perry Gilreath.

The "High Sheriff" was respected and accepted even in the Dark Corner section of the county where independence was fierce and meddlers from outside not generally tolerated. As one 1891 newspaper account related, "The authority of Sheriff Gilreath is yet recognized because he is personally popular, but [Governor] Benjamin R. Tillman and [President] Grover Cleveland are out of date and persons claiming to represent them may expect to be regarded and treated as suspicious strangers."

Sheriff Gilreath may have known the boundaries of so-called Dark Corner, but, if so, he was the only one, for it is an amorphous region somewhere in the general vicinity of Glassy Mountain Township. Outsiders can never quite locate it. Ask a passerby and he will say it's "just over the next hill." Ask again, and its "down the road apiece," just behind you. Nevertheless, it does exist and inhabitants once had a rough-and-tumble reputation for drinking whiskey, toting guns, and fighting hard amidst their sylvan mountain setting.

The name comes from an incident said to have occurred at a Chestnut Springs political rally just after the Civil War. One speaker, who was obviously not pleasing the crowd, happened to be standing on a road cart giving his talk. Two displeased listeners disposed of the lecturer by picking up the shafts of the cart and running with it. The speaker fell off, dusted himself off, and muttered something to the effect that the locals were "in the dark" and didn't understand what was going on in the world. The appellation stuck and that corner of the county was thereafter referred to as "Dark Corner."

Rich soil along the mountain streams and coves in the Dark Corner area gave rise to an abundant growth of corn and vegetables. The sale of corn as a retail crop was not particularly profitable (fifty to sixty cents per bushel), but if it was ground into meal and distilled into moonshine whiskey, the profit margin was improved. A bushel of corn would yield two and a half gallons of whiskey, which sold for one dollar per gallon. Two and a half dollars felt much better in the pocket than sixty cents. Moonshiners generally netted about twenty-five dollars daily. Nevertheless, the economic impetus for the whiskey stills did not lessen the negative side effects: accidents, fights, murders, and general lawlessness.

Writing of his upbringing in the Dark Corner area, J. Dean Crain, a noted minister and educator, ruminated that the geographical area is not dark by nature, because nowhere is the sun brighter, the hills bluer, the sky clearer, the hills more picturesque, or the creeks more sparkling. "It is Dark Corner," he said, "because of what men have done, men ruled by sin and ungovernable passions born of ignorance, men blind to the common blessings of the beauties of life have made it the Dark Corner."

Schooling of any kind was late and slow

MARTIN F. ANSEL

Adopted Greenvillian Martin F. Ansel led an exemplary life of public service for more than sixty years, serving his county and state in all three branches of government. Evidence of the great respect in which he was held is the number of babies who were named for him. It has been said that he had more namesakes than any man who ever lived in Greenville County.

Ansel was one of several children born to Johann Jakob and Frederica Katherine Bauer Ansel, who were natives of Germany. They immigrated to Philadelphia and then to Charleston, where Martin was born on December 12, 1850. In the wake of a yellow fever scare the family later moved to the upcountry, settling in Walhalla. Ansel attended the local schools but any hope of a college education was dashed by the outbreak of the Civil War. However, after the war he studied law under Major James H. Whitner. In 1870, at the tender age of twenty, he was admitted to the bar and thus launched his long and successful career.

After living briefly in North Carolina, Ansel moved to Greenville in 1876 and made it his home for the rest of his long life. He was an ardent supporter of Wade Hampton in his campaign for governor that year. Perhaps this taste of political life dictated his later participation in the governmental world. While serving as Greenville's city attorney in 1880, Ansel compiled a publication containing the city's charter, its amendments, and the city ordi-

Greenvillian Martin F. Ansel served as governor from 1907 to 1911. The Greenville Chamber of Commerce boasted in 1911 that his "residence here speaks as highly for the city to the outside world as any other fact in all the branches of social, industrial, and professional life in the city." From The Gateway to Get There, *1911. Courtesy, Greenville County Library*

nances. The political bug bit him in earnest in 1882 when he was elected to the South Carolina House of Representatives from Greenville County. He was reelected in 1884 and 1886, serving a total of three terms. In 1888 he was elected solicitor of the Eighth Judicial Circuit, a post which he held until 1901, gaining esteem and substantial statewide attention.

Ansel married Ophelia Anne Speights in February 1878. She was the daughter of Archibald McBride Speights, then owner and editor of the Greenville

News. Of their five children, only two lived to adulthood: Gertrude and Frederica. After the death of his wife in 1895, Ansel later married a widow from Pickens, Mrs. Adelaide Rosamond Hollingsworth Harris. It was the second Mrs. Ansel who became first lady of the state.

Undaunted by an unsuccessful gubernatorial bid in 1902, Ansel was elected governor as a Democrat in 1906 from a field of eight candidates in the primary. He was reelected in 1908, defeating Cole L. Blease. His administration was one of steady progress; there were no flashy programs, Ansel explained, simply "straightforward, honest and businesslike" accomplishments. He stood for temperance, urging the General Assembly to repeal the State Dispensary Law and substitute county option on the liquor question. He also stood for improved education on all levels. The governor made a personal visit to almost every public school in the state and encouraged the establishment of 150 additional high schools. Dr. S. C. Mitchell, then president of the University of South Carolina, declared, "This alone is an achievement of which any executive might well be proud and which will give the administration a permanent place in the history of the state for all time."

Honoring heroes and improving the quality of state property were also important to Governor Ansel. In his inaugural address in January 1907 he called for continued pensions to Confederate veterans and the placement of a statue of John C. Calhoun in the U.S. Capitol's Hall of Fame. (The marble statue of Calhoun was unveiled in Washington in 1910.) During his administration the first steps were taken to landscape and beautify the grounds of the State House and to improve the residence of the state's "first family." The Ansel contributions live on in many ways.

As chief executive Ansel not only attended the first Governor's Conference called by President Theodore Roosevelt at the White House in 1908, but served on its executive committee. He was asked to deliver a paper at that same conference in 1910, "A Brief Review of the Law of Extradi-

tion." It was well received, reprinted in pamphlet form and widely distributed, expanding his reputation beyond the boundaries of the state.

Returning to Greenville after leaving the Governor's Mansion, Ansel resumed an active law practice. Yet, at the same time, he continued his enthusiasm for the national Democratic party, making campaign tours in the northern and midwestern states in 1912 and 1916 on behalf of Woodrow Wilson and other Democratic candidates. When the Greenville County Court was established in 1920, Ansel was elected judge and he served in that capacity until his retirement, at age eighty-four, in 1934.

Ansel also followed literary, humanitarian, and religious

pursuits. He was a member of "The 39 Club," a literary organization for men in Greenville. He was a loyal member and elder of the First Presbyterian Church and instrumental in the establishment of Greenville's hospital system. For forty years he was a member of the Board of Trustees of the Thornwell Orphanage in Clinton, S.C., and served as its chairman in his later years.

On his landmark birthdays, Ansel was hailed by newspapers across the state as a wise elder statesman. He died on August 24, 1945, at his Greenville home, at the age of ninety-four. The former judge, legislator, and governor is buried at Springwood Cemetery.

Nancy Vance Ashmore

---

in coming to this part of the county. Crain remembers when the first school—an academy, North Greenville High School—opened in Tigerville in 1893. "People outside the mountains cannot understand the magnitude of this undertaking," he explained in his autobiography, *A Mountain Boy's Life Story*. It was a meager beginning taken on by the North Greenville Baptist Association to combat the ignorance, fear, and superstition of the area. It has done just that. The institution has steadily grown, adding a junior college in 1934 and gaining accreditation in 1957. The minds and habits of the region were tamed and trained, becoming less dark all the time.

At the opposite end of the county is another elusive region generally known as Possum Kingdom. Boundaries are vague; exact

locations impossible to pinpoint. Nevertheless, it is a rich farming area in the southern reaches of the county, home of the Peden clan from early days. Human outsiders have difficulty in learning the area, but the nocturnal animals for whom it is named no doubt know it well.

Nearby, a farm-oriented tradition began in the mid-1880s and continued for some sixty years as an important annual event. The Fairview Stock and Agricultural Show began as a fair for displaying better methods of farming and stock rearing, a move toward progressive farming. Apparently the movement gained momentum when former members of the Ku Klux Klan "desired to do something of lasting value for the community." They sponsored the organization of a club to promote the general welfare of

Above: *The "hero of the Dark Corner," Rev. A.D. Bowers preached throughout the mountain region for forty years without salary. J.D. Crain said of mountain preachers like Bowers, "It will take all eternity to know the good [they] have done...They traveled fearlessly every hog path in the mountains of Greenville County." From J.D. Crain,* A Mountain Boy's Life Story, *1914*

Above right: *An 1880s tin-type reveals the features of Dudley Talley, the former slave who controlled much of the "draying and hacking" business in Greenville in the years following Reconstruction. Supreme Court decisions and segregation ordinances gradually isolated successful black entrepreneurs like Talley from the white community. Courtesy, Greenville Urban League*

farmers in the area. The first show was held on Dunbar's lawn in Fairview Township near Fairview Presbyterian Church in 1886. The affair was popular and new events were continually added, including horse racing, 4-H exhibits, grandstand events, and exhibits of cookery, needlework, and agricultural equipment. Officials claim that the early October event was never marred by bad weather or serious accident.

Consistent with the general pattern of southern history, blacks in Greenville enjoyed a certain latitude in economic and social actions in the latter years of the nineteenth century. While racial segregation was generally practiced on a social level, there were virtually no legal restrictions on the business, housing, and schooling of blacks. Black-owned businesses were common, established by industrious, independent, reliable men. Dudley Talley, a former slave, became the first black in town to operate a hacking business. Others followed in his footsteps, giving blacks a monopoly on that type of business until after the turn of the century. In fact, in 1896 only one white person, Hamp Turner, was engaged in the transportation/hacking field. Other businesses such as barbering, blacksmithing, and catering were controlled by blacks, who also made strong inroads into grocery retailing, general merchandising, meat marketing, brick manufacturing, and the dispensing of drugs. Such businesses were scattered throughout the city with no restriction on their location. As early as 1880 there were five black barbers and one black-operated restaurant on Main Street. These black businessmen formed their own local unions (one for barbers, one for carpenters, and one for bricklayers by 1888) and other professional and benevolent organizations.

There were a surprising number of black property owners and a few who achieved great wealth. In 1881 twenty-one black individuals in the vicinity paid taxes ranging from $200 to $2,300 on real and personal property. Former Representative Wilson Cook paid $2,300 on his possessions. A reporter for the Greenville *Enterprise* claimed that in 1880 Greenville led all South Carolina counties in the percentage of blacks owning farms and homes, with 16 percent ownership. Five other counties were tied for a distant second place, each with only 5 percent ownership.

Housing patterns in the city appear to have been unique to Greenville, according to

Early railroad lines, lured to Greenville by Vardry McBee, improved the county's access to coastal ports and southern urban centers. Individual lines struggled through the economic problems of Reconstruction before being unified into great systems such as the Southern Railway Company, whose busy yards on Washington Street are depicted circa 1895. Courtesy, E.D. Sloan

The Carolina, Knoxville and Western Railway Company crossed the Blue Ridge Mountains by the late 1880s. The line followed the Reedy River west from Greenville through Travelers Rest and Cleveland to River Falls. Principally a logging railroad, it was named the "Swamp Rabbit" because of its low-lying route and the many dips and twists in its track. Engine #110 is seen circa 1968. Photo by Joe Jordan

Opposite page: *Sashes, blinds, insurance, hauling—Gower and Reilly did it all, as this 1884 advertisement proudly proclaims. Most important for the city's growth, however, was their "omnibus" business, which met trains and provided the increasingly commercial Main Street area with customers from throughout the city. From* An Illustrated Guide to South Carolina, *1884. Courtesy, Greenville County Library*

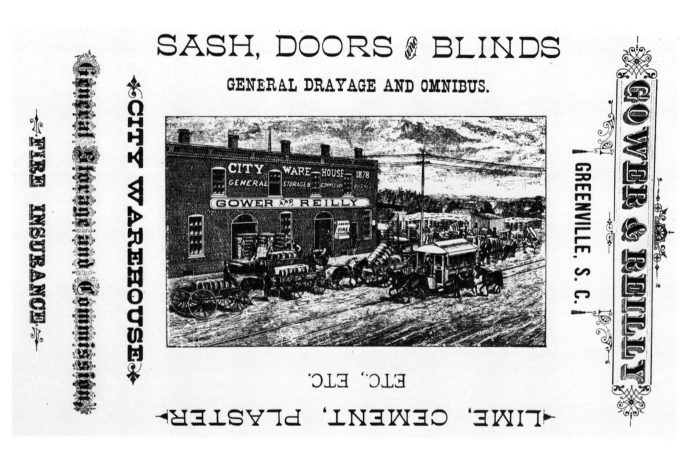

SASH, DOORS & BLINDS

GENERAL DRAYAGE AND OMNIBUS.

FIRE INSURANCE.

General Storage and Commission.

CITY WAREHOUSE

GOWER & REILLY

GREENVILLE, S. C.

LIME, CEMENT, PLASTER.

ETC, ETC.

J.D. Mathis, a student of local race relations. Negro communities were located adjacent to former manor houses; domestics and servants lived in rented or purchased homes in close proximity to their former masters. Blacks lived on almost every street and in every section of town; there was a definite salt-and-pepper flavor.

Perhaps these living arrangements contributed to lingering control that whites maintained over blacks in the community. Subtle influences on black voters and businessmen eroded any real power they might have exerted. Toward the end of the century, advances made by blacks in the commercial world began to slip. As some of the older and respected black leaders died, they were often replaced by whites, especially in the areas of barbering, hacking, and drayage. For example, the Mansion House Barber Shop, which had been black-operated since the hotel opened, advertised in 1898:

"All white tonsorial artist, none but the first class employed." Racial separation and all-white attitudes were gradually creeping into almost every facet of life.

Transportation to and through Greenville began to improve. With two train depots—one at West End and another on West Washington Street—there was need for a shuttle to carry both passengers and freight. Thomas C. Gower established a "streetcar" to fill this need. The new public conveyance was actually a mule-drawn cart, which became an important part of local life for a number of years. The driver was William (Billy) Fronaberger, a colorful black who claimed the route as his own, exchanging greetings, waving at children, and carrying news as well as luggage. One observer noted, "Everybody in town knew William, and to many he was more important than the governor of the state." One of the best known "motors" for the cart was a quick and capri-

ern conveniences as steam heat, electric lights, call bells, and telephone connections. Manager Albion A. Gates appealed with dignity to traveling salesmen and public officials alike. Fine dining was important. "No pains have been spared to make the table equal to any in the country," he advertised. Rates were $2 to $2.50 per day. No doubt the hospitality there was unexcelled, but some visitors who preferred a more rustic setting chose to vacation atop Paris Mountain at the Altamount Hotel. Daily connections were made between the Mansion House and the Altamount by a mule-drawn coach which made the two-hour trek. John Marshbanks, the driver for several summers, added a bit of pageantry to the routine shuttle. When he stopped at the foot of Paris Mountain to rest and water the mules, he would blow his bugle, one blast for each passenger. Thus the hotel management knew the number of guests due to arrive.

Constructed in 1890, the Altamount (or Paris Mountain Hotel, as it was sometimes called) was a large, rambling, three-story wooden structure. There were porches on all four sides to allow maximum exposure to the sights and sounds of the unspoiled mountaintop. The twenty-three-room retreat was popular for several years but was never a financial success. It was sold in 1898 for $5,000 to N.J. Holmes, who opened a Bible Institute there.

A well-known and longtime mountain favorite was the Caesar's Head Hotel, popular since antebellum days. From the highest point in the county, hugging the North Carolina line, guests enjoyed cool air and stimulating views of the Dismal Valley below. The hotel was the site of many dances and parties until the large frame building was destroyed by fire in the 1950s.

Another resort—Chick Springs—actually spawned a new town. The spacious hotel and its enclave were clustered around noted

cious mule named "Lightning." By century's end, however, both Fronaberger and Lightning had been replaced by electric cars and an expanded trolley system.

More and more streets were opened as the city grew, many of them named for early leaders and property owners. Unfortunately, they were frequently muddy beyond all hope. In the words of mill president Mary P. Gridley, "At times mud became so deep along Main Street as to render the thoroughfare almost impassable even to wagons drawn by four-mule teams." There were no sidewalks or paved streets until the 1900s. The mucky streets were a special challenge for the first few automobiles that came to Greenville largely as play toys for the wealthy. In 1904 there were only five autos in the county; they remained curiosities for at least another decade. However, in 1904 one newspaper touted their advantages: the cost was "less than one-fourth the cost of keeping a horse and buggy subject to the same amount of use."

A vital economy, pleasing climate, and the promotion of mineral springs combined to attract vacationers to the Greenville area in the "Gay Nineties." The Mansion House, still the grand dame of Greenville hostelries, was remodeled in 1886 to include such mod-

Opposite page: *Thomas C. Gower, shown here in the 1890s with his marvelous (and much-needed) street cleaning invention, was one of the major forces in Greenville's progress for more than forty years. One of the founders of the Cox and Gower Carriage Factory, he won a hard-fought mayoral race in 1870, established a streetcar line, and was a member of the school board. Courtesy, Greenville County Library*

A crowd gathered to stare when automobiles collided at McPherson Park near Main Street about 1904. This photograph is said to record the first traffic fatality in Greenville County. Courtesy, Gene Eckford/ The Coxe Collection

Left: *Greenville's many mineral springs led to the production of soft drinks at the turn of the century. One of the most popular was Chick Springs Ginger Ale, made from the sparkling waters of one of the county's favorite resort hotels. Courtesy, South Caroliniana Library*

Opposite page: *Whether a crowd gathered to see the photographer or the Standard Oil delivery man, downtown Taylors in 1912 seems to have been busy as well as muddy. Courtesy, Ann Taylor Poole*

Below: *Rocking chairs are poised to receive leisured guests on the veranda of the Caesar's Head Hotel in the late 1940s. For more than seventy-five years the hotel, one of the most popular in the region, was a summer destination for those seeking mountain views and cool breezes. Photo by W.D. Workman, Jr.*

mineral springs, believed to have excellent curative powers. In the 1880s a railroad stop was planned a half-mile away to facilitate travel to the hotel, which had been popular since its opening in 1840. Land for the railroad station and a Baptist Church were donated by Alfred Taylor. A post office was established and "Taylor's Station" began to flourish and take on a life of its own. It soon outgrew and overshadowed Chick Springs, which it had been meant to serve.

Another town in the southeastern section of Greenville County may owe its name, at least, to an old hotel. According to one story, an antebellum inn with a gushing spring-fed fountain in the front yard once stood along the stagecoach route to Columbia. The town of Fountain Inn, chartered in 1886, is named for that old inn.

This was a period of renewed interest in education, culture, and refinement. Educators strengthened existing institutions and initiated new ones. Former Greenvillian Hugh S. Thompson, who served as state superintendent of education from 1877 to 1882 (and later as governor from 1882 to 1886), is considered the founder of the modern public school system in South Carolina. Although the movement did not really take off until the twentieth century, Thompson laid the groundwork for improved teacher certification, "separate but equal" goals for black and white children, and less emphasis on private academies at the secondary level. The State Teachers' Association held its organizational meeting in Greenville in 1881.

Furman University continued to be the pride of local higher education, maintaining

MARY CAMILLA JUDSON

From 1874, when her brother, President Charles Judson, invited her to teach at the Greenville Female College, until she retired as professor emeritus of English in 1910, Mary Camilla Judson served as "Lady Principal" of the Baptist college founded in 1855.

A fervent feminist and a Connecticut Yankee born in 1828, Miss Judson had had a superior education but had not been allowed to enroll at Yale University. She read in the Yale library, however, and developed a good command of French, learned Greek, and studied drawing and higher mathematics. She first came to Greenville in 1857 to visit her brother, and she made her home in South Carolina during the war years. After several years teaching in the North during Reconstruction, she returned to the upstate town with some reluctance.

She found a college of seventy-five students, only two of whom boarded at the school, a neglected campus surrounded by a gateless picket fence, a single dilapidated building furnished with spare wooden benches, and a library consisting of an old bookcase containing her brother's personal books. She gave the next thirty-eight years of her life to this institution.

A superb teacher and an inspirational principal, she brought, a student said, "the wonderful vigor and stern morality and forceful personality of New England to the little struggling school; she breathed into it through her pupils the

will to do and dare for intellectual freedom."

Mary Judson was responsible for beginning training in calisthenics at the college and thus allowed students to loosen their corsets and remove their stays and bustles, and in doing so to become healthier and more poised. She instituted a course in elocution so that they would have the skills to speak in public. She began the first women's club, the college's Judson Literary Society, in Greenville, and thus encouraged intellectual activity among students and helped them learn to argue and debate. She started the college library by assessing Judson Society members dues of twenty-five cents each term, and with the money developed a "choice collection of high-toned literary works." She began a student newspaper and a magazine and with all of this continued to teach nearly every course in the college curriculum until she was eighty-two.

She taught English, French, logic, astronomy, botany, elocution, calisthenics, and drawing. A later president said that "no matter what she taught, no student in her classes left the G.F.C. in those years without carrying away in her mind the lasting impression of a great teacher."

While she was feminist for her time and place, her feminism was necessarily discreet and practical. She favored women's suffrage, but she worked quietly rather than stating her feelings openly. A 1913 graduate recalls that Miss

Mary Camilla Judson was "Lady Principal" of Greenville Female College from 1874 to 1910. Courtesy, Furman University

Judson encouraged her to participate in Greenville's suffragette movement in the early teens; the valedictorian of 1887 said that the "Lady Principal" urged her to speak about women's equality in her commencement address. But southern gentlemen would certainly not knowingly send their daughters to an institution guided by a militant feminist ("May our land be saved from women who are advocates of female suffrage and who clamor for a place in our pulpits and upon the rostrum!" a trustee thundered in 1894), so her feminism was quietly directed at expanding the potential, the independence, and the self-assurance of the young women she taught.

In 1894 the college was threatened when its president, Alexander Townes, unexpectedly resigned and started a private college next door to the older institution. He took half the faculty, many of the students, and all of the furniture with him. Mary Judson wrote an open letter to G.F.C. alumnae asking for their prayers and their dollars to overcome the crisis. She loaned the college her life savings of $3,000 in order for it to continue. It did, with increased support from the South Carolina Baptist Convention. The loan was never paid and she eventually made it a gift. After her retirement she lived on at the college until her death in December 1920, just a month after she voted for the first time.

Alumnae wished to rename the school Judson College, but trustees thought that choice too radical; instead they yielded to pressure and grudgingly changed "Female" to "Woman's" in 1914. Judson Parlor in the Women's Residence Hall at Furman University recalls this outstanding educational leader.

Judith Gatlin Bainbridge

strong ties to the town. In the 1880s one observer noted with pride that students "were
not herded together in dormitories but were
boarded in private homes," giving them an
added identity with Greenville affairs. Such
monthly board would cost a student between ten and sixteen dollars; tuition at
Furman was thirty dollars a term. Charles
Manly was president of the school; professors included James C. Furman, C.H. Judson, H.T. Cook, and G.D. Purinton. History
was made in the athletic world when Furman met neighboring Wofford College on
the gridiron in 1889 in the state's first intercollegiate football game.

Another college entered the scene in 1893
and remained for two decades as a strong
cultural influence in the area. Chicora College, a Presbyterian College for women, was
located on the southwest knoll above the
Reedy River, site of Richard Pearis' old domain. A Greek Revival home was used by
President S.P. Preston and other classroom
and dormitory buildings were added. However, the institution did not succeed. In
1915 it moved to Columbia and was later
absorbed by Queens College in Charlotte,
North Carolina.

The Altamount Bible and Missionary Institute operated on Paris Mountain in the
old hotel building from 1898 to 1918. In
the Dark Corner region, North Greenville
High School (later Junior College) contin-

Above: *Chicora College, a Presbyterian school for
women, was established in 1893. By 1900 the college
had built a lovely campus on "McBee Terrace," over-
looking the Reedy River just across Main Street from
Furman. The college moved to Columbia in 1915,
and the main building burned during World War I.
Courtesy, Greenville County Library*

Page 111: *A gracefully curving drive and imposing
stone pillars welcomed visitors to the old Furman
campus. From this Augusta Road entrance one could
see Old Main with its bell tower (left), the new
(1904) Carnegie Library, homes of faculty members,
and student dormitories and "messes," which preceded a common dining hall. Courtesy, Furman University*

Opposite page: *The bitter winter of 1898-1899 was a
shock to northern troops stationed at Camp Wetherill. Local cartoonist C.A. David reflected the attitudes of the shivering soldiers, who purchased his
drawings and sent them home as mementos. Courtesy, John Baker Cleveland*

Main St. looking South, Greenville, S. C.

Opposite page, top: *After World War I, Greenville was in transition. Looking south down Main Street from the balcony of the Ottaray Hotel, one could see gracious homes and tree-shaded lawns presided over by the Confederate Monument, as well as the numerous stores that were rapidly giving the block a commercial flavor. Courtesy, Furman University*

Opposite page, bottom: *The importance of World War I in Greenville is reflected by the sign on Washington and Main Street: "Our Country First—Then Greenville." Traffic direction by police officers was necessary to sort out frequent conflicts between street trolleys, the rapidly burgeoning population of trucks and automobiles, and the remaining horse-drawn vehicles. Courtesy, Furman University*

Left: *The arrival of Furman University and its seminary undoubtedly provided the impetus for the 1858 construction of the gracious First Baptist Church at River and McBee avenues. The sanctuary's towering steeple, as seen in this 1915 postcard, dominated Greenville's skyline for many years. Courtesy, Furman University*

This view of Furman University's campus with the Reedy River ford below was etched in the late 1850s by an unknown artist. The resort community became something of an upcountry cultural center with the coming of the university and its seminary in 1851, but Vardry McBee's wheat and grist mills, at lower left, suggest the town's future as a manufacturing center. From DeBow's Monthly, *December 1859*

The Old Mill and the New, Greenville, S. C.

Above: *This turn-of-the-century postcard titled "The Old Mill and the New" reflects the importance of waterpower available at the Reedy Falls. The stone grist mill on the left, built circa 1843, illustrates the early use of the falls. On the right, the Camperdown Mill (Huguenot #2), built circa 1876, was one of the last textile mills constructed that used waterpower. Courtesy, Furman University*

Right: *The Southern Railway depot, depicted in this circa 1900 postcard, has served as a major western gateway to the city of Greenville since the 1890s. Although the tower has long been demolished, the station still stands at the west end of Washington Street, serving as the city's Amtrak passenger depot. Courtesy, Furman University*

117

While John William De Forest worried about widows and orphans and doled out clothes and corn to the needy, some Greenvillians obviously flourished during the Reconstruction years. Charles Lanneau built his imposing and flamboyant Italianate Romanesque villa on the crest of Belmont Avenue, where it has been renovated through the years by the Norwood and Funderburk families. Photo by David Jenkins

Above: The gothic revival sanctuary of First Presbyterian Church (seen just before its recent renovations) maintains a commanding presence on land donated to the church by Vardry McBee in 1848. The current building dates from 1883, replacing an earlier structure completed in 1852. Photo by Bob Bainbridge. Courtesy, Greenville Central Area Partnership, Inc.

Opposite page: The Victorian era and textile prosperity influenced residential development in turn-of-the-century neighborhoods. The gingerbread trim and sweeping porches of this elegantly restored home at 317 Hampton Avenue capture the spirit and charm of the "Gay Nineties." Photo by Bob Bainbridge. Courtesy, Greenville Central Area Partnership, Inc.

The Charles E. Graham residence on Broadus Avenue at Petigru Street was one of the first homes built on James Petigru Boyce's farm behind Christ Church. The "Boyce Lawn" subdivision had streets named for seminary faculty John Albert Broadus, Basil Manly, William Williams, and Boyce. Restored in 1983, the house is now the Seven Oaks Restaurant. Photo by Bob Bainbridge. Courtesy, Greenville Central Area Partnership, Inc.

Opposite page: Properly hatted young ladies from the Greenville Female College sketched the falls of the Reedy River near the Camperdown Mill in 1903 for an art class assignment. Their spring uniforms were white shirtwaists and sturdy merino skirts. Courtesy, Furman University

ued to provide appropriate education for its charges.

Other cultural and literary organizations made significant contributions. Begun in 1889, the Thursday Club, a women's organization, developed interests along educational, cultural, and spiritual lines. With Mrs. William Beattie, Mary Putnam Gridley organized the group and served as its president for forty years. It was a serious study group whose concept was emulated by others throughout the state. Some Thursday Club members were also instrumental in establishing the Neblett Free Library, which opened in 1897 on McBee Avenue property donated by Viola Neblett.

In 1900 a Grand Opera House was built on Laurens Street (between Coffee and Buncombe) to accommodate both local and traveling performing groups. Noted theatrical and music companies, traveling by rail from New York to Atlanta, often stopped off for engagements in Greenville. Such ce-

lebrities as Mrs. Fiske, Walter Hampden, and the Flonzaley string quartet made appearances in town. Edwin L. Hughes, Sr., longtime superintendent of public schools, marshalled local talent when he founded and directed a fifteen-member orchestra (1896) and organized the first school band in the area (1904).

Newspapers were increasing in number and influence. Writing in 1903, S.S. Crittenden listed four journals that spoke with progressive voices for the city: *The Mountaineer, Daily News, Evening Herald,* and *Baptist Courier,* which had moved to Greenville in 1879.

Perhaps this era was characterized by a split personality—the best of times and the worst of times. On the one hand there was pride, progress, and patriotism, a forward-looking, industrialized approach to life. On the other hand, there was romanticism about the past, glowing memories of the Confederacy and a "lost cause cult" that

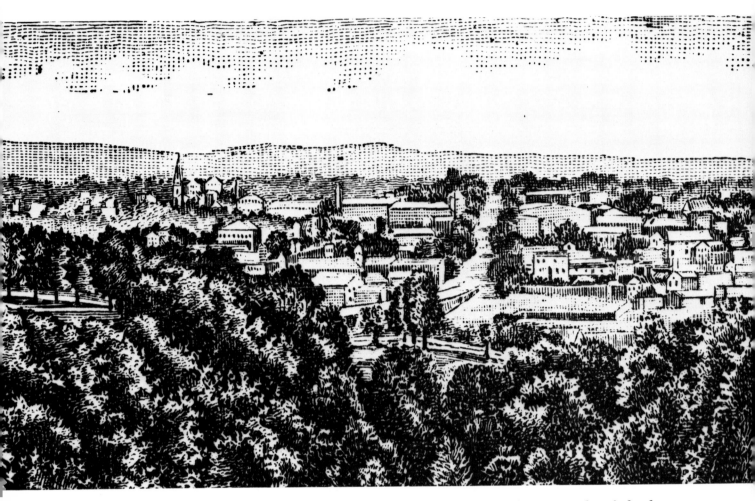

Looking east from the Furman campus in the 1880s, an observer could see, beyond the heavily forested slopes in the foreground, the Reedy River dam, the cluster of industrial buildings on the east riverbank, and beyond them the tree-lined Main Street. Paris Mountain provides the background. From An Illustrated Guide to South Carolina, *1884. Courtesy, Greenville County Library*

would not die. An example of the latter was the unveiling of the Confederate Monument on Main Street in 1892 amidst great ceremony and speechmaking. A marble shaft topped with the figure of a Confederate soldier was dedicated in honor of Greenville County men who had given their lives during the Civil War. The soldier stood high in the center of the intersection of Main and College streets. He faced south, toward the Reedy River, presiding over a bustling town he might not have recognized. Times were changing.

Unlikely as it may seem, the Spanish-American War brought changes to Greenville that could no longer be ignored. President William McKinley's call for volunteers in 1898 was met with a patriotic flurry of activity. Three companies of soldiers were

dwellers of the tent camp experienced bone-chilling living conditions.

There was excitement in the air, an infusion of new life. A patriotic spirit was evident, especially at the Mansion House where proprietor Albion A. Gates displayed a specially made thirty-foot flag for the officers boarding in his hotel. Local merchants enjoyed a boon during the Christmas season; it was the biggest rush shopkeepers had ever experienced. Stores were picked clean of cards, gifts, and warm clothes. There was a new dimension to social life; chaplains made addresses, military musicians performed, and soldiers enjoyed flirting with local girls, although the latter feigned any interest in the pursuit. One young lady described the scene at the Reedy River footbridge where soldiers gathered to girl-watch. "We girls, who had to cross the bridge on the way to Greenville Female Academy, bunched up in groups of about twelve girls to cross the bridge. That way we could get past the soldiers without being teased."

By April 1899 all troops were mustered out and Camp Wetherill became a memory, but it left some lasting effects on Greenville. Provincialism was abandoned in favor of new ideas and expansion. Some soldiers who had enjoyed Greenville remained—or returned later—to make it their home. The economy had received a boost and the effects were lasting. The vacant campsite off Earle Street was auctioned off in lots by Alester G. Furman, creating Greenville's first residential development. The ripple effect went on.

Dreams were being dreamed; new ideas were stirring in Greenville. The sleeping giant was beginning to stretch and claim its full potential. Dr. L.P. Hollis, twentieth-century maverick in education, chose to make Greenville his home. As he later observed, "The town was just beginning to wake up when I came here in 1905."

quickly raised and sent off with "tears and cheers," though none of them ever saw combat. Overtures were made to the War Department about placing an army camp in Greenville. While some local officials feared the negative effects a camp might have, the inherent economic benefits for the community outweighed potential problems, as it was predicted that soldiers would spend a minimum of $150,000 in Greenville each month. By fall Camp Wetherill was established; it had two segments, one on the E.E. Stone property north of Earle Street, and another across the Reedy beyond Anderson Street. Regiments came from the north for training, perhaps expecting a mild southern winter. Those expectations were dashed, however, as the winter of 1898-1899 proved to be one of the coldest ones ever. The

Barefooted school children were clearly aware of the cameraman who photographed them against the background of the Woodside Mill's newly completed expansion in 1908. Textile Crescent mills on the western edge of the city enjoyed prosperous years in the first decade of the twentieth century, and local stores, like Carpenter Brothers, published postcards picturing their rapid growth. Courtesy, South Carolina Historical Society

CHAPTER FIVE

TEXTILE TRIUMPH AND MATURITY
(1905-1945)

An uncommon degree of push, pride, and progressiveness characterized Greenville in the opening years of the twentieth century. It is a trend that has continued. Optimistic, energetic leaders emerged; desire for material progress took hold; belief in the success of the textile industry became dominant. Greenville shifted into passing gear and pulled ahead of other Carolina communities with its own brand of drive and diversity. The Chamber of Commerce placed an electric flag on top of a Main Street bank; its flashing message was perhaps symbolic of the times: "Our Country First, then Greenville."

A braggadocio spirit permeated publications such as Greenville's first history, The Greenville Century Book *(1903), by S.S. Crittenden, and a special souvenir issue of the Greenville* News, *called "The Gateway to Get There" (1911). Praise*

W.H. Balentine established his retail meat market on Pendleton Street in 1900. Expanding rapidly through the addition of a packing house and slaughterhouse, by the 1930s Palmetto brand sausage, bacon, and ham, made from "aristocratic pigs," were being shipped all over the South. Courtesy, Mrs. J.D. Ashmore

for individual leaders and pride in the growing number of textile mills, hands, spindles, and investors filled the pages. Attention was also given to the diversification within the textile industry, such as the establishment of a bleachery and two underwear factories. The 1911 writer was quick to point out, however, that Greenville was·"by no means a 'one industry' city." Among other manufacturers were two roller mills, a cigar factory, a hardwood factory, a machine manufacturing company, two ice foundries, and two cotton compresses. Indeed, an urbanized expansion philosophy prevailed.

Unfortunately, the materialistic impetus

led to hasty, unplanned growth and disregard for some of the area's natural beauty. Urban blight reared its ugly head. Especially hard hit and ignored was the once-picturesque Reedy River and its dramatic falls, which had lured early settlers. As early as 1896 the Greenville *Daily News* lamented the "unsightly pile of buildings" along the river banks. The view of the city's most aesthetic attraction was virtually blocked out. As a customer attraction, the Mansion House lauded its "system of underground sewage and drainage, connecting with the river," but this practice was the kiss of death for the river itself. The deterioration of the unique riverfront caused concern among some local businessmen, especially Thomas Parker and Alester G. Furman. They organized a group called the Greenville Municipal League, which in 1907 commissioned a Boston landscape architecture firm, Kelsey and Guild, to study the river's problems as well as the long-range growth pattern of the

"The largest coach manufacturer south of the Potomac," the Greenville Coach Factory had not yet started to feel the competition from the automobile when it advertised in a 1903 Chamber of Commerce brochure. H.C. Markley and his company were flourishing on the Reedy River at the turn of the century, building a new paint shop and hardware store to serve Greenville's burgeoning population. Courtesy, Greenville County Library

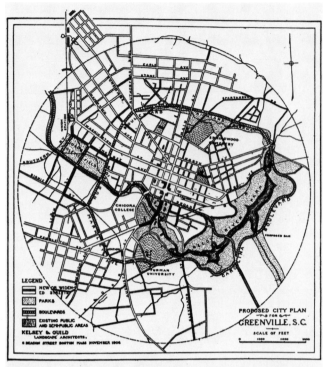

City Plan of Greenville, South Carolina, Showing Proposed
Improvements

Above: *In 1907, the first full plan for Greenville
beautification was prepared by Kelsey and Guild,
Boston landscape architects. The plan, with its
greenways and parks, had little immediate impact,
but led eventually to the donation of Cleveland Park,
the Mayberry Park baseball field, Reedy Falls historic park, and the Broad Street Connector. From
Kelsey and Guild,* A Plan for Greenville, *1907. Courtesy, Greenville County Planning Commission*

Above right: *The new concrete bridge over the Reedy
River at Main Street was the pride of the community
in 1913. The view from its balustrade, however, revealed the "unsightly pile" of industrial buildings
which were destroying the site's natural beauty. On
the left is the Camperdown Mill with its sluice and a
dam that bred malarial mosquitoes; at the center is
the Vardry Mill and mill houses; at the far right are
the roofless remains of Vardry McBee's grist mill.
Courtesy, South Carolina Historical Society*

whole city.

The Kelsey report commended the beauty
of the Reedy River and recommended its redemption and preservation. For reasons of
beauty and health it advised that all sewage
be kept out of the river. The architects
found the Reedy gorge, falls, and stream,
right in the heart of the city, "an object of
scenic beauty, the like of which few cities
can boast; yet it is being rapidly destroyed
and wasted. . ." Unfortunately, the report
was largely unpublicized, unaccepted, and
unheeded. Despite the warning, industries
continued to pour waste into the Reedy and
its tributaries, and businesses dumped ref-
use there. The area around the river contin-

ued its rapid deterioration for another half-century.

In the 1930s one writer found both beauty and beast in the landscape, claiming, "The green beauty of the city is remarkable in a manufacturing center." Yet, one could not ignore the "bare unlovely scenes in the commercial area." In short, industrial progress was a mixed blessing.

The textile industry continued to flourish. Greenville was a mecca in the field. Newer equipment, cheaper labor, and lower taxes attracted management to the area, some coming from northern locations. Some of the world's largest cotton mills were now in Greenville County. In 1915, building on this

"success psychology," W.M. Sherard and Robert F. Bowe staged the first Southern Textile Exposition in the warehouses of the Piedmont and Northern Railway on West Washington Street. Traders in the industry came to view the latest developments in products, machinery, and equipment. This 1915 show began a long and successful tradition in Greenville.

Led by William F. Anderson, Bennett E. Geer, and William G. Sirrine, construction of a large and permanent exposition hall was begun just across the street from the first show. The so-called Textile Hall was completed in 1917 just in time to house the second Southern Textile Exposition. The event was festive and exciting; the regimental band from Camp Sevier played while a heavy snow fell outside. The city accurately declared itself the "Textile Center of the South."

The Textile Exposition has continued to be held biennially, becoming a permanent part of Greenville life. It is an unusual institution that attracts national and international participation. In 1923 the Textile Hall Corporation was formed to oversee both the Hall and the Exposition. William G. Sirrine was its first president, serving until 1950.

Local economic leaders became cultural and civic leaders as well, a typical trend of the time. Historian Albert Sanders has observed that Greenville exemplified the southern paternalistic tradition, the popular philanthropic mode of Vanderbilt, Rockefeller, and Carnegie, and the New South philosophy that industry and education should go hand in hand. Thomas F. Parker was the most outstanding example of such a commercial and social trend setter. A man of vision and compassion, Parker came to Greenville in 1900, organizing and becoming first president of Monaghan Mill. He was soon involved in the lives and welfare of his employees, becoming a trail blazer in social

THE SIRRINE FAMILY

Many families have left a mark on Greenville's growth and development, but few have had the enduring impact of George, William, and J.E. Sirrine. The imprint remains indelible, in business and industry, in community service and leadership.

The story begins in Americus, Georgia, where George Sirrine was raised as the son of a wagon maker who warranted his work "not for six months, nor for twelve months, not ten years, but forever." At the age of sixteen, he joined Forrest's cavalry when his father, wounded in battle, said, "I can no longer serve the Confederacy. There is my pistol in its holster, my horse in the stable and my saddle is in the barn. Take the pistol, horse and saddle and take my place."

At war's end, George returned to find his father's business nearly bankrupt. He married, and moved with his wife and two small sons to Charlotte to establish a new wagon company, but within a year agreed to move to Greenville to manage Thomas C. Gower's flourishing carriage factory.

As manager and later president of the Markley Hardware and Manufacturing Company, he was an influential business leader for many years, but he was also concerned about the community. An 1894 typhoid outbreak showed him the need for a community hospital, and with the Mackay, Goldsmith, Furman, and Ansel families, George Sirrine founded the Greenville Hospital Association

J.E. Sirrine, designer and builder, is pictured circa 1900. From Men of Mark in South Carolina, *1902. Courtesy, Greenville County Library*

(now the Greenville Hospital System) and in 1912 opened the first City Hospital. He served as chairman of the board of the Hospital Association, and later became a trustee for the city schools. With his wife, he started Greenville's first library in their home on West McBee Avenue. Sirrine Elementary School was named in his honor in 1958.

George's son William (Cap'n Billy) Sirrine attended the University of South Carolina, and worked for several years as a reporter before returning to Greenville in 1894 to read law. He served in Cuba in the Spanish-American War before settling down to a life of professional accomplishments and community service. As a lawyer,

he was elected city attorney in 1904 and county attorney in 1908. He was in part responsible for beginning the Municipal League of Greenville which funded (with survey work by his brother, J.E. Sirrine) the first beautification plan for Greenville. He formed the Greenville-Henderson Highway Association which developed easy access to the mountains, and organized the paving of Buncombe Road through subscriptions from mill owners and individuals. His wife, Mary Sirrine, began the Charity Aid Society in 1908 (predecessor of the Community Chest and United Way) to provide emergency medical care in Greenville.

In 1915, Cap'n Billy began his most enduring accomplishment by organizing the first Southern Textile Exposition. The success of the first show led to the construction of Textile Hall (designed again by his brother) and to the international show that has brought worldwide importance to Greenville. He served as president and treasurer of Textile Hall for many years, and organized, from 1923 to 1925, the Southern Exposition, held in Grand Central Place in New York to show off southern manufactured products.

Despite William's accomplishments, his life was overshadowed by the almost legendary accomplishments of his brother, Joseph Emory, (J.E.) Sirrine. J.E. graduated from Furman University in 1890, and immediately began work as a civil engineer. He worked five years as a rodman for a railroad survey, then joined Lockwood Greene Co., a major designer and builder of textile mills. In 1902, he left the company to set up his own business, J.E. Sirrine, Mill Architect and Engineer. He designed the company store for Mills Mill (now renovated for apartments), buildings for the coach factory (C.F. Sauer Building), Textile Hall, and many other projects. By 1920, he had designed sixty-four mills and twenty-two major mill additions plus public buildings, sewer systems, and,

during World War I, Camp Sevier and Fort Bragg. Later projects included Sirrine Stadium, buildings at North Carolina State, the Citadel, and the new Greenville High School. From the end of World War I through World War II, he was noted as the single most influential citizen in Greenville.

When J.E. Sirrine died in 1947, the bells of Furman University tolled all day to honor his memory. His business lives on as CRS-Sirrine, following a 1984 merger with a Houston architectural firm.

The family's great success in

business made it possible to make significant charitable contributions to Greenville's public life. William and J.E. Sirrine made a donation in 1940 to build a new pediatric ward at the hospital, named for their parents. J.E. Sirrine established a scholarship fund that since 1973 has allowed hundreds of Greenville High School students to attend college. Other gifts have aided Shriners Hospital, Camp Greenville, and many other community projects.

Judith Gatlin Bainbridge

---

reform and setting philanthropic precedents. Parker established excellent, well-rounded programs at Monaghan Mill village, which set examples for other mill managers. Monaghan claimed the area's first YMCA; the first community health program in a southern mill village, which had a visiting nurse for workers; and pacesetting mill schools. In the community at large, Parker backed the establishment of the public library and the Phillis Wheatley Center. More than is commonly recognized, Greenville owes its current social welfare and cultural status to the dreams of Thomas Parker.

Managerial pride filtered down to the mill workers. Monaghan employees considered themselves the cream of the crop. As one Mrs. Campbell explained it,

Monaghan Mill people were looked up to— not like other mills. Other mills had people that came from the country and the mountains. They would go around with lint in their hair; we kept ourselves clean, went to church, talked better. They would fight and fuss just the way they were kept at home.

They weren't taught from the beginning.

Monaghan Mill merged with several other mills in 1911 when Lewis Parker (cousin of Thomas) headed a fifteen-million-dollar corporation called the Parker Cotton Mills Company. Other officers in the ambitious project were M.L. Marchant, Alex McBeth, M.M. Trotter, Jr., A.H. Hammond, and Thomas Parker. Unfortunately, Lewis Parker had trouble capitalizing the corporation properly, and it collapsed in the cotton panic at the opening of World War I. Parker's consolidation was ahead of its time; it was another twenty years before such financial mergers were successful.

However, there was another type of mill merger that drew national attention with its success—it was in the field of education. Fourteen independent mill school districts were consolidated in 1923 into the Parker School District. The merger was the largest consolidation of schools in the state's history. The superintendent was Lawrence Peter ("Pete") Hollis, who provided innovative leadership until his retirement in 1950. A

Right: *Born in Charleston, Thomas Parker came to Greenville from Philadelphia in 1900 and quickly became a force for social improvement in the mill village at Monaghan, which he owned, and throughout the city. In addition to establishing the area's YMCA and instituting a public health program, Parker is credited with bringing educational innovator L.P. "Pete" Hollis to the city. Courtesy, John Holmes Collection, Greenville County Library*

Below: *The Monaghan Mill, now a part of J.P. Stevens & Co., is a major anchor in Greenville's "Textile Crescent." This 1940 aerial photograph shows Monaghan at its peak, surrounded by parking, warehouses, a cooling pond, electric generating station, railway spurs, and a mill village. Photo by Joe Jordan*

new concept in public education had begun; a distinctive school district was molded using progressive, flexible methods. Night schools were set up for illiterate mill hands who had never before had the opportunity for an education. Adult education was considered as important as elementary schooling. The curriculum was adjusted to fit the individual rather than vice versa. The needs of the people in the industrial community were met as closely as possible.

In the early years, consultants were brought in to assist the teachers with their challenge. Teachers attended summer school at Columbia University's Teachers College and had the advice of supervisors throughout the school year. However, as time went on, the Parker School District made an outstanding name for itself. The progressive, practical approach of reaching the unlettered was working. The tables were soon turned and educators from afar came to

Monaghan Mill's baseball team poses in 1904. Athletic ability was as cherished by paternalistic mill owners as loom-fixing; for many years victories on the baseball field and the basketball court were almost— but not quite—as important as the end-of-the-year financial statement. Owners built villages, churches, schools, and recreation facilities to attract workers, and, in a style reminiscent of plantation days, evoked a sense of family pride in the mill. Courtesy, Oscar Landing

L.P. "Pete" Hollis was born on a Chester County cotton farm in 1883 and graduated from South Carolina College in 1905, when he came to Greenville as assistant secretary of the Monaghan Mill YMCA. His greatest achievements were made while he was superintendent of the Parker District Schools; he also established the Maternity Shelter and the Singing Christmas Tree. Courtesy, School District of Greenville County

Henry Hammett's Piedmont Mill began Greenville's revitalization through textiles. Situated on the Saluda River on the Anderson County line, it opened in 1876 with 10,000 spindles and grew rapidly during the following years. Hammett was the son-in-law of William Bates, whose Batesville Mill was one of the county's earliest textile factories. From An Illustrated Guide to South Carolina, 1884. Courtesy, Greenville County Library

observe this unusual system in Greenville County. The Parker schools undoubtedly influenced educational practices throughout the nation.

Greenville's distinction in the textile industry continued. In 1921 the New York *Commercial and Financial Chronicle* asked officers of southern textile mills to name the individual who had made the most outstanding contribution to the southern industry. Of the fifteen nominated, three were from Greenville: Ellison Adger Smyth, Lewis W. Parker, and Henry Pinckney Hammett. The largest vote-getter was Smyth, bringing him the designation "Dean of Southern Cotton Manufacturers." Smyth had built, organized, or reorganized several mills in the area and had been an officer in at least thirteen different cotton mills. He organized banks at Pelzer and Belton and controlled the Greenville *News* from 1912 to 1923. His influence was widespread in the community.

Leaders emerged in other areas too, far from the clamor of industry. Greenville claimed another governor when Democrat Martin F. Ansel was elected in 1906 and reelected in 1908. The most significant change that occurred during Ansel's administration was the 1907 repeal of the 1895 State Dispensary Law, which had created a controversial state-owned monopoly for the sale of liquor. The General Assembly followed his recommendation to end the state system, which was fraught with charges of graft and corruption, and substitute a county system which allowed for local option. Upon leaving the Governor's Mansion, Ansel returned to Greenville where he served as judge of the County Court during the 1920s.

Another Greenville lawyer made history in 1918, as Miss James M. ("Miss Jim") Perry became the first woman admitted to the South Carolina Bar. She maintained an active practice for the next fifty years.

During the second decade of the twenti-

The commercial offices of Southern Bell opened in Greenville in 1882, serving sixteen daring subscribers. By 1900 expanding demands for service (there were now 418 working telephones) led the company to move from a crowded office at Laurens and Washington to a new central office at Main and East Washington. By the time of this 1916 photograph, more than 2,000 phones were in operation and four people were employed to keep accounts. Courtesy, Southern Bell

"MISS JIM" PERRY

James Margrave Perry wanted a son. The Greenville Woman's College professor had had two daughters, and he was determined that his third child should bear his name. When his wife, who had taught music at Due West's Woman's College, delivered their third daughter, the professor was undeterred. And James Margrave Perry was named.

Only Freudians can fully assess just what the effects of being "Jim" would have been on a gently bred young lady at the turn of the century in Greenville. But it certainly did not create a southern belle.

After three years of public school education (because she was ill, Miss Jim was taught at home by her mother), she entered the Greenville Female College in 1909.

She was probably thirteen or fourteen at the time, although her age is unclear, since the date of her birth was modestly never mentioned in articles about her or even in her obituary.

After earning her bachelor of arts degree with honors in 1913, Miss Jim made the life-changing decision of entering the University of California at Berkeley, and in 1915 earned her second bachelor of arts degree. That fall she entered Berkeley's law school. This arrangement was not unusual: the woman's college was not accredited and a number of its graduates did one additional year of work before being able to begin graduate or professional school.

The fact that she chose to go

The first woman admitted to legal practice in South Carolina, "Miss Jim" Perry was a highly respected attorney and civic leader in Greenville for more than four decades. Courtesy, Dr. James Pressly, Sr.

3,000 miles away and to study law, however, was extraordinary. There was a small, timid women's suffrage movement in Greenville during her college years, and the woman's college students clearly were aware of the national clamor for votes and equality. But properly reared young ladies, even those who favored the vote, did not consider California or law school an option. One of her classmates, for example, explained that after graduation she returned to her father's home because "In those days a girl didn't take a job out of

home unless her father couldn't support her." It seems probable, however, that Miss Jim's mother's career, her father's encouragement (he had passed the South Carolina bar) and her own ambition, as well as her name, urged her to undertake a thoroughly untraditional career.

The world she encountered at Boalt Hall, the University of California's law school, was far different from the close-knit little southern town she had left. California men, she later remembered, carried gold coins in their money belts rather than paper money in their wallets, and most citizens had contempt for easterners who counted pennies. But she adapted well, although even westerners were confused about her name and her fellow students threatened to change it legally. In 1917 she received her J.D. and was admitted to the California Bar.

When Miss Jim returned to Greenville she joined the firm of Haynsworth & Haynsworth and became, in 1918, the first woman admitted to the practice of law in South Carolina. From 1937 until her death in 1963 she was a member of the successor firm, Haynsworth, Perry, Bryant, Marion & Johnstone.

At first she worked behind the scenes, doing legal research and briefing other lawyers on cases. As women became more accepted in the profession, however, she began to specialize in the organization and financing of corporations and in federal tax laws, in addition to employment regulations and wills and trusts.

In the years that followed, Miss Jim was active in legal associations, professional women's groups, and civic and community affairs.

A member of the South Carolina Bar Association, the National Association of Women Lawyers, and Kappa Beta Pi legal sorority, she was president of the Greenville Bar in 1955, and was one of the first women to chair a local bar association.

A charter member of the Greenville Business and Professional Women's Club immediately after she returned to the city, she served as president during its earliest years (1920-1922) and became deeply involved in the state federation, serving especially on legislative and policy-making committees. She worked consistently for fairness to women in the business world. Always interested in politics, Miss Jim was active in the League of Women Voters and Democratic party politics, serving for one term as vice-chairman of the Greenville County Democrats.

She was involved in the Girl Scouts, the Hopewell Tuberculosis Association, and the development of the Greenville Library, but her most intense community interest and contribution was in beginning a local humane society. An animal lover who had more than thirty cats and a dozen dogs, she worked hard and almost single-handedly to establish the Animal Shelter on Furman Hall Road. She hated cruelty to animals and had great compassion for them. Miss Jim served as president and treasurer of the Greenville Humane Society for many years and was as proud of her contribution to the well-being of animals as she was as a role model for young women.

Judith Gatlin Bainbridge

eth century, the legal status of Greenville's blacks began to shift. Earlier economic and social gains were dealt a setback when a strict ordinance of segregation was added to the city code in 1912. In the name of "preserving peace, preventing conflict and ill feeling between the white and colored races," the regulation called for "the use of separate blocks for residences, restaurants, places of amusement, stores and places of business of all kinds." Later ordinances explicitly called for separation of the races in schools, churches, and public buildings. Integration was considered a misdemeanor; violators could be fined $100 or jailed for thirty days on each count.

Black businessmen now retreated to specific areas of the city to locate their stores and services. In the 1920s the prime black commercial zone existed along East Broad, East Court, and East McBee streets. The heart of the district was the Working Benevolent Building, a three-story structure at the corner of Falls and Broad streets. It became a thriving center of activity, housing seven doctor's offices, two insurance firms, two barbershops, two cafes, one drugstore, and one mortuary.

Nearby, on East Broad Street, was the Phillis Wheatley Center, founded in 1919 by Hattie Logan Duckett as a community center. With encouragement and financial backing from philanthropist Thomas Parker, the hard-working Mrs. Duckett established an organization that provided education, entertainment, and religious programs for the black community. Widowed ten days after her marriage, Mrs. Duckett devoted her life to working with black youth, especially girls.

The advent of World War I increased activity in Greenville, as had earlier wars. The demand for cotton spurred textile mill production and kept the cash registers ringing. Based on the success of Camp Wetherill, Greenvillians were receptive to another military installation in the area, once the United States entered the war. A site was selected five miles northeast of the city, along Rutherford Road, beside the railroad tracks in the Piedmont Park-Paris section. Camp Se-

Sergeant Charles Hill photographed his 787th motorized truck company at Camp Sevier in 1918 while he and his comrades trained for European combat. This early mechanized warfare unit was primarily a supply force, charged with delivering men and materiel to the front lines. From the Charles Hill Collection. Courtesy, South Caroliniana Library

There was dancing in the streets just before Furman's football team played Wofford in October 1914. The young men of the university have clearly engaged the sympathies of Chicora College students during this "pep rally" on Pendleton Street next to the Presbyterian women's college. Even the trolley car and a goat cart have stopped to watch the excitement! Courtesy, Furman University

vier, named for Revolutionary War hero John Sevier, became an important training camp for troops from 1917 to 1919. The 20th, 30th, and 81st divisions trained there before embarking for European battlefields. It was one of three camps in South Carolina; the others were Camp Jackson in Columbia and Camp Wadsworth in Spartanburg.

Camp Sevier was hastily constructed, consisting primarily of tents and temporary shelters. The elements took their toll on

Gold was mined commercially from shafts and placer deposits on the Middle Tyger River in northeast Greenville County for more than sixty years. Vardry McBee is said to have taken $150,000 in gold from the area. This mine shaft, from the Cureton Mine on the Chandler property in the Mount Lebanon Church Road area, was leased to a Pennsylvania mining company from 1906 to World War I. Photo by Bob Bainbridge

many of the soldiers. The winter of 1917-1918 was an especially bitter one—reminiscent of 1898-1899—made worse by the outbreak of influenza, which killed a total of 1,300 people in the county.

Once again citizens responded with patriotism and southern hospitality to the thousands of young men who suddenly became Greenvillians, temporarily at least. Churches had open house; families and clubs provided entertainment; the American Red Cross met social welfare needs. Perhaps those who gave most from the heart were a group of elementary schoolchildren who donated their pets for the war cause. Because rats were such a terrible menace in the warehouses at Camp Sevier, an appeal was made to the children to bring patriotic cats to the site. At least one Greenvillian still remembers traveling with her class in a jitney bus to Camp Sevier, where she and her friends turned loose their cats.

Another section of the county was also used for military training. The War Department leased land at the foot of Glassy and Hogback mountains for use as rifle and artillery ranges for the men at Camp Wadsworth. The reservation included the old "muster ground" where Confederate soldiers

By the 1920s downtown Greenville had become a thriving center of commerce. Its curb market, located behind the old Record Building, overflowed with farmers and craftsmen from across the county who weekly displayed their wares for the increasingly prosperous and sophisticated townspeople. Courtesy, Greenville County Library

had once drilled.

The establishment of Camp Sevier created an increased need for water; the new demands taxed the resources of the privately owned Paris Mountain Water Company. City fathers quickly began negotiations to purchase and expand the system. On August 1, 1918, ownership was transferred to the Commissioners of Public Works, headed by W.C. Cleveland. A million-dollar bond issue covered the purchase and funded a filter plant and pumping station on the Enoree River to supplement the existing water supply. Water was a bit more expensive than in 1827, when the city paid twenty-five dollars to clear Gaol Spring, but it was a wise in-

GREENVILLE PUBLIC LIBRARY

vestment. The commissioners paid close attention to supply and demand and constantly updated pipelines, equipment, and reservoirs, maintaining an excellent water system.

In 1927 the city purchased Blue Ridge Mountain land, which became the Table Rock Reservoir, a gigantic water source (9.5 billion-gallon capacity) for municipal use. A 1940 Chamber of Commerce article described the management of Greenville's unusually soft and palatable water:

By owning every foot of the watershed from which the reservoir is supplied, and guarding the area rigidly against trespassers, the city is able to maintain a water supply so pure that no filtering is necessary to render it fit for human consumption just as it comes from its mountain sources.

The decade of the 1920s roared into Greenville as it did elsewhere with a spirit of change and expansion. The city's population had reached 23,127, according to the census

The same business leaders who brought the mills to the cotton later brought books to the people. The Greenville public library system started in 1922 and expanded rapidly to serve outlying population centers with new branches and bookmobiles. Today, in addition to its main library on Heritage Green, it has eleven branches including a law library, but bookmobiles like this one at Monaghan Mill in the 1930s still tour bestsellers and classics throughout the county. Courtesy, Joe Jordan

The center of Greenville's social life for more than fifty years, the Poinsett Hotel reveals in this 1944 photograph the grace and charm that made it one of the South's leading inns. Constructed by long-time Greenville builder Henry B. McKoy in 1925, the Poinsett hosted debutante balls, high school proms, and visiting dignitaries until well into the 1970s, when it became a residence for elderly citizens. Courtesy, Greenville County Library

of 1920; the county totalled 88,498. Municipal unity and maturity were evidenced through civic organizations and cultural flowering; organizations included the Rotary Club, the Kiwanis Club, and a downtown Y.M.C.A. and Y.W.C.A. City Park and Cleveland Park were available for recreation. In 1922 the Public Library was established with the financial backing of mill and business leaders Thomas Parker and James Wilkins Norwood. In 1926 the Theatre Guild was organized. For social functions there were the Assembly (1923) and the Greenville Country Club (1927). Membership in the Chamber of Commerce swelled to 2,000 by mid-decade, making it one of the largest in the South. The chamber built its own ten-story building on Main Street in 1924 on the site of the old Record Building, which was razed, despite opposition, to make way for progress.

Main Street's appearance was changing in many ways. Its residential emphasis shifted to commerce. Not only did the Record Building drop from sight but so did its neighbor, the Mansion House, whose business had declined in recent years. Torn down in 1924, the Mansion House was reincarnated the next year as the Poinsett Hotel. Directed by proprietor Mason Alexander, the Poinsett perpetuated the early hotel's reputation for grace and hospitality—on a modern scale. The twelve-story hotel did not dominate the skyline, however. That distinction was held by the seventeen-story Woodside Building, which opened in 1923 as the home of the Woodside National Bank (later merged into South Carolina National). At the time, it was the tallest building in South Carolina.

At the other end of Main Street changes were afoot as well. A new and graceful hotel had come on the scene at the "top of Main Street" when the Ottaray Hotel began receiving guests in 1909. Located at the corner of Main and Oak streets, the Ottaray had

THE WOODSIDE BROTHERS

Four brothers in the Woodside family worked as a progressive team leading Greenville and the entire state with their foresight, energy, and ambition. John T., Robert I., J. David, and Edward F. Woodside were born in the lower Greenville County community of "Woodville," four of Dr. John Lawrence and Ellen Charles Woodside's thirteen children. From their humble beginnings the brothers rose to become leaders in business, banking, textiles, and development. Several of their ventures carried the Woodside name— Woodside Mill, Woodside Bank, and Woodside Building—but numerous other projects went unheralded as fruits of their labor.

Working in unison, the four young men often undertook projects that would overwhelm other planners and investors. Explaining their business policy, John T., the eldest who was often the spokesman for the group, once said, "We have always stepped in where the other fellow was holding back." They pooled their talents: John T. was a businessman; Robert I., a banker; and Edward and David, textile manufacturers. Although their attentions were widespread, they centered their enterprises in the Greenville area.

Their first big venture involved organizing Woodside Cotton Mill (1902), which eventually grew to be the largest textile plant under one roof in the world. Similar plants were established later in Simpsonville and Fountain Inn, and a

The four Woodside brothers who changed Greenville are (left to right) Edward F., Robert I., J. David, and John T. Woodside. Courtesy, Mr. James Woodside, Sr.

recreation area in the north Greenville mountains was created for employees and their families. Together the Woodside brothers took the lead in financing a new high-rise hotel on Main Street, the Poinsett, at a cost of $1.5 million. The project had intimidated other financial backers, but the Woodsides willingly jumped in. The Poinsett soon became the state's finest and most respected hotel, attracting many travelers to Greenville. Undeterred by post-World War I scarcity, the Woodsides in 1923 constructed a seventeen-story bank and office building which bore their name. It was the tallest building in the state at the time; its construction required the sanc-

tion of the state legislature.

The brothers assumed a major leadership role far from their home county when they purchased some 66,000 acres in Horry County in 1926. They began extensive development of the isolated coastal area and set the tone for future development of Myrtle Beach as a nationally known, year-round resort. Their pioneering vision for this undeveloped region drew others to take notice of its potential. The Woodsides were praised in a 1928 Kansas City *Star* article as "the type of business men to whom the New South is turning expectantly: men who conduct large scale business undertakings with thoughtful regard for the welfare of the people in the community."

The family leader, John T. (1864-1946), was quiet, soft-spoken, unpretentious, and eager to be of service to others. He began his career with the Reedy River Manufacturing

Company, which was later changed to Conestee Mills. In 1893 he entered the mercantile business in Pelzer and later continued it in Greenville as the owner of a grocery store. He became the first president of the family enterprise, Woodside Cotton Mill, when it was established in 1902. Later he was vice president of Easley Cotton Mills, president of the Greenville Community Hotel Corporation (which built the Poinsett Hotel), and president of Myrtle Beach Estates, Inc. Appreciative of his efforts, the Myrtle Beach *News* described John T. Woodside in 1935 as "the state's greatest benefactor within the past hundred years."

Robert I. (1873-1949) held numerous business and banking positions. He began as assistant postmaster and cashier of Chicora Savings Bank in Pelzer, then moved to Spartanburg where he held two other banking posts. In 1906 he organized the Farmers and Merchants Bank of Greenville which later became Woodside National Bank, of which he was president from 1919 to 1929. In addition, Robert was director of both the Easley Cotton Mills Company and Woodside Cotton Mills. His financial expertise was also sought by others: he served as president of the South Carolina Bankers Association (1924-1925) and was chosen as a member of the American commission to study rural banking systems and branch banking systems in Europe.

J. David (1871-1945) and Edward F. (1874-1943) began their careers in the textile business in Pelzer, as had their older brothers. They joined John T. as the founders of Woodside Mill in 1902. Becoming interested in the converting and sales end of the business, David moved to New York where, for several years, he represented a chain of southern cotton mills including Woodside. Edward remained as manager of the Woodside plants where he was well known and popular with the hands, who called him "Mr. Ed."

Unfortunately, the Great Depression was no respecter of good intentions. It wiped out virtually all the holdings of the Woodside brothers: mills, bank, home, and Myrtle Beach property. As one writer observed, the loss was "enough to break the spirit of the ordinary man." But the Woodsides were far from ordinary; they bore their losses bravely, expressing no bitterness. Many of their enterprises lived on—under new ownership—proving the wisdom of their projects. Their willingness to take risks and to pioneer in new areas mark the Woodside brothers as Greenville's builders who made dreams come true.

Nancy Vance Ashmore

curved and columned porches that provided guests with a close-up look at the Confederate Monument and a more panoramic view down Main Street toward the river. The Confederate Monument itself had been the center of an ongoing controversy; it was considered an anachronism, a bottleneck for traffic. Finally, in 1923, it was removed from the center of Main Street to a less prominent location, approximately one block away, near the entrance of Springwood Cemetery. It has remained in that spot with a little park of its own, a quiet reminder of earlier days.

Improved transportation changed the tone of Greenville. Wider use of the automobile following World War I made suburban living possible and popular. Both homes and businesses began moving futher into outlying areas. New residential areas sprang up; meal hours were changed; lovers lane shifted from the Reedy Falls to Paris Mountain. Streetcars speeded movement in the city and joined it with the numerous mill villages on the city's western side. Streetcars ran around "the belt" connecting the villages with each other and with downtown, reducing their isolation.

An experiment conducted by Judson Mill proved dramatically the value of these mill workers to the Greenville community. For a time, officials at Judson paid all their hands

As late as 1920, visitors could still admire Greenville's Confederate Monument in the middle of North Main Street from the columned veranda of the Ottaray Hotel. Greenville Commons and the Hyatt-Regency Hotel now stand at this location. Courtesy, South Carolina Historical Society

in cash, with silver dollars only. The workers complained of having to carry the heavy money around but in the long run they were the winners. Silver dollars stand out in the cash drawer. Greenville merchants and professionals were made keenly aware of the source of their dollars. The business world quickly learned that without the mills, Greenville would suffer greatly.

Self-awareness was manifested on another level too, through literature and the arts. In 1921 a local play was presented, "Keowee Trail: A Historical Pageant." It was an allegorical pageant based on the colonial history of the piedmont. Neither the prose nor the presentation were remarkable but it rallied

Robert Quillen, the "Sage of Fountain Inn," arrived in Greenville County when he was nineteen, determined to establish a weekly newspaper. His success at the Fountain Inn Tribune *eventually led to national syndication; at the time of his death in 1948, his columns were being published daily in 400 newspapers across the nation. Quillen's newspaper office is a town landmark and has been made into a small museum. From* Cosmopolitan *magazine, October 1933. Courtesy, South Caroliniana Library*

city-wide support from schools, mills, civic groups, churches, and the National Guard. "Keowee Trail" was an outlet for expressing deeply felt regional pride.

Professor Alfred Reid has analyzed three local authors whose works reflect varied aspects of Greenville's self-consciousness in the early twentieth century. S.S. Crittenden's *The Greenville Century Book* (1903) had followed the theme of local pride and achievement. Harvey Toliver Cook wrote a history of Furman University (1912), several biographies of Baptist leaders, and reminiscences filled with Yankee-hating and "lost cause" ideas. J. Dean Crain's *A Mountain Boy's Life Story* (1914) defended and defined the mountaineer character. According to Professor Reid,

Taken together, three men, Crittenden, Crain and Cook reveal three distinctive sides of the Greenville tradition: civic pride; mountaineer humor; and the more narrow-minded religious zeal, which education has not broadened, combined with a dark streak of Southern hate, which time has not enlightened.

Yet another writer made Greenville County his home while gaining a national reputation as a philosopher, humorist, and satirist. Robert Quillen reflected the views and values of many Greenvillians, but his appeal was much wider; he was "everyman," popular with far-flung audiences through his syndicated columns. A native of Kansas, Quillen came to the small town of Fountain Inn in 1906 and made it his much-loved home for the next forty years. He founded a weekly newspaper, the Fountain Inn *Tribune,* in which he published his biting epigrams and essays. His subjects were everyday topics to which he added his special brand of wit, honesty, and common sense. He soon became known as "the Sage of Fountain Inn" and "the Mark Twain of his Time." Quillen and Will Rogers were mutual admirers.

By the time of his death in 1948, Quillen's editorials had been syndicated in some 400 newspapers across the United States and Canada, as well as Manila and Honolulu. His "Aunt Het" was a fictional character (based on Fountain Inn's Aunt Lil Nelson) who freely gave motherly and neighborly advice to anyone within earshot. Through "Letters to Louise, from a Bald-Headed Dad to His Red-Headed Daughter," Quillen published palatable advice on child rearing not only for his daughter, Louise, but for a whole generation of Americans. Many parents clipped his columns and gave them to their children as a message from the heart.

Despite his fame, Quillen chose to continue living in a small southern town. He was often questioned about that choice. He gave his reasons in an article in *American Magazine* titled "Why I Stick to the Sticks." Among them: "I like being Bob instead of Mister"; "I do not like crowds"; "I do not care for fame"; "I like my simple little house"; "I like living where the neighbor yells from the back door wanting to know something"; "I love the friendly people who do not pretend."

Quillen put Fountain Inn on the tourist map as well as the literary one when he erected a monument to Eve on his front lawn. The simple six-foot marble obelisk is believed to be the only monument in the world dedicated to the Biblical character. The brief inscription reads "In memory of Eve, the First Woman." Asked why he honored the mother of mankind in this way, Quillen replied, "She was a relative of mine, on my mother's side."

Nature had rendered Greenville a healthful place to live, with ideal climate and water; every effort was made to capitalize on these natural advantages to perpetuate a high standard of living. One major improvement was the creation of the first sewer district in 1926, which was expanded a decade later to reach suburban areas. By 1929 Greenville was singled out by the U.S. Health Service as "the most sanitary city and county in America."

Interest in health care was a growing concern. City Hospital, established in 1912, later grew into the Greenville Hospital System. In 1915 Mary P. Gridley, through the South Carolina Federation of Women's Clubs, was instrumental in establishing a sanitorium on Piney Mountain for the treatment of tuberculosis. Working through Burgess Charities, local textile magnate W.W. Burgess built and equipped a hospital for crippled children at a cost of $350,000. He deeded the property to the Shriners, who began its op-

Above: *The $250,000 Emma Moss Booth Salvation Army Hospital was dedicated in 1921 by Evangeline Booth, the national commander of the army, with half of the financing provided by local mill owners. The sixty-six-bed hospital operated until 1930 when it became bankrupt and was taken over by the Franciscan Sisters as a private hospital, and renovated as St. Francis Hospital. Courtesy, Oscar Landing*

Opposite page: *Many historic businesses remained active and vital throughout the Depression. Markley-Sullivan Hardware continued to sell horse collars (on column) and corn huskers (lower right) at their prosperous store at 17 West North Street. The building continued as a hardware store until 1983. Courtesy, Greenville County Library*

eration in 1927 as one of sixteen Shriners Hospitals in the country serving indigent crippled children. A county health department was funded in 1936, after many years of working toward that end.

The stock market crash of 1929 and the Great Depression which followed did not wreak the havoc in Greenville that it did in some places, but there were economic repercussions. Some families were without homes, food, or jobs; local charities and federal agencies tried to attend to the most pressing needs. A Civilian Conservation Corps (CCC) camp was located near Greer from July 3, 1934, until the end of the decade. Camp Highland was one of thirty such camps in the state that provided food, lodging, and conservation-oriented projects for approxi-

mately 200 men. For their work the men were paid $30 per month, but $22.50 was deducted and sent home for the support of their families. Much of their work helped stop the erosion of farmland in the piedmont, a common problem at that time.

The Depression heightened the complaints of mill workers in Greenville and throughout the state and nation. Long hours, low pay, and noisy, dusty working conditions had long plagued textile employees. Increased use of the "stretch-out"—the practice of increasing the number of machines

tended by one person—crystallized discontent in 1934. It was a volatile period in which the United Textile Workers (American Federation of Labor) called for a nationwide general textile strike on September 1. For the next three weeks Greenville was caught up in the greater labor-management fracas, but not to the extent of neighboring counties and states.

Discontented local workers, stirred by UTW organizers, went on strike at Dunean Mill, causing it to close down temporarily. Operations at American Spinning, Judson,

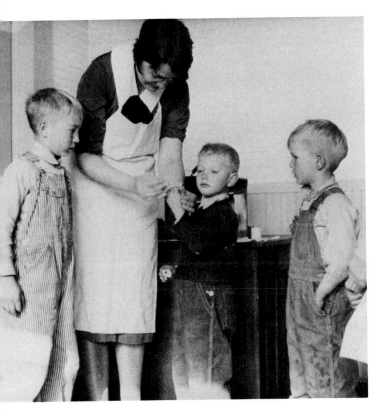

Above: *The Greenville County Council for Community Development studied and surveyed housing, education, health, and recreation, but it also made improvements. Public health nurses, often volunteers, went to small county schools to teach better health habits and inoculate children against disease, as here in the Jordan community north of Greer. Courtesy, Furman University*

Opposite page: *The Greenville County Council for Community Development organized continuing education classes, offered at local schools, which provided Greenvillians with classes in manners, wood-working, English, and current events. In 1940, the third year of the program, more than 1,800 people were enrolled at a cost of fifty cents per course. Courtesy, Furman University*

and Monaghan were slowed or stopped by picketing and occasional fighting. A so-called "flying squadron" of itinerant strikers from Spartanburg, armed with clubs, visited several mills and forced the closing of four plants in Greer. Tear gas was used by National Guardsmen at Woodside Mill to disperse a crowd attempting to prevent workers from being paid. However, violence and bloodshed were kept at a minimum; comparatively, Greenville was the eye of the hurricane hailed by the Greenville *News* on September 5 as the "anti-strike stronghold" of the nation. Only one death resulted in the county, unlike the tragedy in nearby Anderson County, where seven workers were shot and killed by special deputies at Chiquola Mills at Honea Path, an incident which brought the glare of national media.

Settlement of the general textile strike came on the national level with intervention from Secretary of Labor Frances Perkins and President Franklin D. Roosevelt, ending use of the "stretch-out" and calling for study of wage and hour regulations. Rather than encouraging unionization in Greenville, the confusion and violence of the period instilled local workers with a basic distrust of labor organizations. Union leaders have remained largely ineffective in Greenville and throughout the state. South Carolina historian Lewis Jones has observed that the turbulence of the strike era had two results: it delayed union organization and it increased public and management awareness of mill community problems.

Ironically, the arts in Greenville seemed to take on new life during the economically lean years of the 1930s. The wealthy families that once traveled to Atlanta or New York for cultural entertainment now encouraged its development on the home front. The Greenville Symphony Orchestra, the Community Concert Series, the Greenville Art Museum, and the Little Theatre all had

Citizens Education Center

THIRD SESSION

———

Six Monday Nights

beginning

February Nineteenth 1940

———

Greenville Junior High School

Westfield Street, Greenville, S. C.

(Note change of place)

———

Classes for Everyone
at Little Expense

———

Sponsored by the

Exchange, Kiwanis, Lions and Rotary Clubs with the Cooperation of The Greenville County Council for Community Development.

Chairman __ __ __ __ __ R. T. Ashmore, Exchange
Vice Chairman __ __ __ __ __ Dixon Pearce, Rotary
Secretary __ __ __ __ __ J. A. Southern, Lions
Treasurer __ __ __ __ __ R. K. Taylor, Sr., Rotary
Registrar __ __ __ __ J. LaRue Hinson, Exchange

———

REGISTRATION and FIRST CLASSES

MONDAY, FEBRUARY 19th

———

IT'S FUN TO LEARN

their beginnings in the 1930s. The first local radio station went on the air in 1933. Religion and the church continued to be of paramount importance in social and cultural life. One observer wrote in 1940: "Second only to the hum of textile industries is the religious life of Greenville, a city of many churches."

Greenville was the carefully chosen site for a five-year sociological and educational experiment that began in 1936. Initiated by local citizens, the Greenville County Council for Community Development was funded by an $80,000 grant from the Rockefeller Foundation. Furman University president Bennett Eugene Geer and Parker School District superintendent L.P. Hollis led the council, which attempted to study and coordinate all community resources. Farm problems, leisure time, public health, education, social welfare, and Negro communities were analyzed. The study was no panacea for problems but it promoted community unification and the willingness to recognize rather than ignore social shortcomings. Experts have lauded the project as an "experiment in democracy" perhaps ahead of its time.

Greenville was expanding and maturing with every passing year but somehow the growth was not sufficiently reflected in the population figures, a problem that troubled the Chamber of Commerce. The city limits, which had been laid out in 1869, had not changed until 1939; therefore the census figures for the city did not show the tremendous growth that had occurred in that seventy-year period. Most of the population growth—in mill and residential areas—was outside the city proper. However, in 1940 the United States Census Bureau changed its enumeration to include "Metropolitan Greenville" (city plus suburbs), bringing the population up to 74,767.

World War II again speeded mill production and brought Uncle Sam to town in the form of Greenville Air Force Base. (The base was renamed later as Donaldson Air Force Base to honor Major John W. Donaldson, a local son and flying ace.) 1942 proved to be an auspicious year, for in that year construction was begun on the air force base and Daniel Construction Company moved its headquarters from Anderson to Greenville. Both events would prove to be crucially important. The best was yet to come.

151

*By the late 1940s Greenville had become a bustling
city, its streets crowded with cars and pedestrians.
In this view of Main Street looking north from the
Reedy River bridge, only the Poinsett Hotel and the
Insurance Building continue to be downtown land-
marks. The News-Piedmont clock and building have
been replaced by the Multimedia Building, and the
Woodside Building beyond Liberty Life gave way to
SCN. Courtesy, Furman University*

CHAPTER SIX

WARP AND WOOF OF A MODERN METROPOLIS
(1945-1985)

World War II and the following years of rapid change nudged Greenville onto the fast loom of modern American life. The textile city was no longer simply the center of southern acclaim; it earned the title "Textile Center of the World." Yet, at the same time, other interests were afoot with industrial diversity gaining more and more attention. On a social level changes came quickly, challenging old thoughts, prejudices, and habits. The pattern of life in Greenville became as intricate and complex as the fabrics made there. The warp and woof of countless influences were interlaced, creating the unique configuration of a modern metropolis.

The unchallenged leader of much postwar thought and innovation was Charles E. Daniel, builder of an international engineering and construction firm. He was a self-made dynamo who assumed direction of the general southern move toward

Above: *After Charles Daniel's death in 1964, Daniel International has continued to be a major leader in the construction industry under succeeding presidents Buck Mickel (left), Charles Cox (center), and Les McGraw (right). Following the purchase of Daniel by the Fluor Corporation in 1983, Mickel has served in top management positions with Fluor, while playing a major role in new Greenville businesses. Courtesy, Daniel International*

Right: *If Vardry McBee built Greenville in the nineteenth century, Charles E. Daniel was the city's single most influential twentieth-century leader. An Anderson native born in 1895, Daniel moved to Greenville in 1942; by the time of his death in 1964, his company had erected two billion dollars worth of plants and buildings and he had become a missionary to northern industry, persuading corporate leaders to relocate in the South. Courtesy, Daniel Construction Company*

Francis Hipp served as president and chief executive officer of the Liberty Corporation from 1943 to 1977; he remains active today as chairman of the board. One of the region's major insurance companies with diversified interests in communications, Liberty's beginnings can be traced from W. Frank Hipp's acquisition of Southeastern Life Insurance in 1931 and the purchase of WIS radio in Columbia in the mid-1930s. Photo by Mills Steele. Courtesy, the Liberty Corporation

industrialization, fulfilling his own motto as "Builder of the South." Daniel canvassed the northeast, selling executives on the idea of expanding their corporations into the South; at first a few came, and then a few more. Greenville County, the state, and the entire South profited from his tireless recruitment efforts. As new markets were established, Daniel approached related industries or service industries, convincing them of the wisdom of being in proximity to their relocated markets. New jobs resulted. The expansion further led to the need for special and technical training of new employees. Thus economic, social, and educational areas were fertilized by Daniel's efforts.

Industrial plants were not the only fruit of Daniel's labor: scores of hospitals, college buildings, and commercial establishments were constructed by his company. One observer credits Daniel with shifting southern emphasis from "reconstruction" to "construction." His enthusiasm was infectious, his leadership dynamic. Daniel gave of himself generously. He felt that any good citizen should tithe his time and talent, giving at least one-tenth of each to better his community. Daniel set a new example of influential, progressive, and diversified leadership in Greenville. No one man had so dominated the local scene since Vardry McBee a century earlier.

Daniel was not a Lone Ranger, however. There was a cadre of other farsighted, optimistic, problem-solving individuals who wove together their skills and economic leadership for the betterment of the community and state. Alester G. Furman, Jr., Francis Hipp, and Max Heller have been singled out for their wide-ranging influence. (Furman was a community-minded businessman and investor; the latter two both served as chairman of the State Development Board, which concentrates on industrial recruitment statewide.) By the 1950s

Dr. Bob Jones, Sr., shown in 1947, brought "The World's Most Unusual University" to the city after World War II. Now enrolling more than 6,000 students from throughout the nation, the non-denominational, fundamentalist college includes an academy, graduate school, hospital, travel agency, and radio station. It has a widely known Museum of Sacred Art. Photo by W.D. Workman, Jr.

the state government was working closely with the private sector to promote industrial development. At one point Ernest F. (Fritz) Hollings was governor (1959-1963), Francis Hipp was chairing the State Development Board, and Charles Daniel was the chief executive of his construction company. It was said of the new industries, only half in jest, that "Fritz would bring them here; Francis would lend them money, and Charlie would build them a plant."

The paternalistic power-elite were strongly opposed to organized labor of any kind. Daniel was vehement in his belief that "every man and woman, regardless of race, should be privileged to work without paying tribute to any organization." He and others championed the open shop and parlayed their opposition to labor unions into an attraction for industrial leaders throughout the country. In the 1960s one social scientist described Greenville's economic leaders as being "far more anti-labor than anti-integration." As late as 1979 the *New York Times* called Greenville one of the "most relentlessly anti-union cities in the nation." Today less than 2 percent of the county's employees are members of any union.

An addition to the educational and religious scene came in the early postwar years when Bob Jones University moved to Greenville from its former home in Cleveland, Tennessee. Classes began in the fall of 1947 on its 200-acre campus on the northern edge of the city. Bob Jones has come to represent religious conservatism, and is nationally recognized as a bastion of American fundamentalism. Sometimes its stand on social issues has led to a bittersweet relationship with the community at large. Since the opening of its University Art Gallery and Museum in 1951, Bob Jones University has received acclaim for its outstanding collection of European sacred art, which features the works of such masters as Rubens, Titian, Veronese, Botticelli, and Van Dyck. In addition, the Bob Jones University Classic Players have performed hundreds of Shakespearean plays, adding new depth to Greenville's cultural life.

An incident with far-reaching consequences occurred in 1947, when a group of local taxicab drivers lynched a young black man. The victim, Willie Earle, was accused of killing a white taxi driver, Thomas W. Brown. A mob removed him from jail and brutally murdered him on Bramlett Road, near a slaughter yard on the western edge of the county. What made this case different from similar

An Acorn Has Been Planted

GREENVILLE'S EFFORT TO OUTLAW MOB VIOLENCE

International publicity, much of it negative, focused on Greenville during the Willie Earle lynching case in 1947. Some periodicals, the Christian Science Monitor *among them, saw hope for the future when twenty-one white men were prosecuted for the murder. The* Monitor's *cartoon was perceptive: the lynching was the last major act of racial mob violence in South Carolina. Courtesy, Carmack in* The Christian Science Monitor, *copyright 1947 TCSPS*

Sterling High School principal J.S. Beck and teacher Wilfred Walker, who became the first black sportscaster in the South in the 1950s, board a bus for Atlanta and a football game between Sterling and its rival Sims. Walker had a daily variety show on WFBC during the 1950s in addition to his teaching duties at the black high school. Courtesy, Wilfred Walker

ones throughout the South was the fact that the entire lynch mob (thirty-one white men) were arrested and tried for murder and conspiracy. The trial brought the glare of national press and numerous correspondents to the Greenville Courthouse on Main Street. British writer Rebecca West captured the spirit of the entire Greenville community as well as the trial-related events in her *New Yorker* article, "Opera in Greenville."

When the trial ended in acquittal for the accused, the press had no unanimous response. The *Minneapolis Times* found the spirit of justice to be dead in Greenville and its citizens living in the "shadow of a great shame." The *Atlanta Journal* believed the "farcical end . . . compounds the felony" and "Justice has been Lynched." Other journals were far more generous, seeing a silver lining to the immediate gloom. The *New York Times* proclaimed "there was a victory for law" in the proceedings; a precedent was set and lynch mobs were no longer above the law and free to operate as they pleased. *Life* magazine saw a clear message to lynch mobs that they were no longer "100 percent safe" or "100 percent secret." With positive insight, the *Christian Science Monitor* commented on the "solid gains" on behalf of justice, despite the disappointing verdict by the jury; lynch law had been dealt a setback. Indeed, this view proved prophetic. The Willie Earle lynching was the last such mob action in South Carolina. A page in the state's history of criminal justice and race relations had been turned.

A.J. Whittenberg, trial observer and later NAACP leader, believed the trial helped trigger self-help in the black community. He saw the boycott of white taxicabs and the later licensing of black cab companies as an outgrowth of the Earle affair. The trial motivated his own activity in the area of civil rights. "It was the fertilizer for growth," he said. Perhaps the first real legal test of the

CHARLES HARD TOWNES

The Greenvillian who has made the greatest impact on the modern world is undoubtedly Charles Hard Townes, inventor of the maser and laser, a Nobel Laureate in physics, and one of America's most honored scientists.

Born in 1915, the second son of Henry Keith and Ellen Hard Townes, Charles was a curious, active boy who was fascinated by the animals, insects, and birds he found on the family's twenty-acre farm on Sumner Street just outside the city limits. With his brother, he collected bugs, watched birds, did farm chores, and explored the nearby streams and meadows. In later years he said he would have been a biologist like his brother, who became an outstanding entomologist at the University of Michigan, but "Henry had dearly loved biology and was so good that I felt I couldn't top him." And, he admitted, he didn't want to write the papers required.

Instead, when he entered Furman University in the fall of 1931, he studied chemistry, physics, and modern languages. In 1934 he received a B.A. summa cum laude in languages and the following year a B.S. degree in physics. In the fall of 1935, when he was nineteen, he went to Duke University to work on a master's degree in physics, and quickly followed that degree with a Ph.D. at the California Institute of Technology in 1939.

His first job following the end of his academic career was with Bell Telephone Laborato-

ries in New Jersey, where he worked in the Physical Electronics Section of the Physics Research Department. With the coming of World War II, he worked on new problems—helping to perfect radar and radar bombing sights for the War Department. Following the war he went back to Bell to apply his wartime experiences to microwave spectroscopy and absorption—to the question of how atoms and molecules absorb radio waves.

But it was time to return to pure research and to the academic world. In 1948 he left the telephone company and joined the faculty of Columbia University. It was there that he began work on the maser ("Microwave Amplification by Stimulated Emission of Radiation"), which revolutionized radio astronomy and communications. Because the maser "mases" or amplifies incoming radiation, satellite communications become possible. This discovery, made in 1951 when Townes was thirty-five, led to a decade of research, some conducted jointly with his brother-in-law, Arthur Schawlaw, also a distinguished physicist. In a 1958 publication the two scientists described the theory which led to the extension of masers into the optical and infrared region. They patented this idea, which led to the construction in 1960 of the first successful optical maser, or laser.

In the following years Townes followed research opportunities to positions including the vice presidency of the Institute for

Nobel Laureate Charles Hard Townes invented the maser and the laser. Courtesy, Furman University

Defense Analysis, and provost at Massachusetts Institute of Technology. While he was at MIT he received word that he had been awarded a Nobel Prize in physics jointly with two Russian scientists for his invention of the maser and laser. Three years later, in 1967, he went to the West Coast as professor at large at the University of California.

Townes has returned to his Greenville home often, frequently to receive honors for his research and accomplishments. He has been elected to the South Carolina Hall of Fame, to the Science Hall of Fame, and in 1986 was honored by having the science hall at the new South Carolina Museum named in his honor. Still a bird watcher and gardener who cares about the environment, Charles Hard Townes remains the intense observer and question-asker that he was in his Greenville childhood.

Judith Gatlin Bainbridge

Named for Greenville resident Major John Donald-son, Donaldson Air Force Base was first activated as the Greenville Air Force Base in 1942. In the 1950s the base became a permanent installation, flying cargo and men throughout the world. Courtesy, Ron Copsey

Earle trial precedent, and a chance for progress, came eleven years later. In January 1958, four white defendants were convicted of assaulting and beating a black farmer; they were sent to prison. Justice was done.

On an entirely different level, the influence of Willie Earle may still live on. A recent book on South Carolina ghost stories has a chapter called "The Specter of the Slaughter Yards." It reveals that taxi drivers who travel Bramlett Road near Earle's slaughter yard death site often see and hear some horrible things late at night. According to reports, Earle has "appeared" several times through the years, reenacting the events of the lynching. But he is seen only by cab drivers.

Despite growing economic diversity, textiles still triumphed in Greenville's postwar years. By 1950 employment in the area's textile industry had reached 21,000, while the city population was calculated at 58,000. When the new $1.5 million Textile Hall on Exposition Avenue was completed in 1964, it was a fitting monument to the city's claim as the "Textile Center of the World." Greenville was—and still is—recognized internationally as a textile center, for it has more textile mills and related industries within a 100-mile radius than any area of similar size in the world.

In time, however, the textile industry itself began to change and eventually decline. Automation cut the need for increasing numbers of employees. (In 1970 the number of textile employees was still approximately 21,000, unchanged from two decades earlier.) Automobiles and the lure of other jobs lessened the need for clustering mill villages, which had outlived their usefulness as industrial incubators. Competition from foreign textiles threatened profits and caused some mills to close. The demise of one mill was capsulated in a June 1956 Greenville *News* headline which proclaimed: "Camperdown Mill to close, Japs Are Blamed."

International acclaim of another sort came to Greenville by way of Donaldson Air Force Base. The C-124s on its busy runways transported armed forces all over the globe. In the 1950s, Greenville achieved a new distinction as "Airlift Capital of the World." The military installation was an important cog in the local economic machine for twenty years. When it was closed in 1962 as part of federal military cutbacks, there were fears that Greenville's economy would suffer. Not so, however. Creative leadership in the private and governmental sectors came to the fore and converted the 2,400 acres into a business and industrial complex. As Mayor David Traxler said in December 1964, "Donaldson has turned out to be a gold mine instead of a devastating loss to the city's economy."

The success of the Donaldson venture has attracted attention from cities with similar problems, serving as a role model for cooperative projects. Today Donaldson Industrial Center, which operates an 8,000-foot runway, is the state's only air-served industrial park. Its use is reserved exclusively for the center's tenants, which include large tire, aviation, pharmaceutical, and lumber concerns.

As Greenville blossomed as an urban center, its commitment to the arts unfurled. Writing in 1960, some observers noted a lack of creative development in the arts, something of a postwar cultural lag. That hesitation has been overcome, however, with art, theatre, music, and dance finding ever surer footing in the community and comparing favorably with other southern cities. In 1958 the Greenville Art Association purchased the turreted stone Gassaway Mansion for use as a museum. It was a fitting and intriguing home until the County Museum of Art was completed and opened in 1974. It is a striking, modern structure, the first museum built in South Carolina in the twentieth century. Since 1979 the museum has exhibited the noted twenty-six-piece Andrew Wyeth collection, through the generous patronage of Holly and Arthur Magill. Other temporary and traveling exhibits offer variety for art connoisseurs.

The museum has drawn the attention of the art world, just as its next-door neighbor, the Greenville Little Theatre, has received continous acclaim in the field of community theatre. Long directed by Robert H. McLane, the Little Theatre is noted for outstanding productions and for launching the acting careers of Joanne Woodward and Amy Stryker. The Little Theatre has been hailed as "the most indigenous and communal" of all the arts in Greenville. The Greenville County Public Library is the final part of the triad on Heritage Green, the downtown cultural complex on the former site of the Woman's College. The excellent, updated library has recently been recognized as one of eight outstanding libraries in the nation in the field of community relations.

The breadth and depth of cultural participation and appreciation goes on. The Warehouse Theatre, Furman Theatre Guild, Bob Jones Classic Players, and the Savoyards have added variety to theatrical offerings in the 1980s. The Greenville Symphony Orchestra, Bob Jones Symphony Orchestra, Carolina Youth Symphony, Greenville Civic Chorale, and the Community Concert Series provide food for the music-hungry soul. Three ballet companies, one of which is the state's oldest, give performances annually. Indeed, many of the finest cultural activities in the region are enjoyed in Greenville; there is true depth in the city's commitment to the arts.

There is, perhaps, more involvement in

Above: *The Greenville Little Theatre became a starting point for Joanne Woodward, who had performed at Greenville High School in the 1940s and went on to become an Academy Award-winning actress. Ms. Woodward returned to Greenville in the 1950s to visit troops at Donaldson Air Force Base. Courtesy, Ron Copsey*

Left: *Built at a cost of $790,000 in the early 1920s, the Gassaway Mansion, with seventy rooms and a tower constructed of stone from the old Vardry Mill, is a Greenville landmark. In 1958 it became the first home of the Greenville Art Museum. Photo by Joe Jordan. Courtesy, Oscar Landing*

While the arts and a positive industrial climate attracted visitors and new residents, Greenville County, like many others throughout the South, has emphasized tourism through local festivals. Greer's Peach Festival parade in 1959 is an example of the local events that line main streets throughout the region. Courtesy, Southern Bell

literature than is commonly recognized. Professor Alfred Reid said that in the 1960s Greenville was further along than it had been in its first literary heyday in the nineteenth century. He found a rapid increase in the output of both fiction and non-fiction. Mary C. Simms Oliphant and Katharine M. Jones have been cited for their contributions to South Carolina history and southern literary themes. Caroline Coleman wrote nostalgic reminiscences of the "nineties and naughts," which appeared in the Greenville *Piedmont.* Wayne W. Freeman, editor of the Greenville *News* in the 1950s and 1960s, produced clear and vigorous editorials defending the South and opposing school integration. At the opposite end of the political spectrum, Harry S. Ashmore, a native son living in Arkansas, won the Pulitzer Prize for his editorials in the Little Rock *Gazette* during the integration crisis of 1958. In the area of fiction, Lee Fallow was considered "Greenville's latter-day Swift" for the biting satire in his works, *The Ugglians* and *The Ugglians at Large.* However, as Professor Reid observed, Greenville's most gifted contemporary writer is Max Steele. He brought fame to his hometown when he won the coveted Harper's Fiction Award in 1950 for his novel *Debbie.* His storytelling ability is a notable contribution to American literature. In Reid's words, Steele remains "the chief ornament of Greenville letters."

Water—in pure and unpure forms—has continued to play a conspicuous role in Greenville's life. Through the vigilance of three efficient Commissioners of Public Works and a well-guarded watershed, the city's drinking water maintains its reputation as the purest, softest, most desirable water in the world. In addition, it is found in more concentrated abundance than any other place in the nation. Expanding postwar population and the resulting demand for fire protection and water supply created

the need for a new reservoir to supplement the one at Table Rock. Scouting for appropriate land and mountain streams in the North Saluda River area began in the mid-1950s. A dam was constructed; streams were impounded to form a lake. Pipelines connecting the new North Saluda Reservoir with the existing system began service in January 1961. The entire project cost $11.5 million. The supply of fresh, pure water (capacity of ninety-seven million gallons daily) far exceeded the demand.

Ironically, the purity of the drinking water was offset by the continued pollution of the Reedy River. The once-lovely stream, which meanders through the downtown area and bisects the county, suffered from malnutrition. Individuals and industries disposed of waste and trash all along its banks; the formerly fresh white falls turned into a

Left: *An appreciation for quality and beauty in the arts has extended to architecture. "Broad Margin," one of Frank Lloyd Wright's last designs, was built in 1952 on East Avondale Avenue. It is one of only two Wright-designed homes in the state. Courtesy, Greenville County Library*

Below: *In 1956 the Clyde Beattie Circus came to town, and visitors parked along Pleasantburg Drive to go to the Big Top. Pleasantburg Shopping Center is at left beyond the tent; McAlister Square was not yet under construction. The circus was located approximately where the 252 Building is today. Photo by Joe Jordan*

ROGER C. PEACE

Roger Craft Peace had a way with words and the ability to inspire and motivate others with his use of them. His career as a journalist and publisher gave him a broad-based view of the complexities of twentieth-century life; his intelligence, wit, and common sense enabled him to find solutions for many complicated problems. In the life of Greenville and the state he was often a visible and dynamic leader, but more often a behind-the-scenes advisor, counseling those who sought his advice. Either way, his presence was felt. Upon his death in 1968 one columnist mused, "He was like a shepherd—leading at times; at times steering shy."

Peace began early in the newspaper world, first in 1914 as a cub reporter for the Greenville *News.* Roger and his brother Charlie are credited with influencing their father, Bony Hampton Peace, to buy the *News* in 1919. Roger continued as his father's right-hand man in many capacities, moving up through the ranks from sports editor to editor to business manager. After his father's death in 1934, Peace succeeded him as publisher. In 1927 the Peace family had also purchased the evening newspaper, the *Piedmont,* and Peace became president of the new firm, the Greenville News-Piedmont Company. In 1933 the company established the first radio station in town, WFBC.

Gradually Peace and his associates acquired additional newspapers and radio and tele-

News-Piedmont *publisher Roger C. Peace initiated the formation of Multimedia, Inc., in 1967. Courtesy, Greenville* News-Piedmont

vision stations throughout the southeast and guided their growth. He initiated the formation of Multimedia, Inc., in 1967 and led it as chairman of the board.

Foresight and business acumen marked Peace as a strong and stable leader. He was director of Peoples National Bank, Greenville Community Hotel Corporation, and Piedmont and Northern Railway. He served as president of the Greenville Chamber of Commerce and the South Carolina Press Association and as chairman of the Community Chest. He was a long-time trustee and finance chairman of Furman University, from which he graduated in 1919. During World War II Peace chaired the Preparedness for Peace Commission which

made recommendations for postwar industrial development throughout the state. One result was the formation of the State Research, Planning and Development Board which revolutionized South Carolina's economy; he served as an original member of that innovative board.

Only once did Roger Peace hold a political office. In 1941 he was appointed U.S. senator to fill the three remaining months (August to November) of the seat formerly held by James F. Byrnes. He served well but did not seek reelection, deciding that the political arena was not for him. Nevertheless, he was friend and confidante to numerous governmental leaders beginning as early as 1930.

Peace's level-headed counsel was sought by the mighty and the meek and he was "never too busy to help." His newspaper employees—or "associates" as he preferred to call them—were on a first-name basis with their accessible mentor. One story tells of the day the publisher kept a business appointment waiting for quite a time while he chatted with the janitor about gardening.

Writing and editing were Peace's true love. He once said, "No title meant more to me than that of 'Editor.'" His only regret, and that of his reading public, was that as his responsibilities in other areas grew, his time for writing lessened. He never stopped writing, however, and he never lost touch with the man on the street. Peace refused to become isolated in the publisher's office.

One of his greatest joys was to take long walks up and down Main Street, talking to passers-by and absorbing the tenor of the day. He would stroll up one side of the street, perhaps stop for coffee, and then amble down the other side, back to the News-Piedmont Building on South Main. He became dismayed with the mass exodus of downtown businesses to suburban shopping malls, but he did not lose faith in the revitalization of Main Street. Rather than relocate the newspapers, Peace was determined to construct a new multi-million-dollar facility on Main Street. He took great pride in the project, following its every stage of development. Although Peace did not live to see it completed in early 1969, the new Multimedia Building stands as his "legacy to the heart of Greenville."

Nancy Vance Ashmore

slimy green foam; a rank odor of chemicals and sewage caused citizens to refer derisively to the "reeking Reedy." Little was done to improve the situation until the late 1960s, when the Carolina Foothills Garden Club began working with the Greenville County Planning Commission to beautify the area around the historic falls. Land given to the city by Furman University was cleared and turned into the Reedy River Falls Historic Park and Greenway. The club's efforts were well received; a new awareness of the river's potential beauty and value was felt. A tranquil spot of green grass and flowing waters was reclaimed, a faint reminder of what Richard Pearis may have viewed some 200 years earlier. Eliminating the pollution in the river has been a long, slow process; habits die hard. However, by the mid-1980s all major polluters had stopped disposal in the river and plans are underway to expand the Historic Park, the city's birthplace.

Interest in sports and athletics is high in Greenville. Semi-professional textile-industry baseball teams were active for many years; the Greenville Spinners drew crowds to Meadowbrook Park on Mayberry Street. A classic football rivalry between Greenville High School and Parker High School was played annually on Thanksgiving afternoon. Today, a professional baseball team, the Greenville Braves, has adopted Greenville, and Furman hosts its football games in a new 13,200-seat stadium. One of the most exciting moments in sports history came on February 13, 1954, when Furman basketball star Frank Selvy scored 100 points in a game in the old Textile Hall. He broke national collegiate records as a Furman Paladin, creating unbelievable notoriety and excitement. Fans who did not see the actual game relived it in their minds and imagined they were there. Speaking a generation later, Furman basketball coach Joe Williams said, "I'm sure they can never build anything as large as the old Textile Hall. I know it must have been huge because since I've been in Greenville, I've never met anybody who wasn't there the night Frank Selvy scored 100 points."

In the forty years since the close of World War II, public education in Greenville has taken a quantum leap. In 1951 the eighty-seven school districts throughout the county (including Parker District) were merged into one unit, Greenville School District #520, under Superintendent William Francis Loggins. This consolidation was part of a statewide move to equalize schools and upgrade the entire educational system. School bond issues were floated in 1959 and 1963 to help fund the consolidated facilities in the district. Greenville's school system was regarded by many as one of the state's leading systems, and its administrative officials and educational activities received especially

Above: *Furman University political scientist Ernie Harrill headed the citizen's committee that brought peaceful integration to Greenville schools in 1970. Students, parents, and community leaders worked together to dismantle a segregated system in three months. Courtesy, Dr. Ernest E. Harrill*

Opposite page: *The Shriners Hospital for Crippled Children was established in Greenville in 1927; it serves seven southeastern states, providing free medical care for orthopedically handicapped youngsters. By 1956, when this picture was taken, it had treated more than 8,000 children. In 1986, a new hospital is under construction near Memorial Hospital on Grove Road. Photo by Henry Elrod. Courtesy, John Holmes Collection, Greenville County Library*

Frank Selvy set a still unmatched collegiate record when he scored 100 points against Newberry College on February 13, 1954. Photo by Jim Wilson. Courtesy, Greenville News-Piedmont

Four generations of Furmans posed for this 1934 photograph. Their heritage was preaching and teaching, but for nearly 100 years they have been real estate developers who have changed the face of Greenville. The family's relationship with Furman University may be unique nationally: five generations have been involved in its creation, direction, and expansion. Clockwise from lower right: Alester G. Sr.; Charles Manning; Alester G. III; and Alester G. Jr. Courtesy, Mr. and Mrs. A.G. Furman III

high marks.

Token racial integration of the schools began in 1964, about the time desegregation was beginning in all facets of employment and public facilities. At the time, blacks composed 22 percent of the student population (40,676 white and 11,677 black). While there was peaceful acceptance of the desegregation efforts, a conservative attitude continued to permeate the local social and political climate. There was no push to achieve full-scale integration until a federal court order made it mandatory in February 1970. The confusing mid-year transfer of thousands of students, teachers, and administrators was met with amazing calm and success. The required ratio of eighty whites to twenty blacks was accomplished and the business of education went on. In the words of Professor Ernest E. Harrill, the challenge was met "with grace and style," a phrase which was often repeated in the national media. Greenville emerged as a model of integration in the South.

The size and quality of the schools has continued to climb. Today the Greenville School District is the largest in South Carolina with 107 schools and centers, a highly qualified teaching staff, and more than 51,000 students. Emphasis on education is both the cause and result of the influx of new people in the Greenville area, creating a healthy learning atmosphere. Vocational training, advanced placement courses, and the Governor's School for the Arts provide broad offerings for young people. It's a far cry from the educational scene Robert Mills described in 1825.

Having outgrown its inner city campus, Furman University began construction in 1954 on a 1,200-acre tract of land near Travelers Rest and the base of Paris Mountain. The spacious landscaped grounds, which include a thirty-acre lake, had room at last for all Furman students—both male

JESUS ANSWERED, MY KINGDOM IS NOT OF THIS WORLD · JOHN 18:36

and female. Students gradually moved to the new location as buildings were ready; the transition was completed by 1961 under the guidance of President John L. Plyler and Board Chairman Alester G. Furman, Jr. Furman's liberal arts curriculum and general academic stature continues to climb. In 1983 the institution was recognized in *U.S. News and World Report* as the third best comprehensive university east of the Mississippi River, and again in 1985 as one of the nation's "most selective schools emphasizing the liberal arts." Its regional and national reputation are well deserved.

In 1962 another educational institution came on the scene and has had a meteoric rise. Greenville Technical Education College (TEC) was the first such facility in the state; its success inspired a chain of fifteen similar schools throughout South Carolina. TEC provides post-high school career and

The rapidly increasing population in the eastern part of the county has not spoiled the spectacular panorama of the Middle Saluda River valley and the Dark Corner area, as viewed from the Symmes' Chapel at "Pretty Place." Accessible only from North Carolina, the YMCA's Camp Greenville offers a view of the Blue Ridge Mountains to campers, Easter worshipers, and couples seeking the perfect setting for their wedding ceremony. Photo by W.D. Workman, Jr.

technical training for men and women seeking industrial jobs. Its attraction for students is strong, for it gives specific, job-oriented, technical training; its appeal to incoming industries is great because it prepares a pool of skilled workers for the task at hand. Since TEC's opening, over $1.6 billion in capital investment by new and expanding industries has come to Greenville County, as well as more than 26,000 new jobs. Industry and education have worked well together.

One dominant thread in the warp and woof of Greenville life is that of religion. Above government and business, churches are the core around which family and social life revolve. Some say there is more religious interest and activity in Greenville than in any place of comparable size. If the South as a whole is considered the "Bible Belt," then Greenville is the "Buckle" on the Bible Belt. Church membership is high; in 1980 approximately 80 percent of the county's population were members of some organized church. Denomination-wise, the Southern Baptists have been out in front for years. A 1980 survey revealed that of the county's church members, 35.7 percent were Southern Baptist, 9.4 percent Black Baptist, and 7.5 percent United Methodist. (Those with less than 5 percent were Independent Baptist, Presbyterian, Catholic, Episcopalian, Lutheran, and Church of God.)

In spite of the statistics, the Southern Baptist denomination may be losing its firm grip on Greenville. One strong influence is the non-denominational fundamentalist pull of Bob Jones University and its staff and students. The largest single church in the county is Southside Baptist (which is Independent rather than Southern Baptist in affiliation) with 4,700 members, many drawn from the Bob Jones University community. Other independent churches are growing, while the Southern Baptist rate of growth

has slowed. Smaller mainline denominations are growing swiftly, effecting a religious melting pot in Greenville for the first time. The Catholic church is currently the fastest growing denomination (25.6 percent increase), followed by the Episcopal church (14.3 percent), Southern Baptist (8.3 percent), and Church of God (6.1 percent). A religious shift is in the making.

Another obvious change in recent years is the growing influence of international industries and business executives. By 1985 some twenty-one companies with foreign affiliation were located in Greenville County; their products vary from textile machinery to radial tires to grocery store chains, but one thing remains constant: the broadening effect on local attitudes and lifestyles. The same Chamber of Commerce which bragged of "exceedingly few foreign born persons" in 1925 speaks with pride of "cosmopolitan" international influence sixty years later. In fact, an Austrian-born mayor, Max Heller, led the city through crucial growth years from 1970 to 1979. In 1982 a guidebook to "South Carolina's International Greenville" was published in five languages for potential foreign visitors. Greenville adopted a Sister City in 1985, Bergamo, Italy. The two piedmont industrial cities exchanged delegations and visitors, seeking links and similarities while learning from cultural variances.

As with many cities in the postwar years, Greenville's downtown shopping area became less and less vital as businesses retreated to suburban malls. Blocks of Main Street stores stood vacant; a stagnant air hung over the once bustling street. Publisher Roger Peace and Charles Daniel are credited with salvaging the spirit of downtown life when they decided to stand fast and put up new buildings on Main Street. The Multimedia Building and the Daniel Building opened in the mid-1960s as the two new anchors of Main Street. Business leaders and

JESSE JACKSON

The only Greenvillian to try for a presidential nomination, the Reverend Jesse Jackson was born in the city in 1941 and grew up in a warm and loving family. Although his world was a segregated one and money was scarce, the Green Street community in which he lived was stable and valued achievement. "I felt some pain, but I never knew hunger, either for food or for love," he said in a Greenville *News* interview during his campaign for the Democratic nomination in 1984. His mother, Helen Jackson, still lives in the city and his stepbrother, Noah Robinson, was the developer of a Broad Street building for black professionals. The founder of PUSH still votes in the city.

A student leader and starring football quarterback at Sterling High School, he was encouraged by his coach, J.D. Mathis, and his family to attend the University of Illinois on a football scholarship in the fall of 1959. He had selected a midwestern university because he wanted to get a good education and because he wanted to leave the segregated South, but he found at Illinois a huge university controlled by sororities and fraternities where he was considered only an athlete, rather than a student. He was unhappy at Illinois and, as a result, transferred in 1960 to North Carolina A & T in Greensboro, where he proceeded to make a superb record as a sociology major, president of the student body, captain of the football team, and civil rights

The only Greenvillian to be nominated for the presidency, Jesse Jackson has become a force in both national and international politics. Photo by Charles Arbogast. Courtesy, Greenville News-Piedmont

leader. Although he missed the first sit-ins in Greensboro in 1960, he participated in demonstrations against segregated facilities in 1963.

After his first semester at Illinois, he returned to Greenville for Christmas vacation, and when he attempted to write a term paper he found that the books he needed were not available in the Negro library. When he went to the white library (properly, he remembers, through the back door) he was told that it would take more than a week to get the books and that he could not use the stacks. He promised himself that he would change that situation, and in the following summer he was responsible for desegregating the entire library system.

Following his graduation at North Carolina A & T, he en-

tered a seminary in Chicago and was later ordained a Baptist minister. He went to work for Martin Luther King as director of the Southern Christian Leadership Conference Operation Breadbasket. He participated in the march between Selma and Montgomery and was with the Reverend King when he was assassinated in Memphis in April 1968.

In the early 1970s Jackson broke with the Southern Christian Leadership Conference and began his own Chicago-based organization, PUSH (People

173

United to Save Humanity). Combining the old-line Booker T. Washington doctrine of self-help with contemporary appeals to black pride and militant tactics, he is considered the most important black leader to emerge since Martin Luther King. The *Wall Street Journal* has described his Saturday morning PUSH meetings, directed primarily at young blacks, as a "combination of prayer meeting, civics class, and show business spectacular."

In addition to PUSH's emphasis on avoiding drugs, staying in school, and developing a positive self-identity ("I am . . . Somebody," the youngsters roar in response to Jackson's charismatic leadership), the minister-turned-politician has attempted to develop a "Rainbow Coalition" of the disadvantaged; has encouraged black economic strength through announced boycotts and corporate negotiations; and has emphasized voting rights, broadened registration procedures, and election law reforms to eliminate gerrymandering, second primaries, and at-large voting which have tended to diffuse black voting strength.

His surprising showing in several of the 1984 primaries gave Jackson a political springboard for involvement in foreign affairs. His much-publicized personal diplomacy in a successful trip to Syria to free a black American held captive has given him a position as one of the nation's most charismatic black leaders. He has brought, it has been said, "the new politics of Soul to the New South." While Jesse Jackson lives most of the year in Chicago, his is a strong presence in Greenville.

Judith Gatlin Bainbridge

Above: *The twenty-five-story Daniel Building has been a city landmark and the tallest building in the state since its completion in 1965. The building had its genesis in a meeting between Charles Daniel and Roger Peace, who decided to revitalize downtown by building major corporate headquarters at opposite ends of Main Street. Photo by Bob Bainbridge*

Opposite page: *A twenty-member delegation from Bergamo, Italy, Greenville's first Sister City, arrived in October 1985 to formalize the exchange. In ceremonies at City Hall, Mayor William D. Workman III presents a key to the city to Bergamo mayor Giorgio Zaccarelli. Photo by Charles Arbogast. Courtesy,* Greenville News-Piedmont

city officials have worked together as an innovative team to revitalize the downtown area. The approach has worked remarkably well, and, as Mayor W.D. Workman III has observed, other cities are taking note. The new Greenville Commons and the numerous projects planned by the Greenville Central Area Partnership are signs of a strong, forward-looking community with effective ideas.

The census of 1980 found the county population at an all-time high of 287,913; of that total, some 51,000 were black. Gradually these black citizens have made headway into elected offices, despite claims to the contrary by local son Jesse Jackson. By 1981 there was one black representative in the South Carolina House of Representatives, one on County Council, one on the School Board, and two on City Council. Their presence within the establishment has begun to make a difference, but white registered voters still outnumber the blacks. In addition to presidential candidate and peace envoy Jesse Jackson, another black Greenvillian, William F. Gibson, gained prominence in 1985 when he was elected National Chairman of the NAACP.

The 1980s find Greenville in an enviable position: blessed with capable leaders, economically sound, socially progressive, and suffering few of the ills often associated with such progress. A Greenville native, Richard W. Riley, has served two four-year terms as governor of South Carolina, the highest position of leadership and service in the state. The Leadership Greenville project, now in its thirteenth year, identifies a core of young leaders who make the welfare of the community their concern. Access to an almost unlimited quantity of pure drinking water is assured with the opening of a new treatment plant at Lake Keowee. Despite layoffs in textile mills and plant closings, the county's unemployment rate is

Opposite page: *The lone balloon reflected over the waters of Lake Conestee during Freedom Weekend Aloft offers a somewhat misleading impression of serenity. In 1985 Greenville's fifth annual Independence Day balloon festival attracted more than 200,000 people to Donaldson Center to view competitions and mass ascents of 200 colorful balloons, attend jazz and rock concerts, and enjoy fireworks displays. Courtesy, Blake Praytor*

Below: *March 22, 1986, marked the 200th anniversary of Greenville County and provided an excellent reason for community-wide celebration. More than 25,000 people attended the first Greenville Jubilee Parade and stayed for festivities at Heritage Green, which included a Civil War reenactment, a giant birthday cake, and this billboard-sized birthday card to the county. Photo by Bob Bainbridge*

lower than the rest of the nation. The diversified and eclectic economy is bursting with health. In fact, Greenville has been singled out as one of the top Sun Belt cities, combining growth potential with high quality of life. The fast-paced life of Interstate 85 and Donaldson Industrial Center are indeed symbolic of this modern urban center. But the peace and natural beauty of the Cherokee Foothills Scenic Highway and the Mountain Bridge Recreation and Wilderness Area reveal the values of the people who live there.

In short, the fabric of Greenville's development is not simple and is not complete. The design is still on the loom; the finished pattern is still emerging.

Left: *Raven Cliff Falls, just north of Caesar's Head, is one of the many beautiful areas that attracted low-country residents to Greenville County resorts in the nineteenth century. Courtesy, Pat Crawford*

Opposite page: *On a clear spring day, the majesty of Table Rock and the Blue Ridge Mountains is reflected in the waters of Table Rock Reservoir. The reservoir was built betwen 1925 and 1930 by the Greenville Water System to meet the long-range needs of the growing city. Photo by Bob Bainbridge*

Above: *Although Pelham Road is rapidly filling with subdivisions and office parks, a few horses still graze in paddocks, reminding residents of its recent past as a quiet, rural highway. Photo by David Jenkins*

Right: *Sunshine highlights a red barn in northern Greenville County. Cool breezes have brought vacationers to the foothills for generations, but family farms remain central to the region's economy. Courtesy, Ted Ramsaur*

A bicycle rider makes his way over a narrow wooden bridge at Paris Mountain State Park. Located only two miles from downtown Greenville, the park also offers camping sites, beaches, and hiking trails in addition to well-used bicycle paths. Courtesy, South Carolina Department of Parks, Recreation & Tourism

Above: *Students relax near the gates of Furman University. Courtesy, South Carolina Department of Parks, Recreation & Tourism*

Right: *Facilities at Bob Jones University include a 3,500-seat auditorium, a 7,000-seat "amphitorium," a Museum of Sacred Art, and outstanding landscaping including fountain pools and the flags of many nations. The university's conservative Christian teachings are felt strongly in the community. Photo by David Jenkins*

Opposite page: *Brilliant fall foliage highlights the pastoral beauty of Furman University's 750-acre campus at the foot of Paris Mountain. The new campus provided room for consolidation of the men's and women's campuses which completed the move from downtown in 1961. A replica of the original bell tower provides continuity with Furman's long traditions in Greenville. Photo by Bill Henry. Courtesy, Furman University*

Above: *In 1986, Greenville's fifteenth arts festival changed its name—to Riverplace Festival—and its location—from Heritage Green to the banks of the Reedy River near the historic district. In doing so it created a dynamic spring weekend celebration with an international flavor. Four hundred volunteers worked behind the scenes while more than 50,000 residents and tourists enjoyed headliners like jazz trumpeter Wynton Marsalis, the Temptations (seen here), and the Four Tops. Courtesy, Blake Praytor*

Right: *Children in costume enjoy the Riverplace Festival. Courtesy, Blake Praytor*

Left: *Greenville's ethnic communities add spice to the Riverplace Festival. These children from the Philippine-American Association of the Carolinas perform the "tinkling," a regional dance. Courtesy, Blake Praytor*

Summer band concerts by the lake on the Furman University campus attract thousands of Greenvillians. Photo by David Jenkins. Courtesy, Furman University

Greenville's new Museum of Art opened in 1974. It houses the Holly and Arthur Magill collection of Andrew Wyeth paintings and drawings, which has drawn national acclaim. Part of the "Heritage Green" complex, it is flanked by the Greenville Little Theatre and the Greenville County Library. Photo by David Jenkins

Above: *Children enjoy the playground equipment at Cleveland Park. Photo by David Jenkins*

Right: *Progressive leadership by the City of Greenville includes innovative new programs such as mounted police patrols in Cleveland Park. The service has been widely noted for effective law enforcement as well as exceptional community relations that have helped to reestablish respect for law officers in the eyes of Greenville's young citizens. Photo by Bob Bainbridge. Courtesy, Greenville Central Area Partnership, Inc.*

Above: *With a twelve-month recreational climate, both team and individual sports flourish in Greenville County. Parks and playgrounds are found throughout the city, and whether it's a pick-up game after school, a Little League or American Legion team contest, or an adult Textile Tournament, softball and baseball are popular. Photo by David Jenkins*

Left: *Nearly 10,000 Greenvillians have season tickets to watch Furman University's football team play on Saturdays in the fall. The Paladins have been Southern Conference champions for six of the last eight years and were second in the nation in NCAA Division 1-AA in 1985. Photo by Blake Praytor. Courtesy, Furman University*

Above: *For runners, three races—the one-mile fun run, and the three and ten kilometers—are the high point of the Riverplace Festival. More than 1,100 participants in the 1986 10K Reedy River Run followed a course from Heritage Green to Cleveland Park (shown here) through downtown Greenville. Courtesy, Blake Praytor*

Opposite page: *Hot air balloons converge on the landing field at the Freedom Weekend Aloft Festival. Begun in 1981, the Chamber of Commerce's annual Fourth of July event is the second-largest competitive balloon festival in the nation. Courtesy, Blake Praytor*

The Greenville Fire Department's modern training tower on the Mauldin Road is a far cry from the earliest firefighting equipment in the city. The first, hand-drawn fire engine was purchased by city fathers in 1859 and by 1874 the all-volunteer force had purchased a horse-drawn, steam-powered vehicle. The first motorized truck appeared in 1913. Photo by David Jenkins

*Greenville's Main Street has rebounded from vacant
storefronts and deteriorating buildings in the 1970s
to become a tree-lined haven for quality specialty
shops, restaurants, and second-floor apartments.
Photo by David Jenkins*

THE OPEN BOOK

Greenville Woven From the Past is an excellently written history of Greenville. Unfortunately one among the many fine photographs was not taken in Greenville. You will find it on page 192.

We have been in continuous contact with the publisher concerning this mistake. Although the publisher indicates they are committed to remedying this error, we have not been informed of exact details. It will entail our sending books back to the publisher. Our best judgment is that this process cannot be accomplished in time for books to be returned to us by Christmas.

Some customers have indicated that they are happy to have the book as is. We are providing a post card for you to fill in your address if you wish to buy the book now and have us notify you of further details.

Sincerely,

Tom Gower

29602 / 803-235-9651

post office box 93 / 241 north main street / greenville, south carolina

PARTNERS IN PROGRESS

Greenville is, above all, an area built on leadership.

Unquestionably, there were other factors that played significant roles in its growth and progress. Abundant natural resources cannot be overlooked. Neither can luck, fate, and circumstances. But the real story of Greenville is one of people. Individuals who cared not only about the future of their own business enterprise but also about the future of the community itself. Farsighted people who were continually challenged by the problems and opportunities of the day and always looking for a better tomorrow.

Hardy Scotch-Irish settlers came in the 1700s to settle the area. They cleared the land, harnessed the waterpower, and began to build trade and industry.

Soon more pioneering spirits came to profit from these solid beginnings. They built grist mills, then textile mills, and by the early part of the twentieth century textiles were a dominant force in the community—so much so that Greenville became known as the "Textile Center of the World."

Greenville's leadership has guided the area light-years beyond its textile background. But it never left it behind. Textiles continue to play a major role in the economic health and vitality of the area. However, always looking to the future, Greenville leaders diversified the community's economic base early on. And other manufacturing enterprises and regional and national headquarters began to call Greenville County home.

Greenville has been and still is a community in the making. And it will be for as long as its leaders are still being renewed by ideals, still being challenged by problems, and still searching for a better tomorrow.

The organizations whose stories are detailed on the following pages have chosen to support this important literary and civic project. They illustrate the variety of ways in which individuals and their businesses have contributed to the city's growth and development. The civic involvement of Greenville's businesses, institutions of learning, and local government, in cooperation with its citizens, has made the area an excellent place to live and work.

GREATER GREENVILLE CHAMBER OF COMMERCE

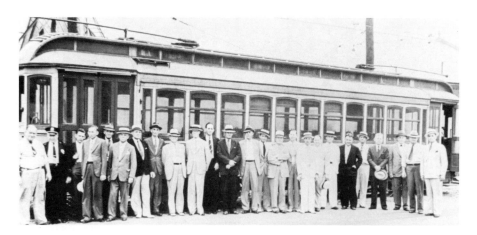

The chamber organized the Greenville State Booster Tour in 1921. Over 100 local businessmen participated in the two-week business recruitment trip, which included travels to Florida cities and Havana, Cuba.

Within the pages of the 1888 *Greenville City Directory,* the formation of an important organization was noted. It was called the Board of Trade and was the forerunner of today's Greater Greenville Chamber of Commerce.

Banded together in the interest of economic and community development, the businessmen who founded the organization wasted no time in getting down to the business of creating a better Greenville. The *City Directory* noted in 1888 that the infant Board of Trade was "... now one of the most important organizations in the city. Already it has done a great deal for the general welfare, and by taking an active interest in everything that pertains to the public good, it has done much to improve the city, to increase the population, and to build up other manufacturing enterprises. It includes in its membership most of the public-spirited businessmen, and active committees are appointed to look after the various interests of the industrial progress of the city."

W.E. Beattie was the organization's first president, and its membership roster contained 31 names. In 1920 the Board of Trade changed its name to the Greater Greenville Association of Commerce, and in 1921 it became known as the Greenville Chamber of Commerce.

One of the organization's first projects was to gain a publicly owned water system for the area. It seemed an impossible task at the time, but around the turn of the century it became a reality. Many other successes followed, and by 1921 Greenville was poised for expansion, and the chamber was ready to go after it.

That year the chamber organized the Greenville State Booster Tour. More than 100 area businessmen gave up two weeks of their own time, boarded a train, and went in search of new business for Greenville. They visited several cities in Florida, including Jacksonville, Miami, and Tampa, and went as far as Havana, Cuba.

The industrial and business growth that the chamber's early leaders sought continued to take place through the next several decades, and by 1978 Greenville was hailed by *Money* magazine as one of the top 10 growth towns in the United States for the 1980s.

Working to expand the area's economic base, solve problems, and improve Greenville's quality of life, the chamber has always been in-

volved in major issues confronting the community. Through the years the organization was involved in the sponsorship of Textile Hall, the promotion of both the downtown and Greenville-Spartanburg airports, the development of Greenville Technical College, and the total desegregation of the Greenville County public schools.

Today, some 3,000 members strong, the organization's objectives include business recruitment, expansion, and retention; promotion and support of good government; enhancement of the area's quality of life; regional cooperation; and community marketing.

It's been nearly a century since the area's business leaders came together to create a better Greenville. And since that time, it has worked. The organization's efforts have grown broader and stronger, but the mission is still the same. The Greater Greenville Chamber of Commerce is still "one of the most important organizations in the city," and it continues "to take an active interest in everything that pertains to the public good."

The Records Building on the corner of Main and Court streets was the chamber's home until 1923, when it moved to the Insurance Building and the Records Building was torn down.

AMERICAN KA-RO CORPORATION

It was the strength of Greenville's textile industry and a 1977 visit from city and chamber of commerce officials that brought Karl Rost's German-based KA-RO Werke to Greenville, where it began to operate as American KA-RO in 1978.

The privately owned corporation is a worldwide leader in the production of plastic yarn carriers for the textile industry. KA-RO produces some 40 million yarn carriers in 500 different sizes each year for sale to textile operations around the globe. The company also manufactures its own molds, employs approximately 180 people, and is capable of meeting any need for yarn carriers through its facilities in Germany, South Africa, and Greenville.

KA-RO's beginnings in 1957, however, were relatively modest. The business got its start as a tool shop in Troisdorf, Germany, a small industrial community about 15 miles southwest of Cologne. The facility, which manufactured plastic injection molds, employed six toolmakers.

In the late 1950s a revolutionary development—the Sulzer shutless loom—took the textile industry by storm. However, there was one problem: There was no existing

yarn carrier on the market that worked well on the loom. It was an invention of Rost's that ultimately solved the problem. Because of that unique development the company expanded its operations to include injection molding, and KA-RO went into the business of producing plastic yarn carriers for the textile industry.

The demand for the KA-RO product grew steadily, and the firm began to get orders from outside Germany. Its first deliveries to the United States were made in 1963. It soon became clear to Rost that the company would do well to expand again and add facilities outside of Germany. He selected South Africa for one additional plant, and cast an eye toward the United States for another.

Rost had become familiar with Greenville's assets from several contacts in the American textile industry, and the 1977 visit by then-Mayor Max Heller and chamber of commerce officials was well timed both for KA-RO and for Greenville.

Rost made a decision to open a plant in Greenville almost immedi-

Karl Rost, founder of American KA-RO.

ately, and less than one year later, in February 1978, construction was begun on the company's $1.5-million Greenville plant. U.S. production began in the 75,000-square-foot American KA-RO plant in September 1978 with two injection-molding machines and 10 employees. The move proved, in a short period of time, to be a wise one, and in 1986 the American KA-RO operation had grown to include 18 machines and 60 employees.

American KA-RO built its 75,000-square-foot Greenville plant in 1978.

DANIEL INTERNATIONAL CORPORATION

In the early part of the twentieth century, when the South lay economically stunned by the Great Depression, Charles E. Daniel envisioned something that few others did—a bright economic future for his homeland. The key, Daniel believed, was industrial development.

That belief, coupled with a knowledge of the construction industry and an almost uncanny ability to move through obstacles toward a goal, provided the base for one of the world's largest engineering, construction, and maintenance companies. Daniel also generated vast economic, industrial, and social gains for the Piedmont Carolina region and the entire South.

Daniel began his construction career in Anderson, South Carolina, with Townsend Lumber Company. Ahead of his time, he acted on his vision, and on December 17, 1934, he filed a charter to form Daniel Construction Company in Anderson.

The first full year of operation for Daniel Construction was a good one, and shortly after its first anniversary, the firm completed its first major project—four barracks at nearby Clemson College. That same year Daniel Construction took the first step toward becoming a national company, with the establishment of a regional office in Birmingham, Alabama, headed by R. Hugh Daniel.

Charles Daniel repeatedly professed that his firm could build "faster, better, and cheaper" than anybody else. The success of projects during World War II firmly cemented the company's reputation for excellence as a builder.

Daniel Construction's first defense project—and its first crash program—was the sprawling Reynolds Metals plant in Sheffield, Alabama. It was recognized as having been completed in a world-record time for a plant of its kind.

Many critical-schedule defense projects followed, including shipyards at Charleston, Savannah, and Brunswick; thousands of military housing units; and Greenville's Donaldson Air Force

Base.

Daniel believed Greenville was the place to be, and in February 1942 the company opened the doors of its new headquarters on North Main Street in the heart of the textile industry.

The industrial boom that Charles Daniel had seen on the horizon arrived immediately after World War II. Because he had seen it all coming, he was prepared not only to take advantage of it, but also to make it happen his way.

Geographically well-positioned, Daniel set out on a mission to bring industry to the South. He persuaded hundreds of businesses to locate in the region, and everyone gained in the process. Em-

ployees, employers, and the area prospered—and Daniel Construction Company began to receive national attention.

The increased work volume and expanding geographic reach of the firm required a strong management team. Daniel solved that problem in typical Daniel fashion—he surrounded himself with others like himself. Key people developed under his leadership included Hugh Daniel, Buck Mickel, Charles Cox, and George McDougall, each of whom would play leading roles in the company.

Daniel Construction was growing at a phenomenal rate, opening regional offices throughout the United States. The company stepped into

the international market, as major U.S. clients such as Monsanto, Eli Lilly, and Phillips asked it to serve them in new locations around the world. International offices were opened in Europe in 1964, and later in the Caribbean, to be close to the work.

Responding to client needs, Daniel Construction's range of services was also expanding, beginning with site location, through turnkey completions and beyond. Daniel Engineering was established, and the company pioneered the "design-build" concept in the industry. Providing equipment installation and continuing maintenance once the facilities were completed was rapidly becoming a major segment of business. In addition, Daniel Realty was created to assist in property management and development.

At the ground-breaking ceremony for the 25-story Daniel Building in downtown Greenville in June 1964, Daniel said, "It is my hope that Daniel Construction Company's expression of faith in a great future for Greenville, in erecting the state's tallest office structure, will cause others to join in building a dynamic new city for the Carolinas." Charles Daniel died on September 13, 1964, but his vision for his business and for Greenville continues.

Just as Daniel Construction Company was serving the major businesses around the world, it continued to play a key role in the growth of Greenville. Throughout the firm's history its clients have made up a Who's Who in the area: Furman University, J.P. Stevens, General Electric, Liberty Life, *Greenville News-Piedmont,* Michelin, The Little Theater, Texize, First Baptist Church, Deering Milliken, Hyatt Regency, Wunda Weve, Stone Manufacturing, Woodside Mills, U.S. Shelter Corporation, and many, many more. It would be difficult to drive for more than a few miles in the Greenville area without seeing a Daniel-built landmark.

On January 1, 1965, Hugh Daniel became chairman and chief executive officer, and Buck Mickel took over the daily operations of the company as president and chief operating officer.

The late 1960s brought important diversification into new, profitable markets, notably chemicals, synthetic fibers, research and development, aluminum, paper, and food processing. Multiple projects for such industry giants as Procter and Gamble, Du Pont, Allied

Chemical, and Eastman Kodak began to dot Daniel's list of successful completions. Another important step during that time period was the firm's move into the electric utilities industry in 1969. The company grew into one of the nation's leading constructors of power stations, providing a wide range of maintenance and technical services to the nuclear and fossil power industry. It was also in that year, on March 19, 1969, that Daniel Construction first offered its stock to the public.

The firm's international reputation continued to grow as major companies from Europe and Japan chose Daniel to serve them, both in the United States and around the world. Names like Hoechst, BASF, Sandoz, Hoffman LaRoche, Degussa, Nissan, Ajinomoto, Mitsubishi, and Toyota have become part of the corporation's day-to-day vocabulary.

In 1970 *Engineering News Record* magazine placed Daniel Construction Company second among all American general building contractors. It was an auspicious start to an eventful decade. In 1971 the firm changed its name to Daniel International Corporation to more accurately reflect its diversified services.

Buck Mickel was elected chairman of the board in 1974, succeeding Hugh Daniel, who remained as chief executive officer and treasurer. Charles Cox was named president and chief operating officer.

Overseas expansion continued in 1976 with new operations in Saudi Arabia, headed by George McDougall. Additional regional offices were opened in the United States.

In 1977 Daniel International Corporation was aligned into two principal divisions—Daniel Con-

struction and Daniel Industrial Services, for all nonconstruction operations. At that time Charles Cox was elected vice-chairman of the entire corporation and chairman of Daniel Construction. Currie Spivey was named president of Daniel Construction, and Greg Rothe became president of Daniel Industrial Services.

In April of that year the company made headlines across the country when it announced that it would be acquired by the Fluor Corporation for approximately $225 million. This marriage of two engineering and construction giants was an excellent move, augmenting the strengths and capabilities of both companies. Daniel International Corporation's identity and operating philosophy remained the same.

During the 1980s the firm assumed worldwide leadership positions in engineering and technical services, construction, maintenance, and project management. Les McCraw was elected president and chief executive officer and is leading Daniel into its second 50 years as a totally diversified services organization. This is certainly in keeping with Charles Daniel's philosophy of listening to clients' needs and responding by delivering "all you say you'll do—and then some."

"Daniel People" are justifiably proud of their history—but more excited about their future. From its headquarters in the downtown Daniel Building and the new Daniel Centre complex on Haywood Road, the company serves a wider range of clients with a broader spectrum of capabilities than ever before. Constantly growing, improving, and stretching to new heights, Daniel International Corporation is committed to "adding value" to Greenville and to the world.

BALLENGER GROUP, INC.

Construction was under way on U.S. 25 in 1929—one of Ballenger's first paving jobs.

The year was 1927, and the automobile was quickly becoming a way of life in America. The number of registered vehicles had skyrocketed during the previous few years, and the need for paved roads was great. The South Carolina Highway Department was ready to undertake a major highway building program, and Charles Pendleton Ballenger saw an opportunity.

In 1927 he opened the doors of Ballenger Paving Company. Success came immediately, and the firm was awarded a number of contracts for roads throughout

North Carolina, South Carolina, and Georgia.

During the next decade Ballenger introduced his two young sons, Charles Jr. and Grady, to the operation, and the schoolboys spent their summers learning the family business. When Charles Sr. died in 1937, Charles Jr. was well prepared to lead the company.

During World War II Ballenger Paving experienced significant growth through government air base contracts, but it was to be in the following two decades that business would soar, primarily as the result of the U.S. Interstate Highway Program. The firm added a number of divisions during those years to diversify and expand its capabilities to encompass grading, bridge building, utilities, hauling, aggregate production, coal mining, landscaping, and erosion control.

In 1967 Ballenger Paving was awarded its first job outside the United States, in Costa Rica. Two years later it changed its name to Ballenger Corporation to more accurately reflect its expanded capabilities.

Ballenger provided concrete paving for Lockheed Aircraft in Marietta, Georgia, in 1956.

Ballenger constructed Greenville's Church Street Bridge in 1958.

As the company entered the 1980s it had to its credit such major projects as the construction of the first diesel-generation power plant in the United States; the Las Americas Expressway and the La-Palmas Viaduct on the side of one of Puerto Rico's roughest mountains; the construction of 300 kilometers of the Inter-American Highway across the Continental Divide in Costa Rica; the construction of a number of water- and waste-treatment plants; numerous building projects, including St. Francis Hospital and student housing facilities at Clemson University; and various bridge-building projects that have earned Ballenger a reputation as one of the premier bridge builders in the Southeast.

In 1984 the Ballenger Corporation was purchased by Currie B. Spivey, Jr., former president of Daniel Construction Company. The corporation was renamed Ballenger Group, Inc., and restructured to become a general contracting firm specializing in commercial, industrial, institutional, and waste- and water-treatment construction; contract maintenance; asphalt and concrete paving; and the construction of highways and bridges.

ERNST & WHINNEY

Ernst & Whinney is the third-largest and one of the fastest growing accounting, tax, and business consulting firms in the world. With international headquarters in New York City and U.S. headquarters in Cleveland, Ohio, the firm's staff exceeds 25,000 located in 359 offices in 77 countries. In the United States, the firm employs approximately 12,000 people in 122 offices. The firm began as Ernst & Ernst in Cleveland three years after the turn of the century and was a new name in Greenville in July 1978. The following year the firm changed its name to Ernst & Whinney with the formation of the international partnership.

In 1926 Robert W. Taylor, an accountant with the Boston firm of Cooley & Marvin, opened a branch office in Greenville in the Franklin National Life Building on West Washington Street. In 1940 the Cooley & Marvin office was moved to the 15th floor of the Woodside Building on the site of the present South Carolina National Bank Building. P.M. Jenness transferred from Boston to the Greenville office in 1930 and remained active until his retirement in 1971. Others who worked for Cooley & Marvin included H.B. Croxton (1934-1942), later an officer of J.P. Stevens & Co., Inc.; J.D. Vann, Jr. (1940-1963), now retired from Belton

Industries, Inc.; and John H. Robinson, who worked in the Greenville office from 1941 until his death in 1967.

Primarily because of merger and acquisition activity in the textile industry, the New York accounting firm of S.D. Leidesdorf & Co. needed to establish a base in the

The current partners in the Greenville office of Ernst & Whinney. Standing (left to right) are Gary V. Sutton, Jack C. Robinson, Michael G. Maxey, and William D. Brigman. Seated (left to right) are Richard E. Parrott and J. Kenyon Lewis. Sitting on the conference table is Carl B. Harper, managing partner.

The only three executives in the history of the Greenville office. The first to hold that position was Robert W. Taylor (above, left), followed by S. Lewis Condron (above, center) and Carl B. Harper (above, right).

Southern Piedmont, and on January 1, 1947, Cooley & Marvin in Greenville became S.D. Leidesdorf & Co. Taylor continued as resident manager of the office. In 1956 the firm's headquarters was moved to the 12th floor of the SCN building, the new name for the Woodside Building.

Not long before Cooley & Marvin became S.D. Leidesdorf & Co., J.M. Burnett, Jr., joined the staff and remained in charge of the tax department until he retired in 1975. George W. Hightower came to work for Cooley & Marvin about the same time. He transferred to the Charlotte office in 1956 and retired as a manager in 1979. S. Lewis Condron joined the firm in 1947, and Charles W. Stowe came in 1952. J. William Davis joined the staff in 1950 and retired as a manager in 1981. Bobbie Gaines worked as typist and bookkeeper from 1952 to 1955 and returned to the

office in 1963, where she continues to serve a vital role as supervisor of report production and tax processing.

In 1957 Taylor retired, and S. Lewis Condron became partner in charge of the Greenville office of S.D. Leidesdorf & Co. A few weeks earlier Carl B. Harper had joined the Greenville staff. He left to open the Spartanburg office in 1965 and returned to Greenville as managing partner when Condron retired on October 1, 1981.

The Greenville office employed about 25 people in 1957. That figure grew to about 35 in 1966 and to 45 in 1978. Condron was the only partner in the office until 1962, when Stowe was admitted to the partnership. Thomas L. McAbee joined the staff in 1959 and became a partner eight years later. Carol D. Vinson, hired in 1963, became a partner in 1971. Both McAbee and Vinson left S.D. Leidesdorf & Co. for executive jobs in industry, McAbee in 1975 and Vinson two years later. Richard E. Parrott came to work for the firm in 1966 and was admitted to the partnership 11 years later. J. Kenyon Lewis became manager

in charge of the Greenville office tax department in 1975 and was admitted to the partnership two years later.

Others who have given long years of service to the Greenville office are Charles S. Bell (1947-1956), John P. Odom (1947-1956), James D. Wiggs (1952-1962), Maurice Brown (1953-1965), Philip S. Brandon (1957-1976), H. Theron Few (1957-1966), James G. Lane, Jr. (1959-1965), N. Barton Tuck, Jr. (1960-1966), Charles Holton (1961-1973), Edward J. Brent (1962-1973), William H. Jarrard, Jr. (1968-1979), Y. Joe Harrington III (1971-1983), Harold P. Hunt, Jr. (1973-1983), James A. Aston (1975-1986), J. Randall Bishop (1976-1984), and Danny Senn, Jr. (1975-1984). James W. Anderson worked in the Greenville office from 1963 to 1973 and remained with the firm in the Spartanburg office until 1979. W. Luther Stancil, who became a partner in 1977 in the Spartanburg office of Ernst & Whinney, served in the Greenville office from 1965 to 1969. Other individuals who have transferred to other offices are James A. Miller (partner, Miami office; Greenville,

J.M. Burnett, Jr., principal in charge of tax.

1968-1982), Ronald D. Wilson (senior manager, Columbia office; Greenville, 1973-1980), W. Hunter Cook (Partner, Charlotte office; Greenville, 1969-1983), and W. Randall Dickerson (senior manager, Charlotte office; Greenville, 1977-1981).

Ernst & Whinney's alumni association is a valuable asset. The firm's policy is and has consistently been to hire outstanding people, provide excellent education and experience for the staff, and maintain contact with those who move on to other careers. The firm is proud of all Ernst & Whinney people.

Gary Sutton (audit-July 1970) and Mike Maxey (tax-September 1976) were admitted to the partnership in 1984. Jack Robinson (audit-May 1973) and Bill Brigman (audit/health care-1972), who transferred from the Charlotte office in 1983, were admitted to the partnership in 1985.

On July 6, 1978, the practice of S.D. Leidesdorf & Co. was merged with the practice of Ernst & Ernst. Just two years later the 60 employees of the Greenville office had outgrown their quarters on the 18th floor of the Daniel Building and a move was made, doubling the office space. The audit staff and general offices took over the entire 16th floor of the building, leaving the tax staff, whose growth had been even greater than that of the audit staff, to occupy most of the space formerly used by the entire office. Further growth demanded that the tax department move to the 15th floor in 1984, at which time Ernst & Whinney occupied almost two floors in the Daniel Building.

The Greenville office of Ernst & Whinney will move to the new Shelter Centre Citizens & Southern Tower in late 1986, where it will occupy approximately 26,000 square feet on the seventh and eighth floors. The office has grown to include approximately 90 peo-

P.M. Jenness, principal audit/textile specialist.

Charles W. Stowe, audit partner.

ple. The Spartanburg office, which operates closely with Greenville, has 25 employees. The South Carolina practice, including the Greenville, Spartanburg, and Columbia offices, employs over 150 people and represents the largest public accounting practice in the state.

South Carolina was second percentage-wise in the nation in the formation of new businesses from 1980 to 1985 and works to provide the best environment for entrepreneurs. Ernst & Whinney people are dedicated to providing excellent accounting, tax, and management consulting services; its people are involved in community leadership and civic affairs. Ernst & Whinney has a strong commitment to South Carolina. Says managing partner Carl B. Harper, "We are very proud of our heritage and look forward with anxious anticipation to the growth and continuing success that we are confident lies ahead."

BI-LO, INC.

Each week more than one million customers are served by BI-LO, Inc. South Carolina's largest food retailer, BI-LO operates more than 150 stores, has over 9,000 employees, and in 1985 reported sales in excess of one billion dollars.

The company's beginning dates back to 1961, when Frank L. Outlaw purchased a 50-percent interest in Greenville's four-store Wrenn & Syracuse grocery operation. Outlaw acquired Wrenn's interest in 1962 and, with several associates, formed BI-LO, Inc. At that time the firm had six stores and five million dollars in sales.

Offering discount prices on quality goods yielded a high sales volume and rapid inventory turnover for the young company. It brought rapid growth as well. By 1968 BI-LO was operating 27 stores and had moved its warehouse and general office to its present location on Industrial Boulevard near Mauldin, South Carolina.

The firm went public in 1970 with the sale of common stock. Seven years later the 97-store operation was purchased by Ahold n.v., an international food retailer headquartered in Zaandam, The Netherlands.

BI-LO took a bold step into the 1980s with a major remodeling program designed to bring all its stores to a modern standard. Service meat markets and bulk produce departments, characteristic of the early days, gave way to large produce departments, self-service meat markets, extensive offerings of frozen foods, and electronic cash registers. Newer stores enticed customers with specialty offerings, including a bakery, deli, cheese island, and seafood counter. And the white-faced Hereford steer that Outlaw had selected as the company symbol nearly 20 years earlier took a prominent place on BI-LO's new logo.

The firm's philosophy of offering quality products at appealing prices remained consistent, and growth continued. Sales topped one billion dollars for the first time in 1984.

To serve its stores in North Carolina, South Carolina, and Georgia, BI-LO operates a 690,000-square-foot warehouse in Mauldin with

Customers are assisted in a typical produce department.

BI-LO operates more than 150 stores in North Carolina, South Carolina, and Georgia.

two shifts of employees and a stock of more than 7,000 items. A fleet of BI-LO tractors and trailers delivers goods to the stores.

Through the years BI-LO has returned much to the community. It was instrumental in the beginning of the Community Food Bank of the Piedmont; it co-sponsored a benefit golf tournament for Meals on Wheels; it has contributed to the nutrition room of the Roper Mountain Science Center; and it is a regular supporter of the United Way and the March of Dimes.

BI-LO, Inc., steps toward the future with 12 additional stores planned for 1986 and a new general office under construction for occupancy in 1987. And the company continues its promise "to deliver maximum value for money by offering quality merchandise at the lowest prices in our marketing area, and by providing a shopping atmosphere of the highest standard characterized by cleanliness, friendliness, and service."

RELIANCE ELECTRIC MECHANICAL GROUP

Reliance Electric Mechanical Group represents a new generation in a long line of industrial pioneers, and its roots run deep into the soil of American innovation. Although the mechanical group was formed in 1969, it actually got its start more than a century ago with three industrial pacesetters and their namesake companies: Dodge®, Master®, and Reeves®.

The story of Reliance Electric Mechanical Group began in a small Indiana factory in 1881. There Wallace Dodge was working on a new invention—a wood split pulley with an interchangeable bushing system. Patented on July 4,

Though Dodge Manufacturing Company of Mishawaka, Indiana, was purchased by Reliance Electric Company as recently as 1961, its history dates back to 1881, when Wallace Dodge invented the wood split pulley with an interchangeable bushing system.

1882, the Independence Wood Split Pulley created sweeping changes in the made-to-order pulley business. His next invention was an improved rope drive for engines. But Dodge saw that the market for the future was in cast iron, so he built a foundry and machine shop, and the Dodge Manufacturing Company was soon producing babbitted bearings, a split friction clutch, shaft couplings, collars, and cast-iron gears. Dodge died in 1894 at the untimely age of 45, but his business went on to become a major manufacturer of mechanical power transmission products.

At about the time of Dodge's death, in the same fertile area of the Midwest, another young inventor named Milton O. Reeves was at work constructing one of the first five automobiles ever to exist in America. He called it the "Motorcycle," and it was a remarkable

development. While other automobiles were able to operate only in stop and go modes, Reeves' vehicle could operate at different speeds. By proving that a standard motor, gearcase, and belt case could be combined for productive mechanical adjustable speed, Reeves' invention changed the way America's motors operated.

Then came the year 1919. It was then that E.P. Larsh and 50 hand-picked engineers formed the Master Electric Company and began to manufacture a profusion of motors and gear motors out of Dayton, Ohio. The gear motor, an original Master invention, found immediate and widespread acceptance and became extensively used in food processing, machine tools, and in materials-handling applications for conveyors and cranes.

When Reliance Electric Company purchased the Reeves Pulley Company of Columbus in 1954, the

Reliance Electric Mechanical Group, headquartered in Greenville, is a powerful organization of plants, warehouses, distributors, and sales offices located throughout the United States, Canada, Mexico, and Brazil.

Master Electric Company of Dayton in 1957, and Dodge Manufacturing Company of Mishawaka, Indiana, in 1967, it folded the three firms into a major operation, which itself was steeped in the American tradition of innovation.

The seeds of Reliance Electric Company were planted in 1904, when a Cleveland industrialist named Peter Hitchcock and an inventor, John Lincoln, opened a shop for electrical experimentation and development. In 1905 they succeeded in developing a direct current motor with adjustable speeds. It was a simple, yet important, discovery, and the variety of practical applications for the new variable speed motor were many.

The firm was incorporated under the name Lincoln Electric Corporation in 1907; two years later its name was changed to Reliance

Electric and Engineering Company. It has since developed into a multidivisional corporation, supplying a broad range of markets with the means for increased productivity through automation. Reliance operates as an independent company, although it is a subsidiary of Exxon Corporation, which acquired the firm in late 1979.

With the purchase of Dodge, Master, and Reeves, Reliance successfully fused an outstanding combination of mechanical power products into a team capable of supplying a full range of top-quality products for drive systems. It also established a network of production centers in America's heartland. Therefore, the stage was set to form the Reliance Electric Mechanical Group in 1969 to take full advantage of both products and markets.

Today, headquartered in Greenville, the Reliance Electric Mechanical Group is a powerful organization of plants, warehouses, distributors, sales offices, and dedicated people located throughout the United States and into Canada, Mexico,

and Brazil. The company manufactures a broad line of industrial products used primarily in mechanical power transmission applications. Many of its products have long been industry leaders. Dodge Type E mounted bearings, Torque-Arm® speed reducers, Para-Flex® couplings, and Taper-Lock® bushings, for example, represent industry standards by which other products are measured. And the group continues to develop innovative new products to meet the ever-changing needs of industrial manufacturers.

The skill and craftsmanship that go into the products of the Reliance Electric Mechanical Group, and the century of tradition from which it all has been built is, in the end, hidden away as integral parts inside machines. Once installed, they are seldom seen; however, the Reliance Electric Mechanical Group finds great pride in that set of circumstances, as the products that it manufactures operate quietly, precisely, and durably in the machinery that keeps America working.

PEAT, MARWICK, MITCHELL & CO.

Founded in 1897, Peat, Marwick, Mitchell & Co. is one of the nation's oldest accounting firms. A multinational copartnership with more than 25,000 partners and employees in over 300 offices, it provides audit, accounting, tax, business advisory, and consulting services to clients all over the world.

Peat Marwick opened its office in Greenville on June 2, 1958. Thomas S. Hudgins was the first managing partner of the three-person Greenville office, which was located in the Insurance Building at the corner of Main and Court streets. With Hudgins in 1958 was Charlie Smith, who later became managing partner of Peat Marwick's Detroit office and a member of the firm's board of directors before retiring in 1986 and again becoming a resident of Greenville. Its initial principal clients, whose South Carolina locations had long been served from other offices, included Dan River, Burlington Industries, Singer, and Winn Dixie.

In 1968 Peat Marwick merged with J. Harlon Riggins & Co., a local accounting firm, and Riggins served as partner in charge of the tax department until retiring in 1976. The merger more than doubled the size of the practice to 30 employees, and the firm moved to larger quarters in the then-new Daniel Building.

Upon Hudgins' retirement in 1969, Robert A. Brown transferred from Greensboro and was appointed managing partner. That same year James R. Talton, Jr., transferred from the firm's Raleigh office as a senior accountant. He became a partner in 1976, and when Brown was transferred back to Greensboro four years later, Talton was appointed managing partner. William Bond also came to Greenville from Miami and served as an audit

partner from 1971 until his retirement in 1980.

The firm again moved in 1974 to the First Federal Building. That same year Robert C. Davis was elected to the partnership and was responsible for the tax department until his transfer to Washington, D.C., in that same role in 1977. Two years later Gerald R. Wicker became an audit partner, and in 1980 Robert E. Hamby, Jr., became a tax partner.

In 1982 Peat Marwick was dealt a blow when Dan River, its largest client based in Greenville, moved its headquarters to Danville, Virginia. However, the office added numerous new clients and led Peat Marwick's 100 U.S. offices in percentage growth during 1982-1983. In 1982 Derrell Hunter transferred from Peat Marwick's executive office to Greenville as an additional audit partner.

In December 1984 the Greenville office's dramatic growth required yet another move, and it almost doubled its space by moving to the First Union Bank Tower at One Shelter Centre. The firm's major client list, which included such companies as Multimedia, U.S. Shelter Corporation, First Federal of South Carolina, American Federal, Builder Marts, Bigelow-

Sanford, Clinton Mills, and many others, was continuing to expand.

The current leadership at Peat Marwick emerged during 1985 and 1986 as a result of promotions within the firm and other opportunities. Tax partner in charge Hamby left to become a member of the top management at client Multimedia; James R. Jones transferred from Nashville to take his place; and Charles P. Butler, Jr., became a tax partner. Wicker became partner in charge of the Tampa office audit department, and audit partner Dale H. Bullen transferred from Memphis. As of July 1, 1986, Cathy R. Faulconer became an audit partner; Talton assumed managing partner responsibility in the Raleigh office; and Hunter replaced Talton as managing partner in Greenville. During Talton's seven-year tenure leading the office, it nearly doubled in size, and Peat, Marwick, Mitchell & Co.'s partners, managers, and professional staff established themselves as leaders in many aspects of the Greenville community.

Partners of the Greenville office of Peat, Marwick, Mitchell & Co. in June 1986 (left to right) James R. Jones, Derrell E. Hunter, James R. Talton, Jr., Charles P. Butler, Jr., and Dale H. Bullen.

DUKE POWER COMPANY

Early construction of distribution lines in downtown Greenville.

It was only a short time after the world's first electric power generating station was established in New York by Thomas Alva Edison that the versatility of electricity was clearly apparent, and people across the country were taking notice.

North Carolina tobacco magnate James Buchanan "Buck" Duke showed particular interest. Duke and his brother, Ben, had invested heavily in textiles in the Carolina Piedmont in the late 1800s, and they knew that hydroelectricity could significantly increase textile productivity.

At about the same time two other brothers, Dr. Walker Gill Wylie and Dr. Robert Wylie, were dreaming of industrializing the Catawba Valley with electricity generated by the Catawba River. The brothers experimented with a hydroelectric plant at Portman Shoals, and soon electricity from that plant was used to drive the machinery of a cotton mill in Anderson. The theory confirmed, construction was begun on the Catawba plant, but toward the turn of the century the project was pressed for financial assistance.

In 1899 Dr. Walter Gill Wylie performed an appendectomy on Ben Duke and later took the op-

portunity to describe the Catawba project. Duke was impressed and made a small investment.

It was five years later, however, when Dr. Gill Wylie was called in to treat Buck Duke for a foot ailment that serious discussions took place as to the advancements being made in hydroelectric development in the Piedmont. William States Lee, the engineer for the Catawba project, was called in to provide Duke with technical details, and the three came together to form Southern Power Company in 1905 with two million dollars in funding from Duke.

The dream of the corporation's founders soon became a reality as the textile industry began to glow with the power gushing out of the Catawba. As demand grew and a number of homes were being serviced in addition to mills, a subsidiary, Southern Public Utilities, was created in 1913. Later that year the company purchased the entire Greenville distribution system. After building several coal-fired plants—including one in Green-

ville—Southern Power merged with Duke Power in 1927.

The firm entered the nuclear age in 1956 when it joined with three neighboring utilities to build a nuclear reactor. Six years later the group opened the Southeast's first atomic plant at Parr Shoals, South Carolina, and in 1973 Duke opened the Oconee plant, which was at the time the world's largest nuclear power plant.

In 1986 Duke provided power to 112,000 customers in Greenville County and 1.4 million customers in the 20,000-square-mile Carolina Piedmont service area. The firm, which currently operates 26 hydro stations, 8 coal-fired stations, and 3 nuclear stations, is the only investor-owned utility in the nation that designs and builds its own plants. In addition, the Duke Power Company generating system consistently ranks as one of the most fuel-efficient generating systems in the country.

Duke Power's first nuclear plant, the Oconee Nuclear Station, located in Seneca, South Carolina, was completed in 1973. The workhorse of the Duke system, Oconee has generated more electricity than any other nuclear plant in the United States.

CRS SIRRINE, INC.

He was one of America's great engineers, one of South Carolina's chief benefactors, and one of Greenville's most remarkable citizens. But perhaps the most lasting and important legacy of Joseph Emory Sirrine is the architectural, engineering, and planning firm that bears his name.

With a staff of six, J.E. Sirrine, Mill Architect and Engineer, began operations in 1902. A former employee of Lockwood Greene Company, Sirrine was well known as an outstanding engineer, and from the beginning his firm's services were in great demand.

Sirrine established divisions within his company almost immediately, employing specialists to concentrate their efforts on the various phases of industrial engineering. By 1908 many of the larger manufacturing plants in the

CRS Sirrine, Inc., carries on the traditions established by its founder, Joseph Emory Sirrine, renowned throughout South Carolina not only as an outstanding engineer and entrepreneur but also for his major civic and charitable contributions.

The 216 Building is the Greenville headquarters for the CRSS Engineering Group.

state were constructed according to Sirrine's plans and under his supervision. His reputation as the foremost mill engineer in South Carolina soon spread beyond the boundaries of the state.

At first the firm was located on the second floor of the Piedmont Shoe Building on the corner of South Main and West McBee Avenue. Growth soon required a move to a larger facility, and in 1913 the company moved to a building across from the old post office.

Business was booming, and the firm entered the decade of the 1920s with the design of 64 new mills and 22 major additions to its credit. But Sirrine wasn't counting past accomplishments; instead, he was looking to the future.

That farsightedness led to the formation of the first Sirrine partnership in 1921. For the business that Sirrine had operated as a sole proprietor until that time, the new partnership and others that would follow in 1937, 1952, and 1954 ensured that the new J.E. Sirrine and Company would continue to operate for decades to come.

The good years of the 1920s turned to bad years in the 1930s as the Depression dealt the firm a heavy blow. It was to be one of only two periods in the company's history in which money was lost and employees laid off. Times were so bad that for a couple of months, Sirrine paid employees from his own pocket.

Some relief came in 1931, when a new law required utility companies to have their properties appraised, and Sirrine found work in appraisals. That new area of the business brought in enough work to carry J.E. Sirrine and Company through the Depression.

Until the late 1930s the firm was involved primarily in the textile business. But a new era was dawning. Textiles were declining, and Sirrine saw the need to diversify the company's operations. Shortly before World War II the diversification sought by the entrepreneur was found in two almost simultaneous ventures: a pulp and paper mill in Texas and an aluminum plant in Alabama.

J.E. Sirrine and Company found much government work during the war, and the majority of its employees who were not called overseas were kept busy designing shipyards. The postwar years brought more opportunities in projects that had been postponed because of the war. Sirrine's paper mill project provided the impetus for continued work in the pulp and paper industry that remains a major market segment today.

Through the years Sirrine was quick to share his success and made regular major civic and charitable contributions. It was a sad day for Greenville when he passed away on August 7, 1947. The bells of Furman Tower tolled all day mourning his death.

He was remembered in one tribute as a man who was uniquely outstanding in three fields: civic affairs, industry, and education. Noted the *Daily News Record,* "It has been said that nothing of consequence has ever been done in the Piedmont over a long period without getting the viewpoint of J.E. Sirrine. He was called in for consultation on practically anything of consequence in this area."

The strong leadership developed

The Patewood Office Building, Greenville.

under Sirrine took the company to new heights in the decade following his death, and in 1956 the partners decide to incorporate. The move, which changed the corporate name to J.E. Sirrine Company, provided the opportunity for more employees to hold stock in the firm and also provided additional work incentives. J.E. Sirrine Company quickly became one of the largest employee-owned businesses of its kind.

The next 20 years proved to be a time of growth, diversification, and expansion. When William L. Carpenter, current vice-chairman, joined J.E. Sirrine Company in the mid-1950s, the pulp and paper industry accounted for 85 to 90 percent of its business. It was clearly time to diversify, and the firm accomplished that successfully with entry into a number of other industries—from chemicals, to research and development, to tobacco.

In 1971 the company began to expand its geographic reach, opening a design center in Houston, Texas, and soon after, its second out-of-state operation in Raleigh, North Carolina. Other design centers were established in Savannah, Georgia, and Summerville, South Carolina. Sales offices were opened in Portland, Oregon, and Chicago, Illinois, and international design efforts were initiated in the 1970s with Mideast and European assignments. Additional international design centers were later opened in Sao Paulo, Brazil, and Winnipeg and Montreal, Canada.

In 1983 J.E. Sirrine Company and Houston-based CRS Group merged to form CRS Sirrine, Inc., a design/construct and management company known worldwide.

In the ever-expanding world of technical services, the future of CRS Sirrine, Inc., the company J.E. Sirrine began in 1902, seems without limits.

CANAL INSURANCE COMPANY

In the decade of the 1930s, when the nation was striving mightily to dig itself out of the worst depression in its history, William R. "Bill" Timmons and T.J. "Pete" Mims were striving mightily to keep a growing industry from being crippled in the Southeast.

Timmons had already built a successful real estate and insurance agency in Greenville when he was introduced to the problems of insuring long-haul motor vehicles. And the problems were many.

The Depression had left the Southeast the poorest of the poor, and its long-haul operators were the riverboat gamblers of the transportation industry. Usually in debt, they fought long odds with overextended equipment. Insurance companies generally held that truckers were much like tornadoes and floods—acts of God for which there was no adequate insurance. When South Carolina passed legislation that mandated long-haul vehicles be properly insured, operators could legitimately ask, "By whom?"

At least one agent was interested. With highways and equipment constantly improving and the need for cheap transportation growing, Timmons saw a promising future for long-haul operators if he could solve their insurance problems. To that end Timmons, with his new agency manager Mims, moved forward and helped the South Carolina Motor Transportation Association set up its own insurance company.

The new venture was successful, but its coverage was limited to South Carolina. When North Carolina and Georgia passed "insure or else" laws, the long-haul operators again turned to the Timmons agency for help.

For nearly eight years Timmons and Mims lobbied and labored in

William R. Timmons, co-founder and first president.

the three-state area to place long-haul business with responsible insurance firms. But mortality among the companies was alarming. In eight years four major insurers went under.

During that critical period Mims watched closely for danger signals, and pulled his clients' business before each collapse. As a result, not a single Timmons client went without coverage or paid an extra premium because an insurer failed.

The company's reputation spread, and by 1942 the Wm. R. Timmons Agency was writing more insurance on long-haul trucks and passenger-carrying vehicles than any other firm in the three-state area. Still, company failures were more than a matter of inconve-

nience for the agency. They were a real danger, setting off rounds of higher rates and wider restrictions.

Mims began to look at casualty companies with a critical eye, and became convinced that firms failed not so much because of the risk involved, but because of poor management and operations. Both Timmons and Mims believed the picture could be altered, but they needed an insurance company to prove their thesis. In December 1942 the pair acquired Canal Insurance Company of Columbia and moved its headquarters to Greenville.

The beginning was not impressive. Canal was a small, virtually inactive firm founded in 1939 under the aegis of the First National Bank. Its original purpose was to insure automobiles financed by the bank, but World War II frustrated both purpose and growth, and Canal stagnated.

The new owners, however, were extraordinarily successful with their acquisition. Then tragedy struck. On the afternoon of June 22, 1948, Timmons was killed in an automobile accident outside Columbia.

The tragedy brought business at Canal to a temporary standstill, but the pioneer spirit that had motivated the team of Mims and Timmons remained intact. At a special meeting of the company's stockholders in July, Mims was elected Canal's new president.

Before Timmons' death, Georgia was on the top of the Canal blueprint for expansion. In less than a year that state was added to the firm's operation. The following year the company picked up Florida and Alabama, and by 1953 Canal was licensed in nine southern and border states. Business was booming.

For the next six years Mims was constantly on the road. Solid insurance for motor transportation vehicles was still the exception, and Canal was welcomed in state after state.

When *Best's Insurance Report* reviewed casualty companies in 1960, Canal was listed as operating in 42 states. *Best's* review of 1960 commended the firm for "excellent" sponsorship, growth, and investments. Mims was singled out as a man of broad experience "in the general agency and executive phases of the fire and casualty business." Assets were listed at close to six million dollars, with a policyholders' surplus of well over one million dollars—a far cry from the original $5,000 capitalization and $17,500 surplus.

Canal Insurance Company continued to extend its operation and increase its volume of premiums written. In the 1960s public service and safety programs were augmented, home office facilities were improved, and client service was fast and efficient as advertised.

Despite the vicissitudes of the national economy during the 1970s, the firm continued to flourish; continued to add staff, technology, and physical facilities; and never recorded a year without substantial growth. For its performance, the company won a rare A+ rating from *Best's Insurance Report,* and continued to hold that rating through subsequent years.

Canal's performance was not only extraordinary, it was unique. Within its specialty, it is the only company in the world that has survived the uncertainties and complexities that have beseiged its own industry and the industry it has served over the past four decades.

Many years ago Mims proved that there was a viable alternative to the restrictions and prohibitions that threatened the operations of the motor transportation industry in the South. A small but vigorous pioneer, Canal made a visible and lasting contribution by helping the industry realize the kind of financial security necessary for growth.

Throughout its history Canal Insurance Company has been a responsible citizen and has played an important role in the resurgence of the South. In Greenville, the firm's commitment and involvement in the community's economic and cultural life has helped make its hometown one of the most attractive and promising cities anywhere.

T.J. Mims, co-founder and current president.

U.S. SHELTER CORPORATION

"Success in the industry is achieved by companies who are flexible enough to offer products and services that meet changing market needs," says U.S. Shelter Corporation's founder, N. Barton Tuck, Jr.

Those words offer a powerful insight into the philosophy that has guided the Greenville-based real estate investment services company toward a position of national growth and prominence since its founding in 1972.

U.S. Shelter organizes public and private partnerships for investing in income-producing real estate, and, by the close of 1985, had raised more than $400 million of equity capital from 32,000 investors for this purpose. In addition, the company develops and constructs multifamily, commercial, and resort properties, and manages more than 60,000 multifamily housing units and approximately 11 million square feet of commer-

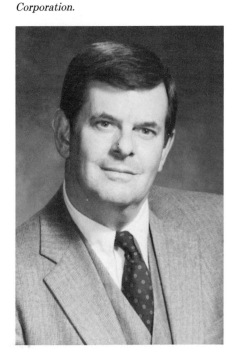

N. Barton Tuck, Jr., founder, is chairman and chief executive officer of U.S. Shelter Corporation.

Buck Mickel, formerly chairman of the board, was named vice-chairman in 1986.

cial space. Beyond its primary businesses of syndication, construction and development, and property management, the firm also engages in mortgage banking, insurance, and real estate brokerage activities. With over 2,000 employees, its operations encompass 28 states.

When ground was broken for U.S. Shelter's gleaming 17-story corporate headquarters in downtown Greenville in 1982, it was difficult for many area residents to recall that it all began rather modestly just 10 years prior.

An investment of $10,000 from local businessmen, coupled with a great deal of foresight, was all it took to form the new company in January 1972. At that time U.S. Shelter employed about 10 people, managed four apartment complexes, and was involved in apartment syndication. Growth began immediately, and by the end of its

first year in business, the firm's revenues were $250,000.

U.S. Shelter's next years were good ones, and by the end of 1974 the company managed 70 apartment complexes. Sullivan Company, Inc., a wholly owned subsidiary of U.S. Shelter and one of the nation's largest independently owned insurance brokers, was organized in 1974.

It was following the 1973-1975 recession, however, that U.S. Shelter's major growth period began. When the recession ended, the firm was able to capitalize on the distressed apartment property business in the region and purchase many projects at bargain prices through syndicating equity funds from investors.

In 1977 the privately held corporation continued its growth when it acquired H.G. Smithy & Co., a Washington, D.C.-based real estate

Carol D. Vinson was named president and chief operating officer of the real estate investment firm in 1986.

and mortgage banking firm that managed apartment units in the Washington area.

That same year marked the beginning of what is now Shelter Contractors, Inc. SCI was organized as a natural extension of U.S. Shelter's involvement in multifamily housing. The division is skilled in construction and condominium conversions, including feasibility studies, site selection and acquisition, regulatory compliance, architectural planning, construction, leasing, and financing.

In November 1979 U.S. Shelter Corporation became a publicly owned company with stock traded in the over-the-counter market.

U.S. Shelter's syndication division, always an integral part of the company's operations, took a major leap in 1980 with its first public offering—a $15-million equity fund called Shelter Properties I. Selling out in six weeks, Shelter Properties I proved that the venture into public offerings was a solid one. It was the first in a series that to date encompasses eight offerings totaling more than $400 million.

Meanwhile, through another business combination in 1981, U.S. Shelter continued to expand its asset base, which now exceeds $200 million. The firm's net worth is approximately $28 million.

It was a proud day in 1984 when the company moved into its new downtown headquarters, Shelter Centre I, now called the First Union Bank Tower. It was only a short time later that the firm announced that construction would begin on the second phase of Shelter Centre, the 12-story Citizens and Southern Bank tower.

At its 1986 meeting the corporation's board of directors elected chief financial officer Carol D. Vinson as president and chief op-

erating officer of U.S. Shelter. Barton Tuck was named chairman and chief executive officer, and Buck Mickel, formerly chairman of the board, was named vice-chairman.

With entrepreneurial spirit and insight into the real estate market, U.S. Shelter Corporation has

achieved steady, solid growth and the flexibility to meet changing market needs. The company also is well positioned for continued growth in the future.

_____

U.S. Shelter Corporation occupied its new 17-story headquarters building in 1984.

WYFF-TV

It was a memorable moment in Greenville's history when Channel 4's first telecast went on the air on December 31, 1953. At one minute before midnight the station's first film aired in an unexpected way—upside down and backwards. Perhaps that beginning was an omen of exciting and adventurous times to come in a business in which the unexpected takes place with some regularity.

It was the second VHF television station in the state, and was created through a merger of radio stations WFBC and WMRC. It operated under the call letters WFBC-TV from studios on Paris Mountain and shared space with its transmitter until new offices and studios were constructed at 505 Rutherford Street in 1955.

WMRC, Inc., later a part of

"Officer Mac" is a robot who's a favorite with children. Operated by local law enforcement agencies in the cities of Greenville, Spartanburg, Asheville, and Anderson, the four robots are sponsored by WYFF in a campaign to increase child safety.

The prestigious Jefferson Awards, sponsored by WYFF, are part of the station's involvement with the community. Here on-location taping takes place for the annual special program with recipient Sam Francis. In the first five years of sponsorship by the station, two local recipients have also won national awards.

Southeastern Broadcasting Company, owned the station until 1967 when, through another merger, Multimedia, Inc., became the station's owner. In 1983 WYFF-TV was traded to the Pulitzer Publishing Company of St. Louis.

Through the years Channel 4 firmly established itself as a pioneer in the market. It telecast the first college basketball game in the area—memorable because Furman University's Frank Selvy scored 100 points and established a record that may never be broken. In the spring of 1954 WFBC was the first VHF station in the state to televise a live church service, and that telecast was followed with the initial airing of the Easter Parade from downtown Greenville. The station also brought such innovative firsts to the market as weather radar, electronic news-gathering equipment, and full stereo broadcasts.

The station has always been affiliated with the NBC Television

Network and produced its first feature for network broadcast in 1955 on the program "Wide Wide World." A year later a feature on Greenville was produced by an NBC special events crew and carried to the nation on the program "Home" through the facilities of WFBC-TV. Channel 4 televised network color programs years before the general advent of color television, and began full-color telecasting during the first week of February 1967.

From the beginning the station has made a healthy commitment to news and community service. From a 15-minute news broadcast, the station expanded to an hour of news, weather, and sports at 6 p.m. in 1976. Daily live news remotes began on a consistent basis in Greenville that same year. As late as 1986 WYFF was still the only station in the state televising an hour of news at 6 p.m.

Since the late 1950s Channel 4 has originated statewide telecasts of the Miss South Carolina Pageant, and has been heavily involved in a number of other community service projects, including the annual Jefferson Awards, Superkids, and an intensive reading program in the Greenville County schools. Freedom Weekend Aloft, the city's

Friendship Four—*the station's hot air balloon appears at station, charitable, and civic events as well as festivals and hot air balloon rallies.*

WYFF was off the air only about one and a half hours, and had recovered well enough to telecast locally by 11 p.m. The late news was broadcast from the station's parking lot—just a few feet from where the fire started.

The station never missed a beat from that moment on. In the weeks that followed WYFF operated from makeshift sets, originating newscasts from the front lawn and from the main lobby. Employees pulled together to get the job done with great enthusiasm, and the community, even competing stations, came forth to help.

Not only did the remarkable outpouring of caring and assistance help get and keep the station on the air, it allowed the local community, of which WYFF has long been an integral part, to let the station know that it too had a friend.

Utilizing techniques developed in the 1970s and widely used in the 1980s, WYFF newscasts originate from on-location sites such as Freedom Weekend Aloft, the giant balloon July Fourth celebration in Greenville.

spectacular Fourth of July hot-air ballooning festival, was first chaired by the station's general manager Doug Smith, and Channel 4 has offered intensive support to the event each year since its inception.

The high level of community service provided by the station has not gone unnoticed. A research project conducted by the station in the late 1970s indicated that a majority of its viewers saw Channel 4 as a friend. That finding led to the creation of a new, and fitting, slogan in 1978—"Your Friend Four." Those words fit so well, in fact, that the station changed its name in 1983 from WFBC-TV to WYFF-TV, an acronym for We're Your Friend Four.

One of the greatest challenges ever faced by WYFF occurred on June 23, 1985, when it was charged with the task of covering a disaster

that hit altogether too close to home. On that Sunday night at approximately 8:15, a major fire broke out in the station's prop room. Fire fighters were quick to extinguish the blaze, but the damage was great, with the final estimate at some $3.5 million.

In spite of the severe damage,

MICHELIN TIRE CORPORATION

The story of Michelin Tire Corporation is a story of remarkable innovation and of solid growth.

It began when Edouard Michelin, owner of a small rubber factory in Clermont-Ferrand, France, repaired the bicycle tire of an English tourist and recognized the need for tires that could be easily repaired by the user. As a result, Edouard and his brother, André, designed such a tire.

Introduced in 1891, it was the world's first detachable pneumatic bicycle tire. Four years later the Michelins introduced the first pneumatic tire for automobiles. Those two innovations were the first in a long and continuous line of outstanding products manufactured by Michelin Tire Corporation, and the company was on its way to becoming a world leader in the tire industry.

The Michelin brothers' rubber factory grew quickly—from an 11-employee operation to an international corporation with 52 plants in 12 countries on four continents. Michelin is now the largest tire manufacturer in Europe and the

Michelin manufactures radial passenger car tires at its Greenville plant located in the South Donaldson Industrial Park.

second-largest tire manufacturer in the world.

Between 1905 and 1939 the company built six plants in Europe, and in the three decades following World War II, plant construction skyrocketed. Four were built in the 1950s, 13 in the 1960s, and 23 in the 1970s.

In 1950 Michelin formed its Commercial Division to sell and distribute tires in the United States. Its beginning was modest, with a small office in New York and a few leased warehouses as distribution centers.

The Commercial Division's first product was the Metalic, a steel-cord tire for trucks. The radial tire, pioneered by Michelin in 1948, appeared progressively on the American market beginning in the mid-1950s, and was used on commercial vehicles and European cars. At that time, however, American-made cars were not designed to take advantage of the Michelin X radial construction.

In 1968 Michelin steel-belted radials entered the original equipment market when Ford made the Michelin XWW standard equip-

ment on the Lincoln Continental Mark III. Other domestic manufacturers soon followed suit, thus opening the door to a dramatic increase in radial tire sales in the 1970s.

As the market expanded, Michelin knew that manufacturing facilities would have to be established in the United States. The firm chose Greenville as the site of its first U.S. passenger tire assembly plant and as headquarters for its entire North American manufacturing operation in 1973. That same year ground was broken for a rubber-compounding plant in Anderson.

Governor John West welcomed Michelin, saying that the plants in Greenville and Anderson represented the largest commercial manufacturing operation in South Carolina, both in dollar investment and in number of jobs created.

Since construction began on the Greenville facility in 1973, it has

Mr. Bib (left), the Michelin tire man, and Francois Michelin, grandson of one of the founders, visit South Carolina often.

been expanded to over 1.1 million square feet. The Anderson plant is today one of the company's largest worldwide, with over 1.8 million square feet of floor space.

And there was to be much more investment in the area. In 1975, as the first Michelin tire bearing the words "Made in U.S.A." rolled off the line at the Greenville plant, an announcement was made by the firm that it would build a plant in Spartanburg to manufacture truck tires. In addition, Michelin announced the purchase of 2,000 acres in Laurens County as the site of its first tire-testing center in North America.

On July 2, 1976, the Manufacturing Division reached a significant milestone—the one-millionth tire was produced at the Greenville plant.

Michelin's fourth U.S. plant was completed in 1979 in Dothan, Alabama, to produce light truck tires. Two years later the company erected an additional passenger tire manufacturing plant in Lexington County, near Columbia, South Carolina. In late 1984, in a move to strengthen its overall efficiency in the United States, Michelin announced plans to relocate its North American headquarters to Greenville. As a result, the company moved its commercial division

In late 1985 the 50,000-square-foot Michelin Sales Training Center was completed on land adjacent to the Greenville plant.

from New York to Greenville in 1985, consolidating it with corporate operations in a temporary location, the CRS Sirrine building at Patewood Executive Park.

In May 1986 Michelin formally opened its new Sales Training Center in Greenville's South Donaldson Industrial Park, on land adjacent to the Greenville plant and to the Michelin Americas Research and Development Corporation (MARC). MARC is charged with the responsibility of maintaining and building upon the worldwide technological edge traditionally enjoyed by Michelin products. Chemists, engineers, and physicists seek new technologies and new materials, and analyze stress and motion to improve tire performance. Other researchers experiment with varied materials to determine how the unique properties of each may be better utilized in tire construction.

In June 1986 Michelin announced plans to build its new corporate headquarters facility in the Pelham Green development, at the intersection of Pelham Road and I-85.

As Michelin Tire Corporation

approaches the close of its first century in the tire business, it continues to depend upon the creative energies of thousands of scientists, engineers, managers, and manufacturing workers to perfect the tire and to continue the strong Michelin tradition of innovation and excellence.

Michelin's Greenville plant manufactures radial passenger car tires such as the XH, which features computer-designed tread, reduced rolling resistance for increased fuel economy, and improved tread compounds for high mileage.

GOLDSMITH COMPANY

As a boy in the 1800s, William Goldsmith used to plow the fields where McAlister Square and Pleasantburg Shopping Center now stand. The soil was fertile and yielded great crops.

He soon found that Greenville was also fertile ground for growing a successful business. His Goldsmith Company, founded in 1884, is still growing strong today. Like the crops he tended, Goldsmith planted the seeds of success for Greenville's oldest insurance and real estate company.

His family moved to Greenville County from Winchester, Virginia, and settled in the Gilder Creek area near Simpsonville, later buying a farm that was the property that now surrounds Pleasantburg Shopping Center. When it came time for schooling, young Goldsmith attended Captain Patrick's Military Academy on what is now Broadus Avenue, the present site of Seven Oaks Restaurant.

Unlike his four brothers who became farmers or worked for the railroad, Goldsmith decided to pursue a career in the insurance and real estate business. He joined Smith's Insurance Company in Greenville, and by 1884, still in his early twenties, Goldsmith bought out his employer and renamed the business.

The Goldsmith Company started out in a small office building on East Court Street in Greenville. Although it outgrew that structure and moved to another location, the firm was never more than two blocks away from its original site until 1972. It was then that the Goldsmith Company moved into a new building on North Main Street.

The Goldsmith Company is the oldest insurance and real estate company in Greenville by four years. The Alester Furman Com-

In 1972 the firm moved to a new building on North Main Street.

pany began in 1888 and, according to Morgan Goldsmith, the older venture good-naturedly called Furman a "junior" organization.

In addition to insurance, Goldsmith also branched out into real estate and banking. He was one of the organizers of First Federal and served as its president, as well as one of the organizers of the Poinett Hotel.

William Goldsmith had several children, three of whom joined the family business. The late Walter W. Goldsmith served as president, and, upon his return from military service, Morgan Goldsmith became vice-president. He retired in 1977. William Goldsmith, Jr., served as secretary/treasurer until his death, and today his son, Paul Goldsmith, serves as president.

When the Goldsmith Company celebrated its 95th anniversary in 1979, it gave silver dollars to everyone 95 years of age or older. It depleted the bank's supply of silver dollars, but it was an important gesture. "It was a 'thank-you' to Greenville," Morgan Goldsmith explains. "Greenville has been very good to us." Several of the silver dollar recipients baked cookies and cakes for the Goldsmith employees. This gave the Goldsmith employees the idea of a Valentine's "tea party" for all of their new, older friends. The Valentine's gathering was one of the most heartwarming events the Goldsmith people had ever experienced, as almost 20 of the new friends came to the party.

The business that William Goldsmith started over 100 years ago is now three separate companies. Paul S. Goldsmith is president of the Wm. Goldsmith Co. and Goldsmith Inc., and Nick A. Theodore is president of Wm. Goldsmith Agency, Inc.

The Goldsmith Company started out in a small office building on East Court Street.

GREENVILLE TECHNICAL COLLEGE

A catalyst for economic development and improved living conditions, Greenville Technical College was established in 1962 on the former landfill site of the City of Greenville. It was an eight-acre campus with one building.

Today Greenville Tech is a showplace for upstate South Carolina—a sprawling, beautifully landscaped, 130-acre campus with 19 buildings and more than a half-million square feet of training space. Because it offers the most advanced technological equipment and facilities in the Southeast, the institution serves as a major attraction for new and expanding business and industry, and enrolls approximately 38,000 individuals each year.

Greenville Tech is the oldest and largest of the 16 institutions in the South Carolina State System for

The 130-acre Greenville Technical College campus.

Technical and Comprehensive Education. It offers associate degrees, diplomas, and certificates in more than 60 programs in eight divisions of study, including a College Transfer Division through which students complete their freshman and sophomore years and transfer to a college or university as juniors. In addition, Clemson University, the University of South Carolina at Spartanburg, and the Medical University of South Carolina offer upper-level courses leading to four-year degrees as well as graduate-level courses on the Greenville Tech campus.

From the days when Greenville Tech was no more than an idea, community support for the school has come from all directions. More than 500 business, industry, medical, and professional representatives form a sophisticated network of advisory committees that function to assure that all programs are relevant to the training needs of the area and the job market. Every program offered by the college is

evaluated annually to see that its curriculum, faculty, equipment, and facilities meet those needs.

The Greenville Area Commission for Technical and Comprehensive Education is involved in the policy-making activities, as well as the college's service to the area. In addition, valuable support comes from elected and appointed local, state, and federal officials and government agencies that recognize the need for diversified technical education and provide the financial means to make it available through local, state, and federal funding.

The founders of Greenville Technical College set forth a goal: to provide "instruction . . . designed to prepare individuals for entering into and progressing in employment and technical pursuits . . . or designed to improve conditions which result in improved citizenship." Without question, the goal has been met, and it continues to be met in a bigger and better way with every passing year.

SNYDER'S AUTO SALES

There is something powerfully alluring about Snyder's Auto Sales' showroom. Perhaps it is the opulent surroundings, richly decorated and elegant. Or maybe it has to do with the automobiles displayed there—luxurious, high-performance vehicles—dream cars.

It is all, unquestionably, impressive. But the showroom at Snyder's is not the whole picture—not by a long shot.

Behind the scenes there is a service area staffed by highly trained technicians, carefully checking, adjusting, and tuning. There are people behind most every door in the offices, smiling as they talk on the telephone. And there are salespeople throughout the building, working to make sure that what they sell is what the customer wants.

This—the unseen effort—is the fabric from which Snyder's was made. And there are five words behind it all: "We'd like to help you." Those words are not a slogan, nor are they a tag line created by some advertising copywriter. Instead, they are the summation of Snyder's Auto Sales trademark: service. And from day one that dedication to service has built a successful business.

A generation ago, at the beginning of the 1950s, Greenville native J. Wesley Snyder opened his automobile dealership at 854 Buncombe Street. It was a modest venture, offering used cars only. But Snyder knew the value of going that extra mile for his customers. He knew that the key to the growth of his business was service, and he was right.

Snyder chalked up one satisfied customer after another, and in just five years the company was awarded the Renault dealership. It was the first dealership in the area devoted entirely to imported cars, and offered parts as well as service by specially trained technicians.

In 1959 the Peugeot line was added, and the firm expanded its Buncombe Street operation with the construction of a new showroom and an enlarged service department. Even in the early days Snyder's service and parts departments were second to none in the imported car business. Snyder sent his service personnel to technical training schools on a regular basis so that they could continue to offer the best service available on the cars they sold.

Snyder's Auto Sales passed one of the most exciting milestones in its history in 1962, when it was selected to represent the Mercedes-Benz line of automobiles. It was an honor not taken lightly, since the Mercedes-Benz name stood for a standard of excellence long recognized the world over. One of the firm's advertisements in the *Greenville News* that year proudly displayed two of the Mercedes models, the 220S Sedan and the 190SL Roadster, with the prices noted as $4,808 and $5,237, respectively.

Other automobile lines were soon added. Snyder's Auto Sales became the dealer for MG in 1963, and gained the Fiat line in 1968, the Mazda line in 1971, and the Jaguar line in 1976.

As the 1980s approached Snyder's had increased its business volume consistently each year, and the corporation was well positioned in 1981 to move into a spacious new office and showroom complex on Laurens Road, in what soon became known as "Motormile." By that time the company's staff had grown to 43.

Snyder's Auto Sales, which began selling used cars, added this impressive showroom when it became the first imported car dealership in the Greenville area.

An extensive computer system is capable of checking every phase of an automobile's operation system to locate any problem.

Things were going well, but Snyder's Auto Sales wasn't resting on its laurels. Ever in search of new and better ways to serve its customers, the firm augmented its already superior service with a unique touch. It became one of the first dealers in the state to introduce 7-day, 24-hour emergency service to its customers. The deal was simple and straightforward: If a Snyder's customer had car trouble within a 30-mile radius of the dealership, a telephone call would bring a fully equipped emergency service vehicle to the customer. The new service not only brought the appreciation of Snyder's customers, but also won the approval of other dealers throughout the nation.

But Snyder's Auto Sales didn't stop there. Next, an extensive computer system was added, capable of checking every phase of an automobile's operating system to locate any problem. The dealership then added Signature Service, which required the person responsible for the work on a particular car to sign off on the work once it was completed. The system was designed to provide extra assurance that all Snyder's work was done properly and with individual pride.

Snyder, now chairman of the board of the company, involved his two sons in the operation of the dealership as soon as they were old enough to work. Today Jimmy Snyder serves as president and general manager, and Richard Snyder serves as vice-president and sales manager. John Finger, a longtime Snyder's employee, serves as vice-president of the critical parts and service area.

Pride in workmanship, state-of-the-art technology, individual responsibility, and a driving desire to be the best—at Snyder's, those characteristics are standard equipment, and they come together nicely in one word: service. It's never an afterthought at Snyder's Auto Sales; it's a principal preoccupation and the company's commitment to the future.

A complete parts and accessories department is maintained as an essential adjunct to providing efficient service.

BIGELOW-SANFORD, INC.

The story of Bigelow-Sanford, Inc., began in 1825, when the United States was barely 50 years old, when New York City ended at 42nd Street, when Chicago consisted of a wooden fort on a river, and when Greenville was a small trading post and summer resort community nestled in the up-country of South Carolina.

The United States government had just enacted a tariff that made importing carpet and certain other goods more expensive. It was an effort to stimulate local production of carpet and other textiles, and dozens of companies sprang up to take advantage of the new opportunity.

But of all the businesses to enter the industry only a few, including the Lowell Manufacturing Company of Lowell, Massachusetts, had the foresight to develop innovative manufacturing methods. And Lowell was the only one to have the luck and wit to hire Erastus Brigham Bigelow as a machinery designer.

Bigelow was an inventor, and from his designs came rope-making machines, stenographic systems, looms that wove decorative lace for stagecoaches, and, ultimately, looms for weaving carpet. The carpet-weaving machine invented by Bigelow was placed in use in 1843 and tripled productivity in the Lowell factory. It soon became a dominant force in the production of a simple, sturdy carpet known as ingrain.

Bigelow soon recognized that his loom could be used to produce more than just ingrain carpet. In partnership with his brother, Horatio Nelson Bigelow, Erastus negotiated a royalty arrangement by which he was allowed to utilize his technology to produce beautiful, elaborate carpets.

His timing was perfect. Over the next 10 years the Bigelows' mills

Erastus Brigham Bigelow, inventor and machinery designer, whose carpet weaving machine planted the seed for the business that is now Bigelow-Sanford, Inc.

grew steadily, and after the Civil War the demand for high-fashion carpets soared. With their fortunes assured, the brothers acquired several firms including the Lowell Manufacturing Company.

The Bigelows operated the business on three basic concepts. The first was to identify the customers' needs and manufacture the products they wanted. Second, Erastus Bigelow saw the importance of total control of the manufacturing process, and operated his own yarn and finishing plants to assure the integrity of the finished product. Finally, the firm was committed to excellence in design, quality, construction, and delivery, and its products took awards at exhibitions as early as 1851.

Through the years the Bigelow Company remained in step with changing times. In the Victorian age, for example, the love of design and decoration led to mechanical innovations enabling the firm to produce highly figured, richly colored carpets. At the turn of the century, when a new respect for the individual worker led to vast improvements in working conditions, the company responded by not only instituting improved working conditions, but also by providing housing and town improvements for its employees. And during World War I the corporation virtually stopped the manufacture of consumer carpet so that its facilities could be used for the production of war materiel.

In 1929 the Bigelow Company merged with Stephen Sanford & Sons, a family-held carpet business founded in 1836, which produced luxurious carpet types. The merger provided modern equipment for the Bigelow Company and necessary leadership for Stephen Sanford & Sons. The result, Bigelow-Sanford, Inc., was the strongest and most innovative firm in its industry.

During World War II Bigelow-Sanford renewed its commitment to national defense, virtually shutting down all consumer production in order to support the war effort. The firm's machine shops, long famed for their precision and accuracy, were used to make parts for fighter planes, submarines, and bomb sights.

The late 1950s brought a revolution in the carpet industry, when a new, homegrown industry sprang up in the mountains of northwest Georgia with rural people turning

out chenille bedspreads, tufted bath mats, and tufted broadloom carpet. It would take a leading-edge manufacturing company to bring those people together and help them make the transition from rural crafts to national industry. That company was Bigelow-Sanford, Inc., the first major manufacturer to embrace tufted carpet and move south.

The firm quickly moved its operations into South Carolina and Georgia, with yarn plants in Calhoun Falls and Belton, South Carolina; two carpet-tufting plants in Lyerly and Summerville, Georgia; and the world's largest carpet-weaving plant in Landrum, South Carolina. The company's national headquarters was moved to Green-

ville in the 1970s.

In 1980 Bigelow-Sanford, Inc., was purchased by a group of its top executives. Corporate headquarters remained in Greenville with C.R. Goulet, chairman of the board; A.O. Kelly, president and chief executive officer; J.P. Kitchens, senior vice-president/manufacturing; R.W. Liptak, senior vice-president/finance and administration; R.E. Guess, senior vice-president/products; and S.K. Bordeaux, senior vice-president/marketing, directing the company's day-to-day operations.

Through the 1980s Bigelow-Sanford has continued to lead the way in the carpet industry. Its products, designed in Greenville and manufactured in five plants in South Carolina and Georgia, set national standards for style and performance.

In 1984 the firm embarked upon the newest phase of the American industrial revolution by developing a worker-involvement Quality Improvement Program. The program is designed to improve all parts of the company's operations by employing the newest educational and operational tools. Other corporations have followed suit, drawing on Bigelow-Sanford's resources for help.

It's all part of the Bigelow-Sanford tradition. Through war and peace, from the North to the South, Bigelow-Sanford, Inc., is a proud inheritor of the American tradition, and an important part of the story of Greenville and of America.

Bigelow carpets have always reflected the tastes of the current times from the ornate rich area rugs of the Victorian era to the thick carpeting in myriads of decorator colors today.

SOUTHERN BELL

The telephone was a revolutionary new development when Southern Bell first brought its service to Greenville on May 21, 1882.

With 16 crank-type telephones and several young men employed as operators, the company set up its switchboard and exchange over a livery stable on Laurens Street near the present site of NCNB Tower. But there was a problem: Customers began to complain about the rudeness of the male operators. Southern Bell promptly dismissed the men and replaced them with more courteous female operators.

With that problem solved, Southern Bell was on its way to meet the growing demand for telephone service, and by 1900 the company was operating 418 telephones in the toll-free calling area. Monthly service fees were set at $3.50.

In 1902 Southern Bell purchased L.W. Floyd's competing Consoli-

These telephone operators worked at the Greenville switchboard in 1916.

dated Telephone Company of South Carolina. The acquisition included the Greenville exchange and the 19-station Greer exchange.

The second floor of Gapin's Cigar Store on the corner of Washington and Main streets became Southern Bell's next headquarters, and in 1913 the firm moved again to a facility at 13 South Laurens Street. That same year Southern Bell converted its service from a magneto system to a common battery system.

The Fountain Inn exchange was purchased in 1950, rebuilt, and opened the following year with 534 stations. The Travelers Rest dial exchange was established the following year and served 1,453 subscribers who had previously been served by the Greenville office.

The city's first electronic office was placed in service in July 1978, serving the downtown Cedar exchange. The Cedar exchange was the first dial office in the county and was installed in a building at 218 College Street in two phases, which began in 1948 and were com-

pleted the following year. Prior to that time operators answered calls with the phrase, "Number please," and then placed the call for the customer. The electronic offices made custom-calling features, optional local-measured service, and international direct-dialing available for the first time.

By 1978 there were 251,750 telephones in the toll-free calling area, which by that time included most towns in the county. That same year Southern Bell began to face increased competition from vendors of telephone equipment, and the Federal Communications Commission ordered that subscribers be allowed to interconnect customer-provided equipment. Because of that order the local telephone company could no longer ensure accurate records of how many telephones a customer had connected to the network, and in 1986 Southern Bell began to measure growth and demand by the number of access lines.

At the end of the first quarter of 1986 there were over 140,000 access lines in service in the Greenville district, with approximately 70 percent of the lines working through electronic switching sys-

The telephone exchange building at South Laurens Street was built in 1913.

This 1930 Ford installation truck, used in Greenville, cost $440 plus bumper, spare tire, freight, gas, oil, and grease—for a total delivery price of $531.50.

tems with digital capabilities being added. The firm plans to have electronic systems operating throughout the county by the early 1990s.

Methods of transmitting telephone conversations have changed drastically over the years. In the early days they were sent over open wires strung on cross arms on telephone poles. Only one subscriber could be served per wire, so party-line service was developed. Next came cables requiring a pair of wires per telephone line, and, depending upon the size of the cable and the materials used, the cables could serve up to 3,600 customers each.

The first fiber-optic installation in Greenville was a 30-mile, long-distance cable between Greenville and Spartanburg. Placed in operation in 1984, the system consists of hair-thin glass fibers over which messages are sent using low-power laser beams. Unlike copper cables, the glass fibers are not affected by water, lightning, or other weather conditions, and are capable of transmitting voice and data at a rate of 2,016 messages per fiber system.

With the divestiture of the Bell System on January 1, 1984, Southern Bell began a new corporate life as a part of BellSouth Corporation, one of seven regional companies created from the original AT&T. Following the divestiture, the firm sought to cut costs and improve its operating efficiency. One measure taken was the consolidation of the Anderson, Greenville, and Spartanburg customer service operations into a new regional office in Green-

ville. In December 1985 that operation and several others located throughout the county began moving into a three-story structure at 10 South Academy Street, just two blocks from the site of the original exchange building.

At the end of 1985 Southern Bell's investment in Greenville County was well in excess of $250 million. The company's investment in civic and community activities is equally strong, and its employees' names appear regularly on committee rosters of the community's special causes. In addition, the Telephone Pioneers of America have filled a special role in providing services for the handicapped.

To the area covered by Southern Bell, service means more than a friendly voice on the phone or a cable able to carry calls with the speed of light. It means a total effort on the part of all its employees to please its customers. It means, according to district manager Arnold Burrell, an effort "to be the best there is in the telecommunications industry."

Southern Bell began moving into the Regional Piedmont Headquarters Operations building at 10 South Academy Street in downtown Greenville in late 1985.

HENDERSON ADVERTISING

Many were dubious in August 1946, when 25-year-old Jim Henderson borrowed $500 from his new bride and opened the Henderson Advertising Agency in Greenville. The doubts increased when they heard the goal he had set for himself: to prove that it was possible to build an outstanding national advertising agency and create outstanding national advertising far away from the so-called "heartlands" of New York and Chicago.

The years that followed have turned those doubts into cheers. For one thing, Henderson Advertising has long since become the largest independent advertising agency in the Southeast. And its success was finally exhibited to the world in 1980 when the firm was named Agency of the Year by *Advertising Age,* the "bible" of the advertising industry. The award marked the first time this prestigious honor had ever been given to

an agency outside of New York or Chicago.

According to *Advertising Age,* "Henderson Advertising was selected as Agency of the Year for its daring concept of building an agency with big-city talent and handling major accounts—far away from the big city; its rapid growth from both old and new clients; new product development work; and its contribution to the growth and success of major clients . . ."

How did the little one-man agency that got its start in a one-room $25-a-month office burst so brightly onto the national scene and into the top one percent of all agencies nationwide?

Fate seems to have been smiling on the venture right from the start. One year earlier, in 1945, another young Greenvillian, Jack Greer, formed a modest chemical company that manufactured sizing compounds for local textile mills. The infant Texize Chemicals operated out of a 60-foot by 120-foot stable-turned-garage. Formulas were mixed and bottles filled by hand. The story goes that the firm doubled production overnight by adding a second spigot to its 55-gallon drum.

Because of Henderson's experience at General Foods, he was able to design and package the cleaner for consumer use. The pair named the product Texize Liquid Cleaner.

Their advertising campaign was lifted from the then-popular Clark Gable movie *The Hucksters.* In the movie, as in the book, "Love that soap!" was used to sell a fictional soap product. Everybody in America knew the line. Henderson, therefore, saturated the market with a "Love that cleaner!" campaign for Texize Liquid Cleaner.

That campaign put Texize on the map. Even more important, however, it taught both agency and

Current chief executive officer Ralph Callahan presides over Henderson Advertising.

client firsthand about marketing consumer package products.

From that initial success Henderson Advertising and Texize have worked closely together. Over the years they've introduced and successfully marketed many fine consumer cleaning and laundry products, among them such household names as Fantastik, Glass Plus, Janitor-in-a-Drum, K2r Spot Lifter, Pine Power, Spray'n Wash, and Vivid All-Fabric Bleach.

Today the agency also handles the advertising for First Atlanta Bank, Folonari Wines, Fotomat, Hanes Activewear, Mount Gay Rum, Quincy's Steak House, St. Pauli Girl Beer, Sylvania Television, and Chris-Craft boats. In addition, Henderson Advertising has had major successes in the recent past with products from Bryan Foods, Miles Laboratories, Orville Redenbacher, Pet Milk, Procter & Gamble, Simoniz, and STP.

Is there a secret? Agency chairman and chief executive officer Ralph Callahan says, "Jim always

Founder Jim Henderson saw his dreams come true before retiring as chairman and chief executive officer in 1986.

The firm's main headquarters building at Pelham Pointe was completed in 1978. Growth and expansion necessitated the construction of a second building in 1984 located across the parking lot.

maintained that the key to success is people. And he was right. I think that's one of our secrets." In fact, the agency has been particularly skillful over the years in attracting top-notch professionals from the advertising centers in New York, Chicago, St. Louis, and Detroit.

One of the firm's most effective recruiting tools is a charming little cartoon booklet entitled "What-in-hell am I doing in Greenville, South Carolina?" It speaks to the fears and frustrations of big-city advertising people, and it counters with the facts of life at Henderson: the same caliber of professionals and professionalism, the same levels of skills, the same or better salaries, the lower cost of living, and the quality of life in Greenville. Few can resist the lure.

At that point, when supply exceeds demand, the agency can afford to become selective. In-depth

interviews and psychological tests over a long weekend weed out all but the top candidates. And when the final decision is made, the firm pays all the relocation expenses and even helps find jobs for spouses.

One result is that most new employees feel an immediate closeness and loyalty—not only to their new agency, but also to their new community. They volunteer for community service on a grand scale, offering their time, talents, and enthusiasm to a variety of local organizations.

Another reason for the agency's success is its policy of centering all advertising on just one message. It's called the OSSI—an acronym for One Strong Selling Idea. It is an approach directed to consumers' self-interest, and it has been fundamental to all of the firm's advertising since day one.

"We think advertising that tries to push a laundry list of product attributes and benefits generally confuses the consumer, who couldn't care less anyway," says Callahan. "But our OSSI approach—presented with some style, flair, and impact—seems to make our adver-

tising work a little harder. We also think it intrudes a little deeper and sells a little stronger."

In addition, to help clients cope with today's higher marketing costs and to help them handle the increasingly tougher, more sophisticated competition, Henderson Advertising has added two important in-house divisions: Henderson Marketing Services, which provides promotion and collateral planning, design, and production; and Henderson Direct, which offers direct marketing planning and execution as well as marketing and project management.

If there's another reason for Henderson Advertising's success, Callahan believes that it may be the firm's size. "We think it's ideal for most clients. We're big enough to deliver all the necessary agency services in depth. We've even added Henderson Marketing Services and Henderson Direct as extras. Yet we're still small enough to guarantee, not just promise, the continuous personal involvement of top management.

"And," vows Callahan, "that's the way it's going to stay!"

YEARGIN CONSTRUCTION COMPANY

From a small rented office on Sevier Street in 1959, the Yeargin Construction Company (now Yeargin, Inc.) team was preparing for its first project. The "team" consisted of founder Bob Yeargin and a secretary, and the job was a $4,000 latticework brick fence for Dr. Paul Hearn. Bigger and better things followed as the firm began to work in the residential construction field. Later, in 1959, Yeargin won its first commercial contract—an office clinic for Dr. George Wilkinson, followed by two branch offices for Liberty Life, the Burgin Motor Company showroom, and the Lake Forest Elementary School.

With business growing at a rapid clip, the company in 1962 was awarded its first industrial contract for the Greenville firm Stylecrafters. The 60,000-square-foot project was also the organization's first design/build package and was contracted for an astonishing four dollars per square foot.

While still a fledgling in the mammoth construction industry, the organization was awarded its first contract with an international company in 1963—Union Carbide's Simpsonville plant. Yeargin made a grand entry into the South's textile market in 1964 with a contract to build the 240,000-square-foot Textile Hall Exposition Center, and broke into major textile plant construction in 1966 with the award of a 285,000-square-foot facility for Clinton Mills followed by a 535,000-square-foot contract to construct twin mills for M. Lowenstein & Sons.

As Yeargin entered the late 1960s, its list of repeat clients was already impressive, including such well-known names as Union Carbide, The Kendall Company, General Electric, and Allied Chemical. However, the need to offer more service to clients became clear.

Yeargin took the first step toward that goal with the acquisition in 1968 of IMPAC, a Charlotte-based mechanical contracting company. Soon thereafter, Yeargin Aviation was formed as a fixed-base aviation service at Greenville Municipal Airport to serve Yeargin's flying needs. To further round out its full-service capabilities, the firm established Yeargin Properties, a real estate development, investment, and brokerage firm, in 1971 followed by organizing the company's Electrical Division. During this period the firm initiated a unique program to assure that the quality of its work remained high. It was named PRIDE, an acronym for Personal Responsibility In Daily Excellence and was designed to motivate employees throughout the organization by recognizing excellent work. As soon as the program was put into place, there were startling improvements in quality, productivity, and speed of completion.

The 1970s were a time of intense growth for Yeargin, which had yet to see its 20th anniversary. A 1.7-million-square-foot facility for Firestone Tire & Rubber Company was among the many major jobs awarded Yeargin. Highlighting the period was a $250-million project for Amoco Chemicals in Charleston—a job requiring a peak work force of more than 1,800 craftspeople. Other major projects included Kerr Glass, Sangamo Weston, Stauffer Chemical, and Alumax of South Carolina, a $400-million project.

Familiar landmarks in the Piedmont region include First Federal Savings & Loan of South Carolina headquarters, Henderson Advertising headquarters, J.E. Sirrine headquarters, McAlister Square shopping center, Clemson Library, Westminster Presbyterian Church,

and many others.

In 1976 Yeargin Construction Company became a wholly owned subsidiary of Perini Corporation of Framingham, Massachusetts, and the client list continued to grow. Yeargin Properties and Yeargin Aviation subsidiaries were not acquired from the Yeargin family and remained privately owned, separate entities.

Yeargin formed a Contract Maintenance and Special Projects Division in 1980. Raytheon Corporation, a major diversified company, acquired Yeargin in 1985. Through that acquisition, Yeargin added design and engineering capabilities conducted from offices in Knoxville and Kingsport, Tennessee, to its already impressive full-service operation. In early 1986 the company name was changed to Yeargin, Inc.

Yeargin has come a long way since it completed its first local job, to stand proudly among the leaders of the U.S. construction industry as well as a cornerstone in Greenville's continued growth and progress.

Today, from this 25,000-square-foot corporate headquarters building in Greenville, the firm conducts business in 22 states.

BAUSCH & LOMB

When John Jacob Bausch, a German immigrant, arrived in the United States at the age of 19, he was practically penniless. He did, however, possess an abundance of hope and ambition.

Four years later he opened a tiny optical goods shop in Rochester, New York. Short on capital, he borrowed $60 from a friend, Henry Lomb, with the promise that if the business ever grew substantially, Lomb would be brought in as a partner. The business did grow, and the partnership was formed. Today it is known as Bausch & Lomb, a name recognized throughout the world as a leader in the development and manufacture of products for the care, correction, and enhancement of vision.

Shortly before the Civil War Bausch made a discovery that sealed his fate. He found that hard rubber called Vulcanite could be used to make eyeglass frames that were more durable and less costly than others currently on the market. By the 1870s the Bausch & Lomb Optical Company had grown enough to open a New York City sales office and move into enlarged facilities in Rochester.

The firm then began to diversify into a variety of optical products, and dozens of developments came out of the operation through the years.

By 1878 the company had begun production of photographic lenses and had won international awards for its microscopes. Shortly after the turn of the century optical-quality glass began to be produced by the firm. In the 1920s Bausch & Lomb developed an absorptive glass that could overcome the brutal glare conditions encountered by U.S. Army Air Corps pilots. The Ray-Ban aviator-style sunglass remains one of the company's best sellers today.

In the 1960s another milestone was passed when the firm acquired the rights to manufacture and market a new contact lens. In 1971 Bausch & Lomb became the first company to receive Food and Drug Administration approval to market soft contact lenses in the United States. The soft lens had a major impact on Bausch & Lomb, as sales of lenses and associated ac-

To meet the growing demand for contact lens solutions, Bausch & Lomb constructed a $25-million solutions-manufacturing plant in Greenville in 1983. The 100,000-square-foot facility is the largest of its kind in the nation.

Bausch & Lomb's Greenville facility offers an advanced design and high product volume, making the company the most efficient producer of contact lens solutions in the industry.

cessory products pushed the company into the *Fortune* 500.

As the demand for soft contact lenses grew, the market expanded for lens solutions and accessory products. To meet the demand, the firm constructed a $25-million solutions-manufacturing plant in Greenville in 1983. At 100,000 square feet, the plant is the largest of its kind in the nation. At year-end 1985 lens solutions had become the company's largest source of operating earnings.

The 1980s brought the end of an era, when the corporation decided to discontinue its eyeglass frame and lens business, as well as its industrial instruments operations.

Today Bausch & Lomb is focusing on the personal health care industry, one of the most rapidly expanding sectors of the U.S. economy. In addition, expansion has taken place in the biomedical and scientific products markets, the ophthalmic pharmaceuticals market, and the professional eye care market.

With manufacturing or marketing operations in 25 countries and distribution of its products in more than 90 nations, Bausch & Lomb still adheres to the legacy of dedication to quality and craftsmanship established by John Jacob Bausch and Henry Lomb.

SHERATON PALMETTO

In 1932 Yates Louis Honey bought the Triple X Restaurant in Charlotte, North Carolina, for $288. He renamed the tiny operation the Goody-Goody Barbeque Service and turned it into a money-making venture despite the turmoil created by the Great Depression.

The Goody-Goody Barbeque Service is a far cry from the plush and sophisticated Sheraton Palmetto in Greenville, but they both represent a continuing dream come true for Honey. And Honey represents what one can do with a dream.

Honey multiplied his original $288 investment, and other successful ventures were not far over the horizon. By 1937 he was operating three restaurants and the Blue Bird Ice Cream Company, a wholesale and retail distributor of his own brand of ice cream.

Honey's Minute Grill was the next venture for the energetic entrepreneur. Featuring the first electronic ordering service in the South, the grill ultimately grew into the 600-seat Honey's Restaurant, an establishment that had grossed a half-million dollars in sales by 1958. And a chain of Li'l Honey's was next on the growing list of operations. Honey ventured into the hotel business in the 1960s with an operation in Gastonia, North Carolina, called Honey's Inn, and built the Sheraton Palmetto at the corner of I-85 and Augusta Road in Greenville in 1973.

An ice sculpture graces the beautifully remodeled banquet room.

The Sheraton Palmetto at the corner of I-85 and Augusta Road in Greenville.

Greenville's rapid growth during the 1970s and early 1980s brought increased competition for the Sheraton for customers and corporate use of its facilities. The hotel began a major renovation in the early 1980s to meet the competition and demand head-on. Each of the Sheraton's 156 rooms and the lobby were redecorated, and its banquet facilities were completely updated.

The community has recognized the Sheraton's accomplishments. Not only did its business volume increase dramatically, but the hotel received a number of important awards. In 1983 it was honored with the chamber's Design Recognition Award for excellence in interior design for the Palmetto Terrace Restaurant and Lobby Lounge, Palmetto Ballroom, executive offices, guest rooms, and main

lobby. Sheraton's world headquarters presented the hotel with its Outstanding New Facility-Existing Property Award for excellence in the lobby and public area renovations. And the Sheraton took the opportunity to show its new facility to the community by hosting Greenville's first "Business After Hours" mixer in the newly remodeled banquet room.

More improvements followed. A new courtyard swimming pool was built to accommodate outdoor events, and in 1985 Tallulah's Supper Club opened in place of the Sheraton's long-standing Palmetto Terrace and Lounge. The all-new Tallulah's was an instant success with updated decor, a new menu, live entertainment, and dancing.

Through the extensive renovation process, the Sheraton Palmetto took great care to ensure that much of its investment remained in Greenville. In fact, some 29 area companies and individuals were involved in the project, and from furniture to equipment, from lighting to landscaping, the Sheraton returned millions of dollars to the community.

The Sheraton Palmetto, since it opened its doors in Greenville in 1973, has positioned itself well through its high level of community involvement with such organizations as the Greater Greenville Convention and Visitors Bureau, the Greater Greenville Chamber of Commerce, and Freedom Weekend

The swimming pool is just one of the amenities available for the hotel's guests.

Business people enjoy the meeting facilities of the Sheraton Palmetto.

Aloft.

Honey's operation has come a long way since he purchased that first $288 restaurant. His business ventures include Honey Properties, Inc., an investment corporation; Y.L. Honey Enterprises; Honey's, Inc., the operating company for Honey's Restaurants and Catering operations; Honey's Inns; and Greenville's Sheraton Palmetto.

His start was small but his dream was large, and Honey has chalked up success after success by delivering a quality product and outstanding service to each of the clients and customers who have come his way since the first plate was served at the Goody-Goody Barbeque Service.

And through the Sheraton Palmetto the Honey tradition of the best in quality and service thrives in Greenville.

BALL UNIMARK PLASTICS DIVISION

Harry B. Ussery, president.

"When you combine quality with low cost you have a winning combination in any industry," says Harry Ussery, president of Ball Unimark Plastics. Unimark Plastics is, without a doubt, a company that has capitalized on that philosophy.

Built from the dream of two Pittsburgh plastics executives who envisioned "the most modern, efficient plastic injection-molding plant in existence," Unimark Plastics was founded in 1973 in Milroy, Pennsylvania, with one 20,000-square-foot plant. Its founders rolled up their sleeves and got down to the business of making high-quality custom plastic products, primarily for the medical, electronic, electrical, and specialty closure industries.

It didn't take long for industry to notice what the little company had to offer, and soon Unimark Plastics was no longer little. The firm built an 11,000-square-foot addition onto its original plant in 1976, constructed a second, 30,000-square-foot plant in 1980, expanded its second plant by 13,000 square feet soon after, and built its 40,000-square-foot Greenville facility in 1984.

Much of the company's growth was fueled by the capital of the Ball Corporation, a diversified *Fortune* 500 firm that purchased Unimark Plastics in 1979. However, its growth would have been impossible without Unimark's continued commitment to quality and service. "The merger has created an ideal marriage of a large corporation's financial strength and a small company's performance," indicates Ussery.

The company's manufacturing facilities are spotless, and Unimark takes great pains to keep them that way. All power and supply lines are underground, eliminating dust collection, and production areas feature brushed aluminum ceilings, epoxy-coated walls, and polyurethane floors. Air in each molding room is filtered, and molded parts are protected during collection and packed into poly bags untouched.

Operating around the clock, each Unimark Plastics plant is highly automated. In fact, it takes only 26 production workers and 10 supervisory and management personnel in each plant to keep the operation going.

Unimark Plastics' long-term growth objectives are supported and ensured by its affiliation with Ball Corporation of Muncie, Indiana. Ball is a billion-dollar packaging, industrial, and technical products company shaped by more than a century of solid business experience. Perhaps best known for its glass fruit jars, the firm produces metal beverage containers for brewers and soft drink fillers; glass containers for commercial food processors and home food preservation; and high-barrier, coextruded plastic sheets and containers for foods and juices.

Ball Corporation's industrial products and services include fabricated zinc, injection-molded and extruded/thermoformed plastics, and the slitting, cutting, coating, and printing of light-gauge steel. The company's high-technology aerospace products include space and instrumentation systems, antennas, and advanced electromechanical devices.

Ball Corporation's Unimark Plastics Division, an ever-growing part of a great American enterprise, continues to build upon its offerings of quality and low cost. They are, after all, the "winning combination."

Unimark's "clean room" operation. With brushed aluminum ceilings, epoxy-coated walls, and polyurethane floors, the manufacturing facilities are virtually dirt and dust free.

PERONE'S RESTAURANTS

In Greenville, the name Perone has been synonymous with fine cuisine for decades. But when Vince Perone came to Greenville, he was not a restaurateur. He was a football player—and he was one of the best.

Perone came to Furman University in 1949 from Hackensack, New Jersey, and immediately racked up an enviable record on the football field. His outstanding ability eventually earned him dozens of honors, including All-State, All-Southern, and Hall of Fame.

Perone married during his college years, and when children entered the picture soon after, he began to look for ways to earn extra money.

Unimpressed with the skimpy sandwiches commonly served at lunch counters, he decided to give Greenville a taste of the Perone version. It was a generous sandwich with spiced ham, bologna, and cheese piled high on a small French bread loaf. The Perone sandwich went like wildfire at the Furman canteen, and soon began to be sold around the city.

Following graduation from Furman, Perone and his wife, Joyce, bought a house and continued the sandwich business out of the basement for several years until they were able to purchase a piece of land at the corner of Route 291 and Laurens Road. The shop was called Vince Perone's Delicatessen and Restaurant. There were no dining facilities at first, but as more and more customers asked to eat there, Perone accommodated them with pickle barrels serving as stools and kitchen work tables as dining tables.

Perone's brother-in-law, Emil Fritz, soon joined the business as a partner, with "Mama" Perone becoming an integral part of the team shortly thereafter.

A native of Sarleno, Italy, Mama Perone set up a card table alongside the sandwiches to sell her homemade spaghetti. Soon she was preparing other Italian favorites, and people came in droves to sit at the pickle barrels and enjoy this

A contemporary view of the Greenville City Club's cocktail lounge.

new adventure in dining.

In 1961 Perone built a new restaurant—this time complete with a dining room. The facility was enlarged three years later to include a formal dining room that offered a wide range of gourmet foods, dinner dancing, and floor shows. It was called the Forum and the VIP Club, and it was a hit.

The establishment was enlarged again in 1972. Now a 450-seat showplace, it was the first restaurant in the area to bring in major entertainment, including such names as Frank Sinatra, Jr., and the Count Basie Orchestra.

In 1985 Perone saw the need to change. He closed the Forum and reorganized the VIP Club. The result was the elegant Greenville City Club. The impressive private club signed some 1,500 members in its first year of operation.

The Perone business is, as it always has been, a family affair. Perone's two sons, Vince Jr. and Steve, along with Vince, Joyce, Mama Perone, and Emil Fritz, are active in its daily operations. Now there are five Perone grandchildren—a development that ensures that the Perone tradition of fine dining will be a part of Greenville for a long time to come.

Perone's opened its deli line in 1961, with partners Vince Perone and Emil Fritz (left foreground) serving hungry customers.

THE FURMAN CO., INC.

The day after Christmas 1888 the Supreme Court of the State of South Carolina issued an order directing that Alester G. Furman be enrolled among the names of the attorneys of the courts of South Carolina.

However, Furman decided not to enter the legal profession. Instead, he chose real estate and insurance as his career. And the date of the court's order marked the beginning of his real estate and insurance firm, Mitchell & Furman. That organization is still a driving force in Greenville today. Known as The Furman Co., Inc., it is one of Greenville's premier real estate firms.

As the communities of the defeated Confederacy were struggling to improve their economic circumstances, Furman was active in Greenville with the Board of Trade (now the Greater Greenville Chamber of Commerce) to attract industry. As New England textile mills began a migration to the Southeast, he was ready and willing to help in the effort. Furman located plant sites and raised equity capital to encourage factory construction and the creation of jobs. Similarly, at the time of the Spanish-American

Alester G. Furman, Jr., joined the firm following graduation from Furman University. He and his father later formed a partnership called The Alester G. Furman Company.

War, he was active in the effort to locate Camp Wetherill in Greenville, and later, prior to World War I, he campaigned successfully for the Army's Camp Sevier.

Recognizing the importance of electric power to Greenville's development, Furman was instrumental in financing, acquiring the land, and constructing a hydroelectric plant on the nearby Saluda River. He also was the first president of the Saluda River Power Company, the firm that operated the plant and distributed power to the city and industry. Duke Power Company still uses power from the generators at Saluda to help meet peak loads.

Upon graduation from Furman University in 1915, Alester G. Furman, Jr., joined his father's business, and the two formed a partnership, the Alester G. Furman Company. The younger Furman took a temporary leave from the business to serve in the Army during World War I, but later returned to the firm as an active partner.

The Great Depression created difficult times for the company,

but strong leadership prevailed. It was during those years that Alester G. Furman, Jr., assumed the management of the business, but his father remained a senior partner until his death in 1956 at the age of 94.

Alester G. Furman III joined the firm in 1946 following overseas service in World War II. At the time of his father's retirement in 1960, a third generation of the Furman family led the company.

Alester G. Furman III not only continued his father's and grandfather's strong tradition of leadership within the corporation, he also continued the tradition of community involvement. He currently serves on the boards of Duke Power Company, J.P. Stevens & Company, Inc., and Liberty Corporation. Upon his retirement in May 1986, Furman's interest in the company was acquired by Junius H. Garrison, Jr.

The decades following 1940 represented a significant turning point in the firm's history. It was in 1940 that the company was asked to assist Greenville's Judson Mills in selling its village houses, which

Until his retirement in May 1986, Alester G. Furman III carried on the traditions of leadership established by his father and grandfather.

Alester G. Furman decided not to practice law. Instead, he set his sights on a career in real estate and insurance.

Junius H. Garrison, Jr., owner and president.

were built at the same time as the mill itself, around 1900.

From that beginning the corporation developed a unique, specialized department that, through the 1960s, handled the sale of more than 26,000 houses in Delaware, Virginia, North Carolina, South Carolina, Georgia, Tennessee, and Alabama for many different textile companies.

Subsequently, the diversified business, which had been incorporated in 1954, was reorganized as a holding company known as The Furman Co., Inc. It had three operating subsidiaries: The Furman Realty Co., The Furman Agency (insurance), and The Furman Securities Co. These corporations were later spun off into separate, independent entities owned by their employees.

In 1975 The Furman Securities Co., the investment banking operation, was acquired by Frost, Johnson, Read & Smith of Charleston. Two years later Marsh & McLennan, the worldwide insurance brokerage firm headquartered in New York, merged with The Furman Agency.

The corporate name for the real estate operation is now The Furman Co., Inc. The firm currently employs 54 people in three divisions: property services, residential sales, and commercial and industrial sales, including development.

Since 1970 Garrison has served as president and chief executive officer of the company and is responsible for its dominant position in the local market. His national professional status is indicated by his designation as a Certified Property Manager by the Institute of Real Estate Management, and

The firm's corporate offices are on the 18th floor of the Daniel Building.

by membership in the Society of Industrial Realtors and the Society of Real Estate Counselors. A graduate of Furman University, Garrison served in the armed forces during World War II and has built his career with The Furman Co. while participating in diverse community projects.

The Furman Co., Inc., has emphasized professional training and expertise for staff members. Today it continues its leadership in the Greenville area, offering a full range of real estate services that emphasize its commitment to the best in property management and leasing, residential sales, commercial and industrial sales, and development.

PYA/MONARCH, INC.

Perhaps the best overall description of the PYA/Monarch, Inc., operation can be found in its slogan, "We're a special breed of cat." The company is, indeed, special.

PYA/Monarch is the product of the marriage of two pioneering organizations in the food distribution industry, each of which brought their own special attributes to the union, and together continue to bring a new dimension to the food-service industry.

The PYA stands for Pearce-Young-Angel, a multibranch southeastern institutional food distributor established in the early part of the century. Monarch's roots date back to a parent company, Reid-Murdock, founded in 1853 in Iowa to supply food to wagon trains participating in the great western migration.

The two firms came together in 1967 when Consolidated Foods Corporation, now Sara Lee Corporation, purchased PYA. The businesses operated separately, however, until 1978, when they were formally combined.

The history of Monarch embraces a number of food industry firsts. A wholesaler of various food products, Reid-Murdock was the first to introduce California oranges to the Midwest and the first to import tea to the area from India and China.

In the early 1880s the company introduced its Monarch brand of coffee, tea, and baking soda. The lion's head emblem, part of the Monarch brand packaging from the beginning, remains an integral part of the PYA/Monarch logo.

Reid-Murdock incorporated in 1891 and began to operate as Reid-Murdock & Co., Monarch Finer Foods. The firm expanded into processing and manufacturing food products in the early part of the twentieth century, and made U.S.

The first branch operation of Pearce-Young-Angel, later to become PYA/Monarch, Inc., in Spartanburg.

food history when it proved that Monarch catsup could be packed without a preservative.

Monarch continued to grow steadily through the first half of the 1900s, both as a manufacturer and distributor, with its business heavily concentrated in the retail trade. However, its direction was soon to change.

The company was acquired in 1946 by Consolidated, and in the mid-1950s was divested of its manufacturing operations. The future for Monarch, Consolidated decided, was in distribution. But times were changing in the distribution business, and it had become evident in the late 1950s that the days of the classic retail food distributor were numbered. The future for food-service distribution, however, looked promising, and Monarch headed down that road. However, the firm soon discovered that riding the winds of change wasn't easy. Retail and food-service distribution were different games altogether.

However, things began to look up for Monarch when a chance meeting took place between Consolidated Foods chairman Nathan

Cummings and R. Roy Pearce, then-president of Pearce-Young-Angel. On his way to the dedication of a new poultry-processing plant in Newberry, South Carolina, Cummings was picked up at the Columbus Airport by Pearce. The two executives exchanged ideas, and Cummings became increasingly interested in the potential of food-service distribution in general and PYA specifically. He wrote to Pearce several weeks later to ask if PYA was willing to sell out and become a part of Consolidated. The answer was affirmative, and in July 1967 Consolidated acquired more than a quarter-century of experience in the food-service distribution field.

Founded in 1903 by C.C. Pearce, PYA began operations in Columbia as a wholesaler of fresh fruit and vegetables, primarily to the retail trade. The enterprise prospered, and the first branch operation was opened in Spartanburg in 1911. Other branches followed, and by

Built in 1920 in Asheville, North Carolina, this warehouse was part of Pearce-Young-Angel's extensive branch warehouse network that served the Carolinas.

the 1920s PYA was a significant presence in the Carolinas. The original branch operated as C.C. Pearce & Co., and the others were labeled Pearce-Young-Angel, featuring the names of two employees holding stock in the firm, but who were subsequently bought out by the Pearce family.

PYA entered the food-service market in 1939. It was a daring move, since there were few food-service outlets in the area at that time. But it held interesting potential, since there were few sources of supplies for operators. Most were buying from absentee distributors and paying extraordinarily high prices.

Initially, PYA offered produce and institutional canned products, grocery specialties, and dried fruits and vegetables. That lineup was expanded in 1937, when PYA became the first distributor in the Carolinas to stock frozen foods. That same year the company took another innovative step, forming an advance sales force when other distributors were selling right off the truck.

Two other moves solidified PYA's position in the food-service industry. The first was its branch warehouse network that placed most of its customers within easy reach.

The second was the fact that since most of its volume was still in produce, PYA was set up for high-frequency delivery when other distributors were not.

The food-service business was climbing, and PYA began to phase out all its retail trade. The process was slow, but by the end of the 1960s the firm was virtually 100 percent into the food service industry, and further expanded its product line to include fresh meat.

The company built what were, at the time, state-of-the-art distribution centers in Columbia and Greenville, and a frozen-food-forwarding in-transit warehouse in Greenville to resupply the North and South Carolina branches—another first in the industry. PYA also expanded significantly with the acquisition of Goodnight Brothers, a Charlotte, North Carolina-based distributor with a dominant position in the

area.

Following its acquisition by Consolidated, PYA's president, R. Roy Pearce, was placed in charge of Consolidated's food-service group, consisting of its PYA and Monarch divisions. In addition, Monarch's headquarters was moved from River Grove, Illinois, to Greenville.

Both PYA and Monarch significantly strengthened their positions in the market through the 1970s, aided to a great extent by the installation of a sophisticated data-processing system.

Meanwhile, Consolidated acquired a number of strong food-service companies, and in mid-1978 the firm reorganized its entire Institutional Foods Group. The move finally brought PYA and Monarch, which had continued to operate as two separate entities, together with a new name—PYA/Monarch, Inc.

With annual sales well in excess of $1.5 billion, and service provided to more than 70,000 food-service operators throughout the nation, PYA/Monarch, Inc., has traveled many roads since its beginning. And, without a doubt, it has proven itself to be "a special breed of cat."

A modern distribution center of PYA/Monarch, Inc., in Greenville.

STEEL HEDDLE

Heddle. As a word, it's an enigma. To those with little knowledge of the textile-weaving business, it probably means nothing. But those in the industry know that it is a critical part of the weaving machinery—the part that holds and guides the individual strands of yarn through the high-speed weaving process. They know that without the heddle, weaving machinery simply could not operate.

For centuries the weaving process utilized a heddle made of twine. But in 1898 there was a breakthrough. A small company in Philadelphia introduced a heddle made of flat steel. The new heddle took the industry by storm, and the tiny operation, which named itself, appropriately enough, Steel Heddle, was on the road to success. Today the name Steel Heddle is known throughout the world as the largest producer of weaving machine accessories and a growing force in the manufacture of non-textile industrial products.

The firm began to expand beyond its original Philadelphia location in 1923, when it purchased a North Carolina loom reed company and formed a Southern Division. The following year the operation was moved to new quarters in Greenville, and in 1930 the small building on McBee Avenue was enlarged so that Steel Heddle could begin to manufacture textile loom shuttles. In 1948 Steel Heddle left the McBee location and moved to its present, sprawling site on Rutherford Road.

The company's expansion in the years that followed was rapid, and from 1948 to 1954 the plant nearly doubled its physical size with the addition of a foundry operation and the relocation of plating and loom reed manufacturing operations from the former location. In 1955 a bobbin manufacturing company in Greensboro, North Carolina, was acquired, and its operations were moved to Greenville four years later.

The Philadelphia facility continued in heddle, reed, and frame production, and industrial wire rolling until 1971. That year the Greenville plant was expanded to accommodate the heddle, frame, and plating departments, which, along with Steel Heddle's corporate offices, were moved from Philadelphia.

In the 1970s the company concentrated on diversification, forming an Industrial Division that operates a foundry, machine shop, and plating department. Products manufactured by the division, unrelated to textiles, include precision parts and assemblies such as machine castings and investment castings. Today approximately 25 percent of Steel Heddle's business is devoted to the manufacture of products for nontextile industries.

Diversified, yet primarily devoted to the textile industry, Steel Heddle, with more than 850 employees, four plants, and more than a half-million feet of manufacturing space, stands ready and well prepared to meet tomorrow's challenges.

This building on McBee Avenue housed Steel Heddle's manufacturing operations from 1923 to 1948.

KEYS PRINTING COMPANY

Keys Printing Company, one of South Carolina's oldest continuously operating businesses, has been closely allied with the growth and progress of Greenville and the Piedmont region for well over a century.

The history of the firm dates to July 1, 1869, and four generations of the Keys family have been associated with it. Operated successfully under their guidance through the years, in depression and difficult war years, the company has become one of the Southeast's most outstanding printing establishments in terms of modern equipment, new methods of production, quality work, and dependability.

For many years Keys Printing owned and printed the *Baptist Courier* until its sale to the South Carolina Baptist Convention in 1921, when the firm adopted the name of Keys Printing Company.

The association of W.W. Keys with the business commenced in 1882. When he died in 1910, his son, James Crawford Keys, was made head of the company and served in that position until his death on August 8, 1935. His widow and sons, J.C. Keys, Jr., and Jack A. Keys, then became the principal figures in the operation. J.C. Keys, Jr., current chairman of the board, was president of the company until he was succeeded by his son, Ben Geer Keys, current president.

Changes in printing production techniques have come in recent years with developments in computers and in other fields, and the 43,000-square-foot plant on Old Congaree Road operates with a battery of sophisticated machines, including a five-color press.

That so many of the organizations and businesses using Keys services have been customers for decades attests to the firm's long record of satisfactory performance and reliability. Some clients have had their printing done by Keys

Keys Printing Company, at Congaree Road and Interstate 385, is one of Greenville's oldest continuously operating businesses.

since before the turn of the century.

The growth of Keys Printing Company parallels in many ways the growth of Greenville itself. The establishment's expansion took it to six different downtown locations. The Old Congaree Road plant was built in 1973 on a five-acre tract near the intersection of I-385 and Roper Mountain Road.

Keys Printing Company, one of Greenville's best-known institutions, also operates a quick print facility, Keys Mini-Print, at its former headquarters location on East McBee Avenue, and a fulfillment center, The Whole Nine Yards, in Northwood Industrial Park.

239

TEXIZE

As World War II was coming to a victorious end and Americans began to dream of a new era of peace and prosperity, Greenvillian W.J. "Jack" Greer had a dream of his own. He wanted to go into business.

While serving textile plants in the area as a salesman, Greer noticed the need for an all-purpose cleaner. He then purchased a building, and in the lab of the 60- by 120-foot stable-turned-warehouse, the company's first chemist formulated the cleaner.

Although it was originally intended for use in textile mills, the cleaner's effectiveness was quickly recognized by homemakers. Therefore, in 1947 Texize Household Cleaner—the first all-purpose household cleaner in the United States—was spawned.

With a brass spigot welded to the base of a drum, the firm's tiny production force filled, capped, labeled, and packaged the bottles by hand. A good day's output was 20 bottles.

From that first cleaner, the company's product line grew quickly. Within a few years it would include bleaches, starches, a floor cleaner, liquid detergent, rug cleaner, and pine oil disinfectant. Texize was on its way to becoming a household name across America.

By 1952 the firm's sales force had grown to 18 in consumer products and 6 in textiles. Three years later the company took a major step forward with the purchase of a new plant, located just outside Greenville in Mauldin to expand its production capability.

By 1958 Texize products were sold in 41 of the 48 continental United States. That same year the firm purchased Industrial Products, Inc., makers of warp sizing and other finishing materials.

In 1965, with sales around $20

million, the company built a 100,000-square-foot plant in New Jersey and continued to serve the still-blooming textile industry with sizing.

Texize was acquired in 1967 by Norwich Pharmacal Company, and it became a division of Morton-Norwich Products, Inc. In 1969 a manufacturing facility in Illinois was added to the two plants already in operation.

Through the decades of the 1960s and 1970s, the firm's product line, and its sales, vaulted, as Americans were introduced to names such as Fantastik, Spray 'n Wash, Grease relief, and Glass Plus.

In 1971 Texize Chemicals, Inc., changed its name to Texize Chemical Co., Division of MortonNorwich Products, Inc., and became totally consumer oriented with the sale of the Commercial, Industrial, and Textile divisions.

After 24 years of service in the company's sales and marketing departments, Jack Mayer was named the third president of Texize in 1975. Shortly thereafter, the firm initiated a million-dollar expansion of its Mauldin plant, significantly furthering its capabilities.

The firm's first plant.

Jack Mayer, Texize president (center); Doug West, senior vice-president, marketing; McGruff; and local youngsters help raise the coveted C-flag, awarded to Texize for its Operation Kidsafe program.

In keeping with its desire to be a good corporate citizen, Texize launched the largest company-sponsored child safety program in the nation in 1985 and raised over $700,000 for national programs to help protect America's children. President Ronald Reagan's coveted C-flag was awarded to Texize in recognition of its community and national accomplishments in the area of child safety in both 1985 and 1986.

Now a member of the Dow Chemical Company and a division of Dow Consumer Products, Inc., Texize continues a solid pattern of growth. It also continues a solid pattern of bringing new and better products to the American consumer.

FIRST UNION NATIONAL BANK OF SOUTH CAROLINA

In February 1984 First Union Corporation executive Ted Sumner called his friend of 40 years, Sam Hunt, president of Southern Bancorporation, to say that First Union was interested in buying 4.9 percent of Southern's stock. At the time 4.9 percent was the most a banking institution could acquire from a bank in another state. Sumner further stated that should interstate banking laws be passed by both states, "It might be a natural to get together someday."

The laws were passed, and the banks did "get together," when First Union Corporation purchased Southern Bancorporation in March 1986. With the purchase, First Union acquired one of South Carolina's financial leaders, and a solid piece of Greenville's history.

Southern Bank began in 1961 as a state-chartered community bank headquartered in Greenville. Its founding officers were Harry R. Stephenson, Jr., who was elected chairman of the board; Thomas C. "Nap" Vandiver, who was selected as president; and Sam H. Hunt, who served as vice-president. It took 18 months and 633 shareholders to raise the $1.5 million required capital.

Southern Bank opened its doors on June 1, 1961, in a converted grocery store on East North Street. By the end of that first year, the bank had more than $5.1 million in deposits, and had opened its first branch office.

In its second year Southern Bank introduced an innovative new concept: payment of 4-percent interest on one-year savings plans. The institution also introduced the state's first bank charge card, the forerunner to MasterCard.

By the end of the decade Southern Bank had become a full-service institution with the addition of a trust department. And, just before

A mixture of innovation and history, First Union National Bank resulted from First Union Corporation's acquisition of Southern Bancorporation. Shown here is the corporate headquarters in Greenville.

celebrating its 10th anniversary, Southern Bank reached the $100-million mark in resources and was in the top 5 percent of all commercial banks in the nation. The institution was serving 15 communities in the western portion of the state through 24 offices.

In 1973 Southern Bancorporation, Inc., a holding company, was formed with subsidiaries that included Southern Bank and World Acceptance Corporation, a Greenville-based consumer finance company. With the purchase of American Bank & Trust Company of Orangeburg in 1974, Southern became a statewide bank overnight, serving an additional 20 cities.

The marriage of First Union and Southern Bancorporation was a natural. The two dynamic, innova-

tive institutions have enjoyed a close association since 1961.

First Union, organized in 1908 in Charlotte as Union National Bank, was a rather conservative operation at first, although it did show early signs of innovative thinking. However, in the early 1950s First Union left its conservative tradition behind in favor of a more aggressive approach, and its growth mounted primarily through mergers and consolidations. Some 30 acquisitions of smaller banks have taken place since its beginning, and a historic window of opportunity opened for First Union in 1985, when regional interstate banking became a reality. First Union seized the opportunity and announced six acquisitions in 1985, including that of Southern Bancorporation.

The 25-year history of Southern Bancorporation has been marked by a number of important events. Clearly, becoming a part of First Union Corporation was the most important.

THE CITIZENS AND SOUTHERN NATIONAL BANK OF SOUTH CAROLINA

"Old Values. New Ideas." Those four words provided the theme for a mid-1980s advertising campaign for the Citizens and Southern National Bank of South Carolina. They were simple words. Yet one would be hard pressed to uncover a more vivid description of the fabric of which the institution was made.

The original bank from which C&S later developed was founded in 1874 by a group of leading Charleston citizens who named their institution the Germania Savings Bank. Building upon the simple virtues of service, hard work, and sound management, the bank thrived. Its success fostered the opening of Germania National Bank in 1916. Two years later the institutions changed their names to Atlantic Savings Bank and Atlantic National Bank. In 1928

The C&S Tower, Citizens and Southern National Bank's latest addition, stands 12 stories tall and overlooks downtown Greenville.

Citizens and Southern president J. Willis Cantey points out a construction site to C.T. Wyche and chairman of the board Hugh C. Lane (left of Wyche) during ground-breaking ceremonies for C&S's first office in Greenville in 1957.

the Citizens and Southern Holding Corporation of Georgia purchased both banks, consolidated several of its offices, and became the Citizens and Southern Bank of South Carolina.

C&S made its first appearance in the upstate area in Spartanburg in 1933. In 1956 C&S merged with Growers Bank and Trust in Inman. The following year C&S opened its first office in Greenville, linking the state with offices in South Carolina's four major cities. During the next several years offices were established in Florence, Camden, Greer, Sumter, Darlington, Rock Hill, Anderson, Conway, Myrtle Beach, and Gaffney.

Old values came together with new ideas in an unprecedented way as the 1960s ushered in the age of computers. The bank be-

came one of the first in the nation to utilize computers to speed the banking process. More new and innovative ways to service its customers followed. In the 1970s C&S was the first bank in South Carolina to use automated teller machines, and the 1980s brought the institution's customers the convenience of banking by phone.

In 1986 C&S reunited with C&S of Georgia to form a three-state company with combined assets of nearly $18 billion and offices in Florida, Georgia, and South Carolina.

Today C&S blankets South Carolina with more than 120 branches and over 100 Financial Wizard machines. In the Greenville area alone, C&S has more than a dozen offices and nine Financial Wizard machines.

A magnificent 12-story office tower in downtown Greenville is the new home base for The Citizens and Southern National Bank of South Carolina as it serves the dynamic Golden Crescent of South Carolina with "Old Values. New Ideas."

DAVIS MECHANICAL CONTRACTORS, INC.

When F. Harold Gillespie became president of Davis Mechanical Contractors in 1965, the company had eight million dollars in sales and extraordinary potential. Gillespie's strategy was to capitalize on that potential. And he did. Today the firm is one of the top four open shops in the mechanical contracting industry and has annual sales in excess of $65 million.

The forerunner of the present company was formed in 1949, when J. Wesley Davis teamed up with Bryant Electric to form Bryant-Davis Contractors, a firm specializing in mechanical contracting. In 1953 Davis purchased Bryant's interest, changed the name to Davis Mechanical Contractors, and expanded the company's service to include both electrical and mechanical work.

Gillespie, owner of Associated Engineers in Greenville, joined Davis in 1963 as head of the firm's mechanical division. Two years later Davis announced his intention to sell the company. It was a golden opportunity for Gillespie. He purchased the mechanical division and merged it with Associated Engineers. The electrical portion of the company was sold to other parties.

The firm continued to operate under the name Davis Mechanical Contractors, Inc., but significant changes began to take place throughout the organization. Operating procedures were revamped, and a number of programs were initiated for growth, diversity, and quality. More important, Gillespie saw to it that employees of the company were treated fairly and with respect, and that clients received more than they expected.

The downturn of the textile industry, a major portion of the firm's client base, created a springboard for substantial diversification during the 1960s and 1970s.

F. Harold Gillespie, chairman and chief executive officer.

The company's growth was rapid as it moved into mechanical contracting service for commercial, industrial, and institutional clients. Davis Mechanical Contractors opened its first branch office in 1973 in Nashville to serve the expanding business in that area.

Constantly seeking to provide its clients with more and better services, the firm opened a 30,000-square-foot specialty metal fabrication shop in 1974. Demand for fabrication was high, and a number of subsequent expansions resulted in what today is a 160,000-square-foot manufacturing operation, including an area recently opened to produce stainless-steel liner plates for nuclear energy plants.

In 1983 the company opened a Sanford, Florida, branch to serve its growing business in nearby Orlando and the surrounding areas. During this same year Ray Cobb was

W. Ray Cobb, president.

appointed president and chief operating officer of the firm, and Gillespie became chairman of the board and chief executive officer.

As Davis Mechanical Contractors, Inc., continued to grow, so did its reputation for high-quality work, on-time completions, cost control, and integrity. And behind that reputation are some 1,200 Davis office, manufacturing, and field employees who have flourished in the close, family atmosphere created by Gillespie—people who believe that you don't just promise more than everyone else, you *do* more.

J.P. STEVENS & CO., INC.

The history of American business is rich with success stories. There are stories of innovation and initiative, tales of grit and gumption, and striking examples of courage. But of all of this nation's great corporations, one would be hard pressed to find a more dramatic illustration of the strength of the free-enterprise system than J.P. Stevens & Co., Inc.

The oldest diversified firm in the venerable textile industry, Stevens has maintained its management within the family since 1813, when Nathaniel Stevens began weaving woolen broadcloth in a converted gristmill in North Andover, Massachusetts.

Like most new business owners, Stevens and his two partners found the going tough. For one thing, the War of 1812 cut off vital supplies and new equipment. And peace brought its own problems, including a flood of imports. While many new mills gave up and shut down, Stevens found it a challenge and diversified from broadcloth to flannel. No one up to that time had successfully produced flannel in the United States, but Stevens chalked up his first success and re-invested the profits.

As the years passed Stevens parted company with his two partners, served a term in the Massachusetts legislature, fathered nine children, and continued to improve his mill.

Stevens' sons and, eventually, his grandsons, joined the business. And the resourcefulness that ran thick in the Stevens bloodline began to yield both new products and a mounting business volume.

One grandson, John P., decided to learn the family business in a different way. In 1883 he went to work in the selling house that handled the goods for the Stevens mills. With solid experience in merchandising, John P. joined with the principals of the original Stevens mills on August 1, 1899, and formed J.P. Stevens & Co.

The expansion from manufacturing into merchandising proved to be a good move for the family, and John P. traveled the rapidly expanding South lining up cotton mills for the selling house. Soon the company became a selling agent for other mills and found fertile ground in South Carolina. Over the next three decades J.P. Stevens & Co. became associated with a number of South Carolina mills, including Watts Mill in Laurens; Glenn Lowry Manufacturing Company, which later became the Whitmire Plant of Aragon-Baldwin Mills; Dunean Mills of Greenville; Victor Monaghan Company, with plants in Greenville and Greer; and Slater Manufacturing Company in Slater.

Stevens continued to propel itself ahead of its competitors by starting an organized textile research and development program in 1937. In a laboratory in one of the firm's many New York City units, its scientists began analyzing and testing cotton and rayon cloths. Years later this effort led to such developments as a superior wash-and-wear finish process and a variety of unique fabrics, produced without spinning or weaving, which became known as nonwovens.

In September 1946 a merger united the J.P. Stevens selling house and mill company with eight other firms. The newly created corporation then became known as J.P. Stevens & Co., Inc., operating 29 mills with corporate offices in New York City. The firm's presence in South Carolina deepened with the merger, with 15 of the 29 mills located in the state. More were soon added, including a finishing plant of the Delta Company; the Appleton Company in Anderson; and Utica-Mohawk in Clemson.

By the early 1960s the J.P. Stevens presence in Greenville was clearly permanent. The firm set up administrative offices of its cotton division in the city in 1951 to oversee the operation of six area plants. The Utica-Mohawk Group's administrative offices were in nearby Clemson, and Raw Cotton & Wooltop Procurement Services were also handled out of Greenville.

The company had diversified its line by that time to include cotton goods for clothing, upholstery, woolens and worsteds, rayon and wool-blend fabrics, automobile upholstery fabric, and filament and spun rayon.

In 1966 J.P. Stevens & Co., Inc., leased two floors of the Daniel Building to house the firm's southern headquarters. As the 1980s approached, the company decided to consolidate various management functions previously located in New Jersey and throughout the

Stevens was started in this converted gristmill on Lake Cochichewick in North Andover, Massachusetts.

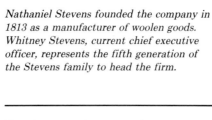

Nathaniel Stevens founded the company in 1813 as a manufacturer of woolen goods. Whitney Stevens, current chief executive officer, represents the fifth generation of the Stevens family to head the firm.

Southeast to improve the operation of all manufacturing processes and increase productivity. The end result was the purchase and renovation of two former Sears buildings, located next to each other in downtown Greenville. The complex is called Stevens Center, and it became home for many corporate management functions in 1981.

However, Stevens Center wasn't the only new thing that year. In fact, the entire company was awash with a fresh new look brought about by a strategic identity program. The firm's trademark was updated, and the change was reflected everywhere. From its packaging to the tractor-trailers carrying Stevens goods, the new design was at the heart of the system, and it reflected the company's stronger, more unified image. And, although it did not change its legal name, the corporation began to call itself simply Stevens.

The company's administrative offices in Greenville are located at 400 East Stone Avenue. Formerly occupied by Sears, Roebuck and Co., Stevens bought the building in 1980 and, after extensive remodeling, occupied the facility one year later.

The Stevens of the 1980s was changing rapidly with the times. A new corporate strategy focused on home fashions and industrial fabrics, and the two would take the company to new heights.

Striving to create a "total fashion environment for the home," the firm began to market a line of home products created by such noted designers as Ralph Lauren and Gloria Vanderbilt. Stevens' acquisition of the Domestics Division of Burlington Industries in 1986 added the Laura Ashley label.

Stevens Industrial Products Division, whose marketing, product development, and manufacturing staff moved to Greenville in 1982, continued to grow as a major supplier of fabrics to a number of industrial markets, including automotive, aircraft, construction, electrical, and aerospace. And Stevens Aviation, a growing part of the company since 1950, prospered as a corporate, executive, and aero center for Beechcraft airplanes and associated products.

Today some 23,000 people are employed by J.P. Stevens & Co., Inc. They continue to build on the firm foundation laid long, long ago, and they continue to write a great American success story.

Two mills of Piedmont Manufacturing Company, one on each side of the river in nearby Piedmont, were among those acquired in the 1946 merger that created J.P. Stevens & Co., Inc. The mills, typical of those of the early part of the century, were surrounded by "mill villages," built by textile companies to house employees and their families.

STONE MANUFACTURING COMPANY

Five people reported for work at 154 Rivers Street on July 9, 1933. It was the first day of business for Stone Manufacturing Company.

As the clatter of eight sewing machines and one elastic machine filled the third-floor room, and stitch after stitch took its place in the first lot of ladies' cotton jersey bloomers, the business that Eugene E. "Gene" Stone founded was on its way. Under Stone's leadership, and with the help of his energetic wife, Allene "Linky" Wyman Stone, the company has grown to become one of the leading apparel firms in an industry of over 16,000 such operations.

In the early days, just as today, the emphasis at Stone Manufacturing was on producing a quality garment at an affordable price. It was a policy that was quickly recognized by a growing number of customers, and within a year the company was producing dresses, slips, and sunsuits in addition to bloomers. It didn't take long to outgrow the second-floor facility, and the firm soon expanded its operations to both the first and second floors of the Rivers Street property.

The late 1930s and early 1940s were years of explosive growth for Stone Manufacturing Company. Expansions to Cox Street, Falls Street, and Court Street took place during those years, and an office and showroom were opened in New York. Today the renovated Court Street facility, first occupied by Stone Manufacturing in 1942, houses the Activewear and Umbro divisions.

Located on 55 acres of rolling lawns and wooded terrain, the Stone residence, Cherrydale, is listed on the National Register of Historic Places.

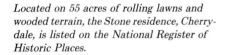

Eugene E. Stone III (seated), chairman; with Jack Stone, chief executive officer (left); and Charles Rivers Stone, president.

With the outbreak of World War II, the firm added military mattress covers and aprons for the Women's Army Corps to its rapidly expanding product line. It was during that time that the "boxer short," a product designed by Linky Stone for her son in 1938, became a commercial success.

In 1939 Stone purchased 55 acres of land and a beautiful, old home, located at Poinsett Highway and North Pleasantburg Drive, from the heirs of the Furman family. It was called Cherrydale. In 1951 Stone returned from a special assignment for the State Department in Europe and found that Linky had moved the family to Cherrydale. The home, which is listed on the National Register of Historic Places, continues to be the Stones' residence.

In 1952 Stone built a plant on land adjacent to Cherrydale. It was a magnificent facility, and at the time was known as the largest and finest apparel plant in the world. The facility, with cutting tables as long as football fields, can accommodate the spreading of 300 miles of cloth and houses 2,000 sewing machines.

Stone is well known and respected throughout the apparel industry for the efficiency with which his plants operate. In fact, he has invented many labor-saving devices to streamline the work process, and builds them at the Cree Division, adjacent to the Cherrydale plant.

During the 1950s and 1960s the name "Stoneswear" was rapidly becoming a household word across the nation. As the company grew, so did the spectrum of its products, which had expanded to include childrens' playwear and lingerie. In December 1965 the firm announced the production of its one-billionth garment—a snappy girls' sailor short set.

A national quest for physical fitness took the country by storm

The River Street plant—Stone's first manufacturing facility.

during the 1970s, and Stone Manufacturing responded with the creation of its Activewear Division. In the same building where a generation earlier aprons and sunsuits rolled off the line, merchandisers and marketers began to combine their talents to meet the burgeoning needs of this new life-style.

Stone Manufacturing Company has always been a family business. Both sons of Gene and Linky Stone have been active in the operation since boyhood, and in 1976 Charles Rivers Stone was appointed president of the firm. He officially joined Stone Manufacturing in 1960 following his attendance at Clemson University. Jack Stone returned to the business in 1977, following an absence during which time he served in the U.S. Navy, received an M.B.A. from Stanford University, and held executive positions at Levi Strauss and Hang Ten in California. Today Jack Stone is chief executive officer with responsibility for the firm's marketing efforts, while his brother oversees the manufacturing operations.

In keeping with the family atmosphere of the business, the Stones got the name for the Cree Division by combining the initials of their two sons. And Maros, the com-

pany's executive office, consists of the first three letters of the names of their daughters, Mary and Rosalie.

Stone Manufacturing Company currently has plants in South Carolina, North Carolina, and Georgia, and regional offices in New York, Chicago, Atlanta, Dallas, Los Angeles, and Miami. Through its International Division, the Stone brand's acclaim is rising in an increasing number of foreign countries. "Stone Apparel, the brand you can believe in," offers an exciting line of activewear under the Harbor Town label, as well as a line of soccer uniforms under the Umbro name and children's wear under the well-known Stone Youthwear label.

From a handful of workers producing ladies' bloomers to the worldwide operations of today, Stone Manufacturing Company has been enhanced by the catalyst of innovation and the drive for excellence, and it continues to excel through "a brand you can believe in." The firm presently has 21 plants and approximately 8,000 employees.

Today the Court Street facility, first occupied by Stone Manufacturing in 1942, houses the Activewear and Umbro divisions.

FIRST FEDERAL OF SOUTH CAROLINA

In December 1933 First Federal of Greenville became one of the first federally chartered savings and loan associations in the nation when it was issued Charter No. 41 by the U.S. government. As the first federally chartered savings and loan in South Carolina, First Federal of Greenville began its operations with paid-in capital of $5,000 and the simple purpose of promoting thrift and providing home loans to the area's citizens.

The association's growth during the early years was unspectacular but solid, and at the end of its 15th year in business, assets totaled $5.7 million. It is interesting to note that during that time the organization had no borrowers who defaulted on their home loans—an enviable record unequaled by any other financial institution in the Southeast. In addition, the association never paid less than

The architecturally unique nine-story First Federal headquarters building, completed in 1974, was constructed of native materials, and the interior features the work of South Carolina artists.

3-percent annual dividends to its savers.

First Federal has occupied five different home office buildings since its inception, with each office being within a four-block radius of its present site. The first three offices were located on West McBee Avenue in downtown Greenville. In 1954 the association moved to its newly constructed headquarters at 320 Buncombe Street, where it remained for the next 20 years. In order to better serve the needs of its customers, a decision was made to construct its first branch office, which was opened in 1962 on Wade Hampton Boulevard directly across from one of Greenville's first shopping centers, the Wade Hampton Mall. The manager of First Federal of Greenville's first branch office was H. Ray Davis, who, interestingly enough, was later to become chairman of the board and chief executive officer of the association.

In keeping with the accelerated growth of the Greater Greenville area during the late 1960s, First Federal of Greenville began marching to a quickened pace under the leadership of Walter P. White,

First Federal's home office was located at 320 Buncombe Street from 1954 to 1974.

chairman of the board, and Charles W. Scales, Jr., president, and in 1971 a major milestone was achieved when management proudly announced the attainment of $100 million in assets.

Meanwhile, Scales, who had taken the reins in 1968, was busy working on the dream of a new corporate headquarters building that would enable the association to keep pace with the demands of a rapidly growing metropolitan area. It took six years from the intricacies of acquiring additional property (adjacent to its existing location) to the actual design and construction, but Scales's patience and perseverance paid off for all First Federal employees, when, in 1974, they were able to call a beautiful, unique, architecturally award-winning nine-story building on College Street "home." In keeping with its desire for South Carolinians to keep their money in-state, First Federal made certain that the majority of materials used to construct the building was from South Carolina. The interior decor was also enhanced by the purchase of over 100 pieces of art from South Carolina residents that were prominently displayed throughout the building.

Those were exciting days! But the quickening pace of the 1970s was to become a full gallop in the years to follow.

The credit crunch of 1975 gave birth to some intense economic pressures as the calendar turned to the 1980s. And the outlook was just as bleak, with the advent of deregulation, more high interest rates, and a worsening economy predicted. It was clear to management that the savings and loan business would never be the same again. First Federal needed to make some tough decisions, and it needed to make them quickly.

Under the leadership of H. Ray Davis, chairman of the board and chief executive officer, a multifaceted plan was put together to make First Federal a financially strong and viable financial institution fully capable of meeting all challenges of the future. An important component of the plan, Davis concluded, was to consummate mergers with other associations throughout the state having a strong net worth, proper geographical positioning, and sound management. A list of 20 of the most desirable merger candidates was compiled. Then the state was divided into 12 regions, each one surrounding a key community into which First Federal hoped to expand and which contained a likely merger prospect. Next, comprehensive guidelines were set for each candidate.

But there was one more critical item on the agenda before Davis could hit the merger trail. The association needed to change its name from First Federal of Greenville to First Federal of South Carolina to more properly reflect its

future statewide presence. The Federal Home Loan Bank Board in Washington, D.C., was petitioned, and, for the first time ever in the case of a First Federal, the FHLB Board allowed an association to change its name to that of the state. All systems were go!

Chairman Davis made the first merger proposal to Fort Hill Federal in Clemson, an association with $52 million in assets, a net worth of about 11 percent, and, in 1980, one of the top 10 strongest organizations in the United States within its asset category. Fort Hill accepted the proposal, and the merger was announced in May 1981.

Within 60 days Davis announced another merger—this time with Piedmont Federal of Spartanburg, a profitable $110-million association. Two good mergers, as they say, deserve a few more. More did follow, in fact, as the total reached nine within the next 12 months.

The numbers looked great! From the mergers, the institution had more than doubled its assets— from $440 million to over $900 million, and its number of employees went from 160 to 445. First Federal of South Carolina had 30 branches strategically located across the state.

While the association had made gigantic strides in becoming a statewide financial institution in

an unprecedented period of time, Davis realized that the job was not over, as servicing gaps still existed in important areas throughout the state. Almost immediately First Federal purchased 16 offices from 5 other South Carolina banking institutions, finished its climb well above the one-billion-dollar mark, became the largest savings and loan in the Carolinas, and made the *American Banker* magazine's list of the top 100 savings and loans in the United States. Another important milestone was achieved in 1983, when the association converted from a mutual to a publicly owned financial institution through the sale of 2.6 million shares of common stock.

Today, as the Carolinas' largest savings and loan with assets of $1.85 billion, First Federal of South Carolina has completed its transition to the era of the "modern thrift," fully capable of handling the needs of individuals and businesses in a personal but professional manner. From its civic involvement in the communities it now serves to its highly regarded position within the financial industry, First Federal of South Carolina truly is "The First."

First Federal, the first association to be federally chartered in South Carolina, began operations in this building on West McBee Avenue in 1933.

SLOAN CONSTRUCTION COMPANY

Greenville, like the rest of the nation, was left stricken by the Great Depression, and in 1934 hope was all that many had left.

E.D. "Ed" Sloan had plenty of hope as he salvaged two trucks, borrowed $600 from his schoolteacher sister, and opened the door of Sloan Construction Company (Sloco) that year. Today the Greenville-based firm operates primarily as a public works contractor in upper South Carolina and Florida.

Sloan graduated from Clemson University in 1918. Following service in the Navy, he was employed by the then-new State Highway Department and soon became its Greenville District Engineer. Sloan left the Highway Department to manage the Charlotte-based Carolina Road Surfacing Company,

which had a yard behind the Southern Railway Yard on Greenville's Kelly Avenue. When Carolina Road Surfacing Company collapsed during the Depression, Sloan ventured out on his own.

With a performance bond signed by his Greenville friends, J. Will Hunter, Charles P. Ballenger, and Sydney Bruce, Sloan contracted for his first project—repairing a hurricane-damaged wharf at the Key West Naval Base. The company's founding was just in time

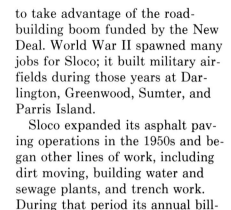

Willis H. Duininck, 1985 National Asphalt Pavement Association's chairman of the board (center), presents the national first place award plaques to V.L. Ashmore, Jr. (left), president, and W.W. Mims (right), vice-president, of Sloan Construction Company.

to take advantage of the road-building boom funded by the New Deal. World War II spawned many jobs for Sloco; it built military airfields during those years at Darlington, Greenwood, Sumter, and Parris Island.

Sloco expanded its asphalt paving operations in the 1950s and began other lines of work, including dirt moving, building water and sewage plants, and trench work. During that period its annual billings reached approximately three million dollars.

When E.D. "Ned" Sloan, Jr., was discharged from the Army and joined the firm in 1953, hot-mix asphalt was in great demand. The company was performing more than half of all such work in South Carolina during that time, operating three hot-mix asphalt spreads.

Sloco's asphalt paving operations expanded to 13 spreads in the next decade. The firm also constructed six bridges during that time and began work offshore on the Eastern Missile Tracking Range. In 1963 the company was awarded its first job at Guantanamo Bay Naval Base; more work followed on that base over the next 17 years.

A fixed-price Navy contract to rebuild the airfield on Ascension Island between Brazil and Africa was awarded to the firm in 1965. It was a complex job, and the one on which Sloco grew up.

Because of the lack of port facilities at Ascension, Sloco chartered landing ships and beached them in the surf on the isolated island—1,000 miles from the nearest tugboat. Despite the obstacles, the company maintained air traffic throughout the project, and was awarded the Navy's highest commendation for the job.

More offshore work followed on Ascension and in the Azores, Antigua, Grand Turk, the Panama Ca-

nal Zone, Puerto Rico, and Key West. The firm also participated heavily in the interstate highway building program. Sloco paved, with only a few exceptions, all of I-85 and I-26 in upper South Carolina. By 1970 annual billings had reached $15 million.

During the 1970s Sloco contracted numerous paving jobs in Florida and began quarrying and crushing stone at Sandy Flat in upper Greenville County and at Inman, above Spartanburg. In 1977 the company contracted to resurface the one-runway Greenville-Spartanburg Airport designed by Alex Crouch. The job was completed over the July 4 weekend in a fraction of the time necessary for a multiple runway airfield where one runway can be closed and air traffic maintained on others. Sloco earned the maximum bonus for early completion of the job and repeated the act on the then single-runway Columbia airfield two years later. Business was growing at a rapid pace, and the firm's annual billings reached approximately $40 million by the end of the 1970s.

Because the company is primarily a public works contractor and competes only on a price basis, it has earned a reputation for being contentious about its rights. In 1959 Sloco successfully sued the State Highway Department over interpretation on contract specifications. In 1984 the Supreme Court found in the company's favor in a Department of Health and Environmental Control trade secret/permit case. That same year the Supreme Court ruled that Sloco—not the state—owned a riverbed. In 1986 DHEC abandoned a prosecution when Sloco attacked DHEC's regulation promulgation process.

In the early 1980s the public

Previously called New Mountain Road and maintained as a public highway on Ascension Island, Sloan Construction resurfaced it in March 1980 as a gift to the island. As a result it is now called Sloan Freeway.

works industry nationwide was beset by criminal charges of violation of the Sherman Anti-Trust Act by bid rigging. Sloco was indicted on two counts; the court found the company not guilty on one and declared a mistrial on the other. Those were trying times.

As often happens in the construction business, many Sloco employees have left the company to form their own firms. Among those businesses whose owners were former Sloco employees are Terry Construction Company, Singleton Construction Company, Castles and Sloan Construction Company, Mustard-Coleman Construction Company, Jeter Construction Company, Hicks Construction Company, Childress Construction Company, and Wham Construction Company.

Sloco's officers have served in various capacities and on numerous committees of trade associations over the years. The National Asphalt Pavement Association gave Sloco its Best in America project award in 1977 for work on I-95 in Chatham County, Georgia;

the runner-up for Best in America overlay in 1979 for I-26 in Richland County, South Carolina; Best in America airfield in 1979 for Columbia Metropolitan; and Best in America overlay in 1985 for I-26 in Richland-Lexington counties, South Carolina. Florida honored Sloco in 1984 with its best interstate award for I-95 in Broward County.

In 1984 the Sloan family sold the firm to Koppers Company of Pittsburgh. Since that time Koppers has invested additional capital in the business and has encouraged expansion of its Florida operations.

Today V.L. "Billy" Ashmore, Jr., is president of Sloan Construction Company; Paul F. Haigler, Jr., is executive vice-president; J.M. "Jim" French, Jr., is controller; and W.W. "Bill" Mims is chief estimator.

GREENVILLE HOSPITAL SYSTEM

The typhoid fever epidemic that ran through Greenville in 1896 made one thing tragically apparent: Greenville needed a hospital.

But action did not come quickly. Thirteen years passed before the city council approved funds for a first aid building. It was a start, but it wasn't enough, so in 1912 Greenville City Hospital was established. Its board, the Greenville Hospital Association, sold stock at $10 a share. A Women's Hospital Board gave $4,000 to help get the institution running and to purchase the old Corbitt Building on Memminger Street. The option on the building was secured when William Goldsmith contributed $16,000 to the cause.

World War I and the growth of the textile industry brought new demands for increased health care, and the hospital began to grow. In 1920 the institution's first addition was built. A surgical wing was added 10 years later, and a wing for nursery and maternity facilities was built in 1936. The previous year the name had been changed to Greenville General Hospital.

In the mid-1940s it became clear that one hospital for the growing county was not sufficient. A study committee's recommendation that hospital services be provided for all residents of Greenville County led to the passage of State Act 432 in 1947, creating the Greenville General Hospital System and a seven-member board to govern it. The system's name was changed in 1966 to Greenville Hospital System.

Meanwhile, new facilities were being built throughout the county. Allen Bennett Memorial Hospital was established in 1952 to serve the Greer area, followed by the Roger Huntington Nursing Center, which was built next door in 1963. Hillcrest Hospital opened that same year to serve the growing

An aerial view of Greenville Memorial Medical Center, the hub of the countywide Greenville Hospital System.

communities of Mauldin, Simpsonville, and Fountain Inn.

In 1966 development began on what was to become a regional medical center on Grove Road. Following the purchase of 128 acres, Vice-President Hubert Humphrey broke ground on September 21, 1967, for the first facility on the site. It was called Marshall I. Pickens Hospital, named in honor of the vice-chairman of the Duke Endowment, a man whose association with hospital efforts dated back to 1928.

Other facilities followed, including Greenville Memorial Hospital and the Roger C. Peace Rehabilitation Hospital in 1972; the Center for Family Medicine and Ambulatory Care Center (Medical Center

Clinics) and North Greenville Hospital in 1975; and The Cancer Treatment Center in 1978.

By the 1980s the demand for high technology and sophisticated facilities had outgrown Greenville General Hospital's capabilities. Greenville Memorial Hospital was enlarged and, by December 1982, was ready to accept most of Greenville General Hospital's services. With the move of the obstetrics department and nurseries in June 1983, Greenville Memorial became the state's largest acute care hospital, and Greenville General Hospital began a new era as a multiservice health care facility.

Today the Greenville Hospital System continues developing into an even more comprehensive health care provider with a broad range of preventive health and medical inpatient and outpatient services and facilities positioned to meet the changing demands of a growing region.

THE CLINE COMPANY, INC.

The opportunity to start a business from scratch and build from the ground up appealed to N.Q. Cline, Sr., and his wife, Martha, when they started their fledgling business venture in 1948. In fact, the Clines remember that they were "beaming with enthusiasm."

In the early days The Cline Company operated out of a small house at 5 Atwood Street in downtown Greenville. The front porch was used as a loading dock, and the family worked feverishly inside, making hose assemblies with a hand hacksaw, a pair of pliers, and a knife to cut and peel off rubber covers. (At present this is called skiving a rubber hose.)

Their enthusiasm soon paid off. As business from individuals and industry both in the immediate area and beyond began to roll in, The Cline Company found it necessary to expand several times. However, each expansion enlarged its commitment to the Greenville area, which is still the focal point of all facets of the Cline operation.

In 1950, when hydraulic hose

and fittings were becoming increasingly popular for replacing wire cables and winches on bulldozers and front-end loaders, the firm became distributors for the leading manufacturers of hose, fittings, adapters, and couplings.

Today, as a highly regarded replacement parts supplier of hydraulic and mill products, The Cline Company operates through two divisions. The sale, assembly and fabrication, and product knowledge of the hydraulic demands of industry make up the Hose and Hydraulics Division. The firm's Mill Products Division supports the nation's pulp and paper, steel, and textile industries with the sale of drive shafts, power take-offs, clutches, specially designed brakes, and other products. The majority of the mill products sold and distributed by The Cline Company are designed and tested by the firm and fabricated at its complete in-house machine shops.

The corporate motto of the Hose and Hydraulic Division— "Need a hose in a hurry? We're ready to serve you"—is prominently displayed throughout The Cline Company's operation, which includes a 50,000-square-foot, four-building complex on Buncombe

The officers of The Cline Company, Inc. Seated (left to right) are David M. Cline, vice-president and general manager; N.Q. Cline, Jr., vice-president and sales manager; and Mrs. Martha Cline, vice-president and secretary. Seated is N.Q. Cline, Sr., president.

Street in downtown Greenville, as well as an 8,000-square-foot full-service branch in Charleston, South Carolina. The firm, through the leadership of its founder, has continued to invest heavily in its "Service First" philosophy throughout the years with staff members trained and experienced in each field in which The Cline Company is involved, and sales and engineering representatives in the field to provide the latest in product knowledge as well as assistance in making the most advantageous use of the products in the most economical way for users of Cline's products.

N.Q. Cline, Sr., heads the service-oriented company that bears his family name. The other members of the family serve in major roles: Mrs. Martha Cline is vice-president and secretary; N.Q. Cline, Jr., serves as vice-president and sales manager; and another son, David M. Cline, is vice-president and general manager.

The Cline Company is headquartered in a 50,000-square-foot, four-building complex on Buncombe Street.

TEXTUBE CORPORATION

Twenty-four hours a day, seven days a week, 30 sophisticated injection-molding machines at Textube Corporation's plant in Greer work endlessly. The machines are massive, ranging in size from 150 to 440 tons. They are also efficient. While being fed resin from outside storage silos, the giant creatures deftly melt and form the raw material into products with exacting specifications. The entire process takes only seconds.

Textube produces textile yarn carriers and food and beverage containers. The work requires an 80,000-square-foot facility, including a fully equipped machine shop, 90 employees working in three shifts, and some of the most advanced equipment in the area. The plant and the process are an engaging study in high-tech manufacturing.

However, back in 1949 when Textube got its start, manufacturing was not on the agenda. The company began as a United States sales agent for Emil Adolff Works, a manufacturer of yarn carriers, located in Reutlingen, West Germany. Emil Adolff was established in 1874, and is still controlled by the same family.

Works Hofen, a division of Emil Adolff of Reutlingen, West Germany, which had been in operation since 1924, was shut down temporarily in early 1945 when the French Armed Forces occupied the village of Kleinweiler-Hofen. In September of that year Paul Fallscheer, a member of the controlling family and an engineer, obtained permission from the Allied Forces to reopen the plant, and production was under way once again. The company produced toys until 1948, when bobbin manufacturing was brought back as an integral part of Works Hofen's operation.

With bobbin production back at a solid pace, Fallscheer set his sights on the lucrative U.S. textile market, and opened a sales agency in New Jersey for the distribution of Works Hofen and Reutlingen products. The new agency was called American Bobbin Company.

In 1954 the firm decided to enter the manufacturing arena in the United States. With Americans as principal stockholders and Emil Adolff holding minority interest, Textube Corporation was formed. The company had a small manufacturing plant in Pawtucket, Rhode Island, and, operating in conjunction with the New England Paper Tube Company, produced paper yarn carriers exclusively for the textile industry. In 1958 Emil Adolff purchased controlling interest of Textube Corporation.

Since textile industries, Textube's customers, were heavily concentrated in the upstate area, the corporation decided in 1968 to move its operations to a location just outside of Greenville, in Greer.

The plant was relatively small in those days, with 15,000 square feet of floor space and three employees. But the company had positioned itself well in its new headquarters,

with 95 percent of its customers located within a 300-mile radius of Greer. Expansion would come rapidly for Textube, in spite of trying times ahead.

In the years immediately following Textube's move, textile machinery began to change, making yarn carriers of paper, wood, and metal increasingly obsolete. The market of the future was to be in plastic. Textube was quick to meet the changing demands, phasing out paper carriers and turning the majority of its production efforts toward plastic yarn carriers.

Changes continued to sweep through the textile industry throughout the 1970s. New spinning, weaving, and winding machinery required new designs in yarn carriers. And the textile market as a whole was shrinking—brought to its knees by the heavy influx of imported finished goods.

However, Textube was not to be outdone by less-than-ideal market conditions, and the company's

Textube's Greenville, South Carolina, facility has been expanded four times since the company moved to the area in 1968. The plant now encompasses more than 80,000 square feet of floor space.

An eight-cavity mold equipped with a robot and automatic stacking device streamlines the production process at the Textube plant.

management began to investigate the possibilities of diversifying its product line. An extensive market study was initiated, searching specifically for a nontextile product that could be manufactured using the firm's existing equipment. Possibility after possibility was painstakingly analyzed, and a decision was finally made to enter the food and beverage packaging market.

The decision proved to be a good one. Textube found dozens of customers and potential customers in the same 300-mile radius in which the majority of its textile customers were located. Within just a few years food and beverage packaging represented some 40 percent of the firm's total sales volume.

Textube has clearly demonstrated the ability to not only keep up with changing times, but also to grow and prosper with them—and sometimes in spite of them.

The company's physical facilities have been expanded four times since Textube was moved to Greenville in 1968, and now the plant exceeds 80,000 square feet. Its staff has grown from three to 90, and its equipment represents the industry's finest.

The firm's toolroom features one of the few electric discharge machines in the area, allowing Textube to cut metal in an oil bath to precision within fractions of a millimeter. In addition, three of the yarn carrier machines in the company's operation are equipped with robots and automatic stacking devices.

Textube Corporation's strong and experienced management team has played a leading role in the firm's continued growth and success through the years. President Jules P. Fratturo, who joined the company in the early 1950s, leads the effort; vice-president of sales Hans Fretag is also a longtime employee; and vice-president of manufacturing Rolf Mueller and treasurer and controller Charles Bolin round out the solid team.

Advanced injection-molding machines in Textube's production facility range in size from 150 to 440 tons and have the capability to produce plastic yarn carriers and food and beverage containers in seconds.

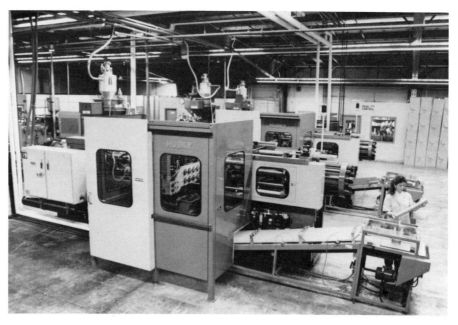

BOB JONES UNIVERSITY

Founded in 1927 by internationally known evangelist Dr. Bob Jones, Sr., Bob Jones University began with one purpose: to train Christian leaders for all walks of life. Through 60 years the institution has not deviated from that original goal.

The college began in Florida, but a growing student body required two moves. The first was to Cleveland, Tennessee, in 1933, and the second was to Greenville in 1947. Now located on a 200-acre campus noted as one of the most attractive and modern in the nation, Bob Jones University, "The Opportunity Place," attracts thousands of visitors from around the world every year.

Through the years more than 50,000 students have attended BJU. They come from every state in the union and more than 40 foreign countries to take advantage of the institution's spiritual emphasis, high academic standards, and cultural atmosphere. Students may choose from more than 70 major

The university family meets regularly in the 7,000-seat Founder's Memorial Amphitorium and the Rodeheaver Auditorium, which seats 2,600.

programs and 40 minor concentrations in the schools of Religion, Education, Business Administration, and Fine Arts, as well as the College of Arts and Sciences. In addition, the School of Applied Studies offers one-, two-, and three-year programs leading to certificates and associate degrees. Courses in music, speech, and art are available without additional cost to students. Graduate degrees are offered in some 40 programs in the schools of Religion, Fine Arts, and Education.

In connection with Bob Jones University, standard curricula are taught in Bob Jones Academy, Junior High, and Elementary School, which are located on the college's campus.

Selflessness, a sense of calling, and the pursuit of excellence mark the faculty at BJU. And the 15-to-one student/faculty ratio ensures individual attention.

The cultural climate of the campus is exemplified by the university's Collection of Sacred Art, consisting of more than 400 original paintings. Known as one of the foremost American collections of religious art, the gallery contains representative works of Flemish,

Dutch, German, French, Italian, and Spanish painters from the thirteenth through nineteenth centuries.

Hundreds of students are involved each year in the institution's large and active fine arts program. The Bob Jones University Shakespeare repertoire group, the Classic Players, is listed by the international *Shakespeare Survey* as one of the "noteworthy classic repertoire companies" in the country. The college also produces grand operas each year, in which the world's leading singers appear with the University Opera Association chorus and orchestra. In addition, students and community lovers of fine art have the opportunity to see a number of outstanding artists perform in the Concert, Opera, and Drama Series.

Students who participate in the plays and operas perform on one of the best equipped stages in the country, the 2,600-seat Rodeheaver Auditorium. The facility includes turntables, hundreds of lights, and the largest stage elevators of their type ever manufactured. Three other performance halls are available, along with more than 100 art, music, and speech studios.

Students participating in plays and operas at BJU perform on one of the finest stages in the country in Rodeheaver Auditorium. The facility includes turntables, hundreds of lights, and the largest stage elevators of their type ever manufactured. Photo circa 1952

The Division of Cinema and its production unit, Unusual Films, have been recognized throughout the world for the excellence of their Christian and educational motion pictures and for the quality of training offered. Cinema students have the opportunity to use the equipment of Unusual Films and to work on actual Unusual Films productions. In addition, BJU offers modern, fully equipped radio and television studios. The university's radio ministry extends worldwide through taped programs produced and distributed each week to scores of stations.

Among the other facilities located on the campus is the 200,000-volume Mack Memorial Library. The library utilizes SOLINET's (Southeastern Library Network) LAMBDA on-line catalog service combined with the Burroughs automated circulation system, which gives students access to the institution's collection as well as SOLINET's consortium of 430 libraries. Through this arrangement, students have catalog access to 1.2 million titles, as well as to DIALOG—185 indexes that provide on-line computer search, including magazine and other nonbook information.

Other BJU facilities include the 7,000-seat Founder's Memorial Amphitorium, where the university family meets regularly for chapel; the Howell Memorial Science Building, which houses modern laboratories and the Spitz Planetarium; over 125 lecture rooms and classrooms with seating for 7,275; a state-of-the-art computer lab; a fully equipped audiovisual learning resource center; a 62,000-square-foot student center complete with snack shop, bookstore, photo studio, travel agency, game room, and several meeting rooms; a 3,000-seat soccer stadium with a paved quarter-mile track; two gymnasiums; an olympic-size indoor swimming pool; 10 lighted tennis courts; a 4,000-seat dining hall; a 79-bed fully licensed general hospital with a staff of board-certified physicians and surgeons; and a 609-acre beef and dairy farm.

The Bob Jones University Press includes a large production unit and printing facility, and is one of the leading publishers of scripturally reliable textbooks for Christian schools.

Practical Biblical Christianity is lived and taught both in the classrooms and in the campus atmosphere at the university. Each week literally hundreds of students hold Bible Clubs, minister in nursing homes, and work in local churches. And to show that the institution cares about the community, hundreds of students do volunteer work for the elderly and infirm, deliver food to the needy at Thanksgiving and gifts at Christmas, and participate in various civic projects. All these activities combine to give Bob Jones University a spirit all its own, bringing together an atmosphere of culture, scriptural discipline, high academic standards, and practical Christianity.

Displayed upon the Bob Jones University seal are the words, *petimus credimus*, "We seek, we trust." University president Dr. Bob Jones III explains: "We seek to inculcate into our students a desire for knowledge of the arts and sciences, and we seek to satisfy that desire. We trust the Bible as the inspired word of God, the Lord Jesus Christ as the only hope of the world, and His gospel as the solution to the problems of our day."

The 62,000-square-foot student center at Bob Jones offers a snack shop, bookstore, photo studio, travel agency, game room, and several meeting rooms.

ST. FRANCIS HOSPITAL

When St. Francis first opened its doors in 1932, it was a dream realized for the Franciscan Sisters of the Poor.

In 1921 a hospital was built in Greenville with the understanding that its management would be placed in the hands of Catholic Sisterhood. Right away there was a problem. No Sisterhood willing to take on the formidable task could be found. As a result, the institution, named Emma Booth Memorial Hospital, was entrusted to the Salvation Army. However, when the Great Depression hit, it proved to be too much for the hospital, and the Salvation Army shut Emma Booth Memorial down.

Greenville's medical society again looked to the Catholic Church for help, and help was there. The Franciscan Sisters of the Poor were interested. Negotiations began with the Salvation Army, and a deal was struck. The Sisters paid $50,000 for the 50-bed facility.

The Sisters had two purposes in mind when they purchased the hospital. First, they could administer to the health needs of the community, and second, they could carry out the congregation's own objective of caring for the needs of the poor.

In what was a relatively small Catholic community at the time, the Catholic diocese also saw opportunity in the hospital. The institution, they decided, could certainly provide for the physical needs of the "flock" in Greenville. What's more, it could possibly win converts to the Catholic faith through the examples set by the Sisters.

Sister Camilla was installed as the first superior, and in May 1932 the Franciscan Sisters of the Poor opened St. Francis Hospital. The medical community and all of Greenville welcomed the new addition to the area, and in July 1932, following two months of renovations, a dedication was held for the hospital. More than 6,000 people attended.

On July 18 the institution admitted its first patient. The next day four more patients were ad-

The Sisters help to perpetuate the compassionate, caring attitude of St. Francis. Shown here is Sister M. Bernardine Kirchhoff, S.F.P. (center), with two of her staff members posing in front of the original facility, circa 1965.

mitted, and the first surgery was performed. By year-end 1932 the hospital had taken in 426 patients. After a full year in operation, St. Francis had cared for more than 2,000 patients, including 1,300 surgery and 200 maternity cases.

The institution was soon filled to capacity, and on November 7, 1934, plans were announced for a four-story addition atop the brick and stucco structure. The addition would double the bed capacity and significantly relieve overcrowded conditions.

The hospital received full accreditation in 1956, and the following year the Sisters celebrated the 25th anniversary of its opening. But the Sisters were not looking back. Instead, with a keen eye to the future, they purchased 14 acres of land from the H.K. Townes estate for future expansion.

When Sister M. Bernardine Kirchhoff came to St. Francis in 1964, she had plans for a new facility. The new hospital opened in 1971 and was one of the first all-private-room facilities in the Southeast. By 1973 the institution

After completing a $30-million expansion program in 1985, St. Francis has continued to expand both physically and technologically to meet the increasing needs of the community.

was operating at full capacity, and the old structure came under the wreckers' ball two years later. It was an exciting decade for the hospital, whose name had been changed in 1968 to St. Francis Hospital.

St. Francis celebrated its golden anniversary in 1982, and it continued to grow, expanding physically and technologically to meet the increasing medical needs of the community.

A high point in the history of the hospital came on August 19, 1985. It was on that day that hundreds of employees, state and local dignitaries, and friends of the institution gathered at the front

steps of St. Francis for a ceremony marking the culmination of a three-year, $30-million expansion program. It was a program through which St. Francis grew by leaps and bounds, adding new technologies and new services to better meet the needs of an ever-growing Greenville.

The expansion brought St. Francis the capability, through nuclear medicine technology, to see 3-D pictures of internal organs or blood vessels in motion. A CT scanner allows medical professionals to detect cancer in its earliest stages, and a catheterization laboratory enables cardiologists to perform advanced heart studies.

St. Francis now offers a specialized outpatient surgery center. It also expanded its laboratory capabilities in hematology, blood bank, microbiology, and histology. New lasers were also added in the expansion—one breaks apart tumors and cysts, and the other allows certain eye patients to see again.

St. Francis' new and expanded services list grew substantially with the physical and technological expansion. The hospital now offers

specialized programs for those suffering chronic pulmonary problems; corporate "shape-up" programs with courses on stress management, weight loss, how to stop smoking, and other wellness-related topics; seminars on women's health issues; and a medically supervised exercise program for expectant mothers.

Those new and expanded offerings earned St. Francis the Governor's Award for Worksite Health Promotion for 1985. It was the second year in a row that the institution won the award.

It is hard to imagine that the St. Francis Hospital of today struggled from such humble beginnings, growing initially on hopes and

With four special types of lasers, St. Francis is capable of performing any type of laser surgery being done today.

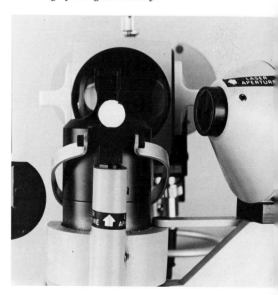

prayers. Today the growth, modernization, and innovation have created an altogether new look for St. Francis. However, the commitment to broad-spectrum, high-quality care at a reasonable cost remains the same as it was long ago, as the Sisters continue to accept responsibility for the sick and all who are involved in their care.

CAINE COMPANY

The timing was right. Greenville's real estate market was ready for a dose of innovation, and Robert M. "Bubber" Caine was just the person to provide it.

A graduate of Furman University, Caine worked for a number of years as a real estate salesman in Greenville, and eventually became a partner in the firm of Zimmerman, Chandler, and Caine. He set out on his own in 1933, forming Caine Realty and Mortgage Company. The firm, located on the second floor of the Beattie Building on the corner of West Washington and Main streets, was in the business of providing mortgage loans, as well as selling and managing real estate.

Romayne Barnes, H.D. Burgiss, Shuman Gerald, and Jimmie Curtis were Caine's earliest associates; Mary Lou Shaw, who is still with the company, was hired in 1934 as secretary and bookkeeper.

Things went well for Caine from the onset, particularly in the area of commercial property leasing and sales, and in 1935 he consummated

Robert M. "Bubber" Caine set out on his own in 1933 to form Caine Realty and Mortgage Company, which later became Caine Company.

his first big deal—a long-term lease on property for the F.W. Woolworth Company on the site Woolworth occupies today.

Caine's creativity, energy, and dedication spawned accelerated growth, and the company began to compile an impressive list of "firsts," beginning with Tuten Mart, Greenville's first strip shopping center across from Sirrine Stadium on Cleveland Street. Forest Hills, one of the city's first planned residential subdivisions, was also an early Caine development. In addition, the firm acquired the land and assisted Malcombe Davenport with the construction and leasing of University Ridge Homes, which consists of 48 apartments located on University Ridge Drive.

When World War II broke out in 1942, Caine left his flourishing business to volunteer to serve time in the United States Navy. In the meantime, Albert J. Quigley and Mary Lou Shaw kept the daily operations of the company going, while W.M. Rast saw to the details of the insurance business.

When hostilities ceased in 1945, Caine came back to Greenville with some great ideas. While stationed on the West Coast, Caine was impressed with the shopping centers there. As a result, he developed a burning desire to build one in Greenville. And he did. Lewis Plaza was Greenville's first regular shopping center, and with the apartments that Caine developed in back of the center—Plaza Apartments and Lewis Village Apartments—the property was well ahead of its time. During this time Calvin F. Teague served as vice-president and general manager of the Caine Company operations.

Meanwhile, with newfound mobility and a baby boom brewing, postwar consumers were drafting

Frank Halter has served as the chairman and chief executive officer of Caine Company since 1968.

their demands. High on the list were three bedrooms, two baths, and a garage. Caine got into the act quickly, and in 1947 he and Belton R. O'Neall announced plans for a $2.7-million planned community to be known as Woodfields. Set on a 165-acre tract of land off Augusta Road, Woodfields was the American Dream, with five- and six-room homes priced at $8,500 to $10,000.

The firm continued apartment development and management in a strong way through the late 1940s and early 1950s, including the land acquisition and development of Park Heights Apartments and the impressive $2.4-million, 260-unit Calhoun Towers apartment/hotel complex, which opened in 1950 and held claim as the state's largest building of its type. Frank B. Halter, who would later become president of Caine Company, joined the firm to manage Calhoun Towers.

The new residential housing demand during those years resulted in a new emphasis on the residential side of Caine's business, headed by Barnes and Halter. Employing three people at the outset, the division would ultimately employ 21 and produce millions of dollars in sales for the company.

As real estate projects grew larger and more complex in scope, Caine Company reinforced its leadership stature in retail development, and played a major role in the development of downtown Greenville in the 1950s. It was during that time that the firm leased the old Cleveland Building on the corner of South Main and East McBee Avenue from W.C. Cleveland to S.H. Kress & Co. Caine later handled the sale of the property to Kress and leased property on North Main Street to a number of other businesses, including JCPenney and Lerner Shops.

Caine and Estes, an insurance firm headed by Joe Estes, became a part of the Caine operation in the 1950s. The agency merged in 1978 into the national insurance brokerage firm of Corroon and Black, but remains Caine's insurance affiliate. Martha Gallemore joined the firm during the early 1950s to manage Caine's financial affairs. She is still with the company.

The next decade brought major activity in the development of shopping centers and malls. Pleasantburg Shopping Center and Richland Mall in Columbia, which was at the time the state's largest

Lewis Plaza, an early Caine Company development, under construction in 1948.

shopping center, were developed during that time. They were followed by McAlister Square, a joint project between Halter and Ned Apperson, which held claim as the state's first enclosed mall. Many other shopping center and mall projects came Caine's way during the next years, including Dutch Square in Columbia and Myrtle Square in Myrtle Beach. Today the firm consults for and manages

McAlister Square on opening day in March 1968. A joint project between Frank Halter and Ned Apperson, this Caine Company development was the state's first enclosed mall.

more than a dozen centers, with a combined total of 2.3 million square feet of leasable area. In addition, the company leases and manages a variety of industrial and office property, with a leasable area well in excess of a half-million square feet.

Caine's proven strength in property management yielded even more business when condominium development in Greenville vaulted in the 1980s. Today the company is the area's largest manager of condominiums, with a major share of the market.

Caine Company tradition of excellence continues, not only through its professional employees, but through families. George Zimmerman, grandson of one of Caine's original partners, Sam Zimmerman, heads the firm's Commercial Division. And Frank B. "Brad" Halter, Jr., Caine Halter, and Debbie Bell, children of the Caine president, play vital roles in the Leasing and Property Management, Commercial, and Condominium Management divisions, respectively.

From commercial to industrial property, from residential to retail, Caine Company continues to be a major part of the Greenville success story.

FURMAN UNIVERSITY

Almost without exception, first impressions of Greenville's Furman University are positive ones. And there is good reason. Furman's 750-acre campus, located just five miles north of Greenville, is without question one of the most beautiful in the nation.

Located at the foot of Paris Mountain and within sight of the Blue Ridge Mountains, Furman's campus includes a 30-acre lake and an 18-hole golf course. A rose garden, Japanese garden, fountains, and beautiful modified colonial architecture add to the beauty of the landscape.

One of America's 64 oldest colleges and the oldest affiliated with the Southern Baptist denomination, Furman is a coeducational institution with 2,400 undergraduates and a full-time faculty of over 160. Its students come from approximately 35 states and 15 foreign countries.

Its facilities for study and research are exceptional and include a Hewlett Packard 3000-68 computer, a network of microcom-

The main building on the Furman University campus in downtown Greenville was Richard Furman Hall, an Italian Renaissance structure that was completed in 1854.

puters, and sophisticated scientific equipment. Faculty members possess academic interests ranging from Middle English, to the sociology of the future, to high-temperature chemistry. Some 87 percent of the faculty hold doctorate degrees. And the college's fine academic reputation is substantiated by chapters of the leading honorary societies, including one of only 234 Phi Beta Kappa chapters in the nation.

Furman University also has a tradition of excellence in intercollegiate athletic competition. As a member of the National Collegiate Athletic Association (NCAA) Division I, Furman competes in men's baseball, basketball, cross country, football, golf, soccer, swimming, wrestling, tennis, and track and field. Women compete in intercollegiate basketball, golf, softball, swimming, tennis, volleyball, and track and field.

Founded in Edgefield in 1825-1826 as a training ground for Baptist ministers, the school was chartered as a full-fledged university in 1850 and was moved to Greenville. Its theological school branched off in 1858 as the Southern Baptist Seminary and eventually was moved to Louisville, Ken-

tucky. Plans for a law school were made during that period, but were deferred until after the Civil War. In 1920 the law school became a reality, but only for a 12-year period.

During the 1920s Furman completed a building program that made it a residential institution. It became an accredited member of the Southern Association of Colleges and a recipient of the Duke Endowment.

In 1933 Furman University was coordinated with the Greenville Woman's College and became permanently coeducational. Operations continued on separate crosstown campuses, however, until female students moved to the new campus in 1961.

In recent years Furman University has earned the reputation for being one of the finest liberal arts colleges in the nation. A high percentage of its graduates attend graduate and professional schools, and many alumni serve in leadership positions throughout the country.

The James Buchanan Duke Library, located at the center of Furman's present campus, houses more than 300,000 volumes and 1,550 periodicals. Photo by Peter Vanderwarker

BELK SIMPSON COMPANY

William Henry Belk was 26 years old when he decided to go into business for himself. With 12 years' experience as a store clerk, $750 in savings, and a $500 loan, he opened his own general store in Monroe, North Carolina, in 1888. He called it the New York Racket.

Belk's store was different from those of his competitors. For one thing, his sales were strictly cash, and all merchandise was clearly marked with a price. In addition, he allowed customers to return merchandise if they were not satisfied. He advertised his operation as "The Cheapest Store on Earth." It worked. Enough customers came to the New York Racket that first year for Belk to turn a profit of $3,300.

The business became known as Belk Brothers in 1891, when Henry persuaded his brother John to leave medical practice and join him. In 1893 the brothers established their first branch, setting up a cousin in a store in Chester, South Carolina. Two years later an operation was established in Charlotte.

The Belk brothers found the success of their three stores motivating, and they began selecting capable employees and setting them up as partners/managers in new stores. Establishments with names such as Belk Simpson, Belk Hudson, Belk Tyler, Parks Belk, and Belk Lindsey began to appear throughout the Southeast.

By setting up each store as a separate corporation or part of a multistore corporation owned by the Belks and various partners, each establishment was able to retain its individual identity and was locally managed. In addition, the Belk organization made it clear that it never was, nor did it intend to become, a "chain."

There were five stores in 1900,

The Belk name has been an entity in North Carolina merchandising since before the turn of the century, and the firm's roots have grown deep in the Greenville area, with six stores. Shown here is the Belk Simpson Company's 187,000-square-foot Haywood Mall store.

and 16 just five years later. In 1916 the Belk operation came to Greenville. Its first store, called Belk Kirkpatrick Company, was located in the 100 block of South Main Street and employed 18 people.

Four years later the Belk brothers called upon their half-brother, Dr. W.D. Simpson, to close his medical practice in Abbeville, South Carolina, and join the business. In 1923 Simpson bought an interest in the Greenville store, and on March 1, 1924, its name was changed to the Belk Simpson Company.

The firm's roots have grown deep in the Greenville area since that time. It has grown from one store to six, and has made signifi-

cant and lasting contributions to the community. Belk Simpson has long been one of the area's major employers, and has added greatly to the economy by providing jobs for hundreds of area residents.

Because Belk Simpson is a home-owned and homegrown operation, it has placed much emphasis through the years on service, efficiency, and guaranteed satisfaction for its customers. In its stores—located at Haywood Mall, McAlister Square, Lewis Plaza, Pleasantburg Shopping Center, Greer, and Easley—there is something for everyone. Its variety, quality, and service paid off as Belk Simpson became the number one retailer in the Upstate.

The firm's Greenville-area president, Jack Kuhne, and its vice-chairman, W.H.B. Simpson, oversee the daily operations of the stores, and continually ensure that the Belk Simpson Company remains an important part of the community—repaying a debt of gratitude to its customers and the communities in which it is a part.

ARGO CONSTRUCTION COMPANY, INC.

The Professional Medical Center at St. Francis Community Hospital is physically connected to the hospital by an enclosed, suspended pedestrian bridge, keeping physicians in close touch with the institution. The three-story, 51,000-square-foot steel-and-glass structure provides offices and examination rooms for some 30 physicians.

"In pursuit of excellence" was the founding theme for Argo Construction Company, Inc., in 1974. Dedication to that pursuit has resulted in steady growth and a reputation for excellence in upstate South Carolina. The firm has made its mark through outstanding projects, including the Thomas A. Roe Fine Arts Building at Furman University, Alcoa Fujikura in Liberty Properties' Ridgeview Center, and the Professional Medical Center at St. Francis Community Hospital.

Argo was formed in 1974 by Morris E. Nichols, who sought to create a quality-oriented company that, through its commitment to excellence, could offer the growing upstate market a wide range of construction services.

But a business without customers is really not a business at all. In 1974 Argo was awarded its first job by Bigelow-Sanford Inc., thanks to the confidence of Bigelow-Sanford's chief engineer, Lou Keeney. Despite the firm's lack of a track record, Keeney believed in Nichols and job superintendent Hobart Smith, and Argo was awarded the contract. Keeney's confidence was confirmed when the company successfully completed the project.

Over the years Argo's resume of successful and prestigious projects

has grown steadily. However, throughout its growth, no aspect of management's original philosophy has been neglected. And no area of operation has been given stronger emphasis than employee safety. The firm has consistently been at or near the top of the list in its division for accident-free operation in the annual awards given by the Associated General Contractors.

Argo's excellent reputation brought it to the attention of M.B. Kahn Construction Company Inc. of Columbia, South Carolina. Kahn was seeking to acquire an upstate organization with a dedication to the basics, a proven track record, and a strong potential for growth. Argo fit Kahn's requirements, and in 1983 the acquisition took place. From that point forward Argo has operated as a division of Kahn under the Argo name. The combined companies rank in the top 400 in-

dustrial and commercial construction firms in the United States.

Argo's client list reads like a "who's who" with names such as Michelin Tire Corporation, Southern Bell, 3M, J.P. Stevens, Dan River, Union Underwear, Westinghouse Air Brake Company, General Electric, Alcoa, Union Carbide, Piedmont Airlines, Dayco, and Liberty Properties.

Add parent company M.B. Kahn, and the list grows even more impressive, with such names as Mack Truck, Dana Corporation, McCrory Stores, Bankers Trust, Clemson University, the University of South Carolina, Bendix, Kirsch, Allied, Kimberly-Clark, and W.R. Grace.

Its work in the industrial, commercial, and institutional contracting business and its commitment to approach each job "in pursuit of excellence" has earned Argo Construction Company, Inc., a prominent position in the Greenville business community.

The neoclassic design of the distinctive Thomas A. Roe Visual Arts Building at Furman University provides an architecturally stimulating environment that is also visually appropriate to the Furman campus.

ALICE MANUFACTURING COMPANY, INC.

It started with one small mill, built in 1910, named Alice. Today, with five large, modern textile plants, Alice Manufacturing Company, Inc., is a case study in teamwork.

Foster McKissick and his son, Ellison Smyth McKissick, Sr., purchased the Alice plant in 1923. With Ellison serving as president and his father as vice-president, the business grew quickly.

By 1926 the plant's size had doubled, and, as more employees joined the company, new families moved into the surrounding community. The hallmark of Alice Manufacturing, its family atmosphere, would gain strength from that time on.

Concurrent with the plant's expansion, plans were under way for a new facility. Built in 1928, the new plant was named Arial for the hill it crested and the family that once lived there. As new homes, churches, and schools were built around the plants, the Alice "family" grew.

In 1953 a third plant was built. The new facility, called the Elli-jean plant, brought the total annual production of Alice fabrics to some 60 million yards.

When Ellison Smyth McKissick, Jr., took over the presidency of the operation in 1955, his goal was to enter the broadcloth market. The Foster plant was built in 1959 for that purpose, and immediately the company, long known as a leader in the print cloth market, gained recognition as a producer of top-quality broadcloth. It topped its own records soon afterward, when annual cloth production exceeded 100 million yards.

Increased public interest in polyester cotton blends resulted in additional expansion for Alice Manufacturing. The Ellison plant, built in 1966, led the company into the production of custom blends, and soon each plant was producing blends in addition to its other cloth products.

By the 1960s mill villages no longer existed, and the family atmosphere that had been built around textile plants through the villages disappeared at many mills. However, not at Alice.

Through the years of change in the company's operation, Alice employees have consistently devoted time, energy, and effort to manufacture a product of which they and their children can be proud. And it is common to find several generations of a family working in Alice plants.

Some 2,000 Pickens County citizens are employed by Alice Manufacturing. More than 10 percent of those have been with the firm for over 25 years, and 37 have celebrated their 50th anniversary of employment with the company.

Alice Manufacturing views itself not only as a vital industry in Pickens County, but also as an integral part of the life of the county itself. And for good reason: Through good times and bad, area citizens, Alice employees, and the McKissick family have worked, planned, and grown together. Through mutual concern, interest, loyalty, and support, the "family" of Alice Manufacturing Company, Inc., will continue down the road of success for generations to come.

The Ellison plant.

PATRONS

The following individuals, companies, and organizations have made a valuable commitment to the quality of this publication. Windsor Publications and the Greater Greenville Chamber of Commerce gratefully acknowledge their participation in *Greenville: Woven From the Past.*

Alice Manufacturing Company, Inc.*
Alliance Mortgage Co.
American KA-RO Corporation*
American Liba, Inc.
Argo Construction Company, Inc.*
Ballenger Group, Inc.*
Ball Unimark Plastics Division*
Bausch & Lomb*
Belk Simpson Company*
Bigelow-Sanford, Inc.*
Bi-Lo, Inc.*
Blue Cross Blue Shield of S.C.
Buddy's Nursery & Greenhouse
Caine Company*
Canal Insurance Company*
Canteen of Dixie, Inc.
Century Lincoln Mercury, Inc.
John G. Cheros, Attorney at Law
The Citizens and Southern National Bank of South
    Carolina*
City of Greenville
The Cline Company, Inc.*
Corroon & Black of the Carolinas
CRS Sirrine, Inc.*
Daniel International Corporation*
Davis Mechanical Contractors, Inc.*
Del-co Real Estate, Inc.
De Witt International Corp.
Digital Equipment Corp.
Jim Dodds Pontiac-GMC Truck, Inc.
Dr. & Mrs. E. Arthur Dreskin
Duke Power Company*
Fred W. & Joyce H. Ellis
Ernst & Whinney*
First Federal of South Carolina*
First Union National Bank of South Carolina*
Lucius S. Fowler, Jr.
The Furman Co., Inc.*
Furman University*
Goldsmith Company*
Graham Photo Supply, Inc.
Greenville Board of REALTORS, Inc.
Greenville County Museum of Art
Greenville Hospital System*
Greenville National Bank
Greenville Technical College*

Joseph E. Harrison
Henderson Advertising*
Hillandale Acres Community Club
IBM Corp.
Bob Jones University*
Jurgens Corporation
Kent Inc.
Keys Printing Company*
Leroy Cannon Motors
Lucas CAV
Michelin Tire Corporation*
National Car Rental
Norwich Eaton Pharmaceuticals, Inc.
Old Mill Stream Inn, Inc.
Palmetto Chemicals, Inc.
Peat Marwick Mitchell & Co.*
PEBBLE CREEK COUNTRY CLUB
John W. Peden Co., Inc.
Perone's Restaurants*
Picanol of America, Inc.
Puckett-Scheetz Insurance Agency
PYA/Monarch, Inc.*
Lynne & Niles Ray
Reliance Electric Mechanical Group*
The Residence Inn
Robinson Company of Greenville, Inc.
St. Francis Hospital*
Olin and Carolyn Sawyer
Seidman & Seidman
Siempelkamp Corporation
Sheraton Palmetto*
Sloan Construction Company*
Mr. & Mrs. Luther B. Smith, Jr.
Snyder's Auto Sales*
South Carolina National Bank
Southern Bell*
Steel Heddle*
J.P. Stevens & Co., Inc.*
Stone Manufacturing Company*
Stone Plaza Books & Gifts
Texize*
Textube Corporation*
U.S. Shelter Corporation*
J.W. Vaughan Company, Inc.
Wangner Systems Corporation
WYFF-TV*
Yeargin Construction Company*
Arthur Young & Company

*Partners in Progress of *Greenville: Woven From the Past.* The histories of these companies and organizations appear in Chapter Seven, beginning on page 193.

266

CHRONOLOGY

Compiled by Penny Forrester, Tinie Freeman, Choice McCoin, and Albert Sanders

Courtesy, Greenville County Library

1768 — Richard Pearis arrived in Greenville and settled near Reedy River Falls.

1786 — Greenville County established by act of the South Carolina General Assembly.

1795 — United States post office opened in Greenville village.

1797 — "Pleasantburg" (quickly known as "Greenville Court House") laid out on his land at Reedy River Falls by Lemuel J. Alston (Greenville County Plat Book E., p. 62).

1799 — Greenville County abolished and reorganized as Greenville District by the General Assembly in state-wide reorganization of local government and court systems.

1800 — First Criminal Court held in Greenville District in the new, two-story, log courthouse in the village square.

1813 — "Whitehall," the oldest house in the city, built by Governor Henry Middleton.

c. 1815 — Adam Carruth manufactured muskets for the state at his arsenal on the Reedy River below Greenville.

1816 — Vardry McBee purchased lands of Lemuel J. Alston and surveyed additional streets for the village. (The deed was signed November 15, 1815, but was recorded in 1816.)

1820 — Lester's Mill (as it came to be called), a textile mill, opened by Rev. Thomas Hutchings. Sheribal F. Arnold opened a yarn mill (known as Berry's Mill). John Weaver opened a third yarn mill at Thompson's Beaverdam in the upper district.

1820 — Poinsett Bridge, spanning Gap Creek, completed as part of the state road from Charleston to the mountains. Joel Roberts Poinsett was engineer for the state road west of Columbia.

1820 — The Greenville Academies built on thirty acres of land deeded to the trustees by Vardry McBee on August 20, 1820.

1820 — St. James Mission (predecessor to Christ Episcopal Church) organized and erected its first building on land donated by Vardry McBee.

1823 — First petition to charter the village of Greenville filed with the General Assembly.

1824 — The Mansion House, a resort hotel, built by Colonel William Toney on the northwest corner of the village square.

1824 — The Record Building, Greenville District's second courthouse, built on eastern side of the village square. Robert Mills probably designed the building.

1826 — *The Greenville Republican,* the village's first known newspaper, began publication.

1829 — The *Greenville Mountaineer,* the village's famous antebellum newspaper, began publication. Under the editorship of Benjamin F. Perry it became the leading Unionist newspaper in the upstate.

1829 — Springwood Cemetery opened as the village's first public burying ground.

1831 — Greenville Baptist Church constituted and erected a building on land donated by Vardry McBee. (This was the first Baptist church in the village.)

1831 — Greenville chartered as a village by the South Carolina General Assembly on December 17.

1832 — Vardry McBee opened a textile mill at Conestee.

1833 — Batesville Mill, erected by William Bates, began operation in Greenville District, manufacturing both yarn and cloth.

1834 — Predecessor to Buncombe Street United Methodist Church organized and built its first building on land donated by Vardry McBee.

1835 — Carriage factory established by Ebenezer Gower and Thomas Cox utilizing water power of Reedy River.

1840 — Chick Springs Hotel opened by Dr. Burwell Chick.

1841 — The octagonal McBee Chapel (Methodist) completed at Conestee.

1848 — Predecessor to the First Presbyterian Church organized and built its first building on land donated by Vardry McBee.

1851 — Furman University moved to Greenville (its fourth location) from Winnsboro.

1852 — Columbia and Greenville Railroad reached its western terminus on Augusta Street.

1855 — Third Greenville Courthouse erected on southwestern corner of the town square opposite the Mansion House.

1855 — Greenville Female College (later Greenville Woman's College and even later the Woman's College of Furman University) opened on the site of the Greenville Academies on College Street.

1855 — Markley Dam across Reedy River between Main and River streets built to increase power needed by the carriage works. (The dam was torn away April 4, 1913.)

1859 — Baptist Theological Seminary opened.

1860 — South Carolina seceded from the United States on December 20. The Butler Guards, local militia, soon travel to the theater of war.

1862 — The Ladies' Association in Aid of the Volunteers of the Confederacy opened a Soldier's Rest in the Boys Academy Building on the Greenville Female College campus.

1862 — The State Military Works for the repair and manufacture of ordnance began operations on present-day Green Avenue on land donated by Vardry McBee.

1865 — Elements of Stoneman's Brigade raided Greenville on May 2.

1865 — Benjamin F. Perry appointed provisional governor of South Carolina.

1866 — Predecessor to John Wesley United Methodist Church organized with Rev. J.R. Rosemond as pastor.

1866-1867 — Major John William De Forest, author of *A Union Officer During Reconstruction,* stationed in Greenville as commander of the occupying Federal troops and head of the Freedman's Bureau District.

1868 — Springfield Baptist Church organized with Rev. Gabriel Poole as pastor.

1868-1869 — Greenville designated as a "city" rather than a "village" by the South Carolina General Assembly.

1872 — The Atlanta and Charlotte Airline Railroad (later absorbed in turn into the Richmond and Danville and the Southern Railway System) began operation with its station on West Washington Street. Contemporary comment proclaimed that this new railroad made "Greenville the best mart for trade in the upper part of the state."

1872 — Greenville Cotton Oil Company established.

1872 — National Bank of Greenville (now merged into the South Carolina National) opened.

1872 — Saint Mary's Catholic Church organized.

1872 — Dantzler and Mackey Mortuary began operations at corner of Main and McBee.

1873 — Thomas Claghorn Gower laid lines and began operating a horse-drawn street railway between the Columbia and Greenville Railroad station on Augusta Street, up Main Street to Washington and out West Washington to the Air Line Railroad station. This business built the first bridge across Reedy River at Main Street. It operated until 1897.

1874 — *Greenville Daily News* began publication.

1875 — Camperdown Mill, the first textile plant within the city, began operations.

1876-1877 — Redemption election in South Carolina: October 17, 1876: Federal troops occupied Greenville to support the Carpetbagger Republican, Daniel Chamberlain, for governor; November 7, 1876: Wade Hampton, Conservative Democrat, elected governor; and April 10, 1877: Federal troops withdrawn from Greenville as part of the settlement by which Rutherford B. Hayes became president.

1877 — Baptist Theological Seminary became the Southern Baptist Theological Seminary and moved to Louisville, Kentucky.

1878 — Mattoon Presbyterian Church organized by Rev. Dr. S. Mattoon.

1879 — *Baptist Courier* moved to Greenville.

1882 — Mount Zion Baptist Church organized with Rev. F. Brown as pastor.

1882 — Huguenot Mill, second intra-city textile plant, began operations.

1882 — Telephone service inaugurated with about thirty subscribers by the end of the year.

1882 — Hugh Smith Thompson, one-time Greenville resident, elected governor. He served from 1882 to 1886.

1882 — Home mail delivery began in the city.

1885 — City School District of Greenville created as result of a movement led by Thomas Claghorn Gower.

1890 — Carpenter Brothers Drug Store established by A.B., T.S., and W.B. Carpenter. It is still operated by members of the same family.

1890 — Paris Mountain Reservoir built and lines run into the city the following year by the Paris Mountain Water Company.

1891 — Greenville Gas, Electric Light, and Power Company began operations.

1892 — Greenville Post Office built at the corner of Main and West Broad streets. This facility eventually became the third City Hall. It was demolished in 1972 to make way for the parking garage now on that corner.

1892 — Greenville's second City Hall built.

1893 — North Greenville High School began classes. The school later took the name North Greenville Academy (1904). The Academy became North Greenville Junior College in 1936.

1895 — Chicora College, a Presbyterian college for women, began operations.

1896 — Greenville City Hospital, forerunner of the Greenville Hospital System, admitted its first patients on June 17.

1897 — Neblett Free Library established on McBee Avenue on property donated by Mrs.

Viola Neblett.

1898 — Altamont Bible and Missionary Institute, predecessor of Holmes College of the Bible, began its first term on Paris Mountain.

1898-1899 — Camp Wetherill, a training camp for Spanish-American War soldiers, operated by the United States Army.

1900 — Greenville Traction Company began building the first electric street railway. The first streetcar ran on January 12, 1901.

1900 — Grand Opera House built on Laurens Street between Coffee and Buncombe.

1902 — Southern Bell purchased the local telephone exchange.

1902 — Coca-Cola Company of Greenville began operations.

1903 — American Cigar Company moved to its new building on East Court Street.

1906 — Martin F. Ansel, Charleston-born citizen of Greenville, elected governor. He served from 1907 to 1911.

1908 — "Shoeless Joe" Jackson became a national figure in professional baseball.

1909 — Ottaray Hotel at the "top of Main Street" began to receive guests.

1911 — Beth Israel Congregation founded when Charles Zaglin was asked to Greenville as the first Rabbi. The first synagogue was constructed on Townes Street in 1920.

1911 — Main Street Bridge over Reedy River opened for traffic.

1913 — Thomas McAfee estab-

lished his funeral home at 123 South Main Street.

1915 — County road-building program began with a $950,000 road bond issue. These were the first county bonds sold.

1915 — First motor ambulance brought to Greenville by Thomas McAfee.

1915 — Tornado struck southeastern part of the city on August 20, killing one person and damaging much property.

1915 — Southern Textile Exposition, Greenville's first textile show, held in November.

1916 — Fourth Greenville County Courthouse opened on Main at Court Street. This building is presently used as a county office building.

1917 — First Textile Hall opened on West Washington Street to house the Second Southern Textile Exposition. In this exposition Greenville proclaims itself the "Textile Center of the South."

1917 — Camp Sevier opened to train World War I troops. Operations continued until 1919.

1917 — First weather bureau in Greenville opened on September 2.

1917 — Chick Springs Hotel burned on September 30.

1918 — Miss James Margrave ("Miss Jim") Perry became the first woman admitted to the South Carolina Bar.

1918 — City of Greenville acquired title to the water works heretofore owned and operated by the Paris Mountain Water Company.

1919 — Phillis Wheatley Association organized by Mrs. Hattie Duckett.

1921 — Greenville Public Library established through the philanthropy of Thomas F. Parker and James Wilkins Norwood.

1923 — Woodside Building, the tallest building in South Carolina at the time, opened as the home of the Woodside National Bank (now merged into the South Carolina National).

1925 — The Poinsett Hotel opened on the site of the Mansion House, which had been razed in 1924.

1926 — Fuller Normal Industrial Institute moved to Greenville from Toccoa, Georgia. The school was founded April 12, 1912 by Rev. William E. Fuller.

1926 — Greater Greenville Sewer District created.

1927 — Greenville Juvenile Court established.

1928 — Greenville Municipal Airport opened and air mail service began.

1929 — Greenville declared "The most sanitary city and county in America" by the United States Health Service.

1929-1930 — Buncombe Road paved to provide a "ribbon of newly-laid concrete over the mountains to bind Greenville County closely with the many resorts of Western North Carolina."

1934 — A month-long General Textile strike disrupted Greenville with violence and bloodshed.

1936 — Rey's Jewelers founded by William S. Reyner and Stanley Goldblatt.

1942 — Greenville Air Force Base opened. The base was renamed in 1951 as Donaldson Air Force Base to honor Major John W. Donaldson, a flying ace from Greenville.

1945 — On April 13, 15,000 people viewed the train carrying the body of Franklin Delano Roosevelt to Washington. The train stopped briefly in Greenville.

1945 — *S.S. Greenville Victory,* a merchant freighter, launched.

1946 — Ideal Laundry explosion on November 19 killed six and injured 150.

1946 — Dunean Mills and Victor Monaghan's four plants merged with J.P. Stevens and Company in one of the larger mergers in southern textile history.

1947 — Bob Jones University moved from its Tennessee campus to its new facility in Greenville.

1948 — College Street "boulevard" with four lanes opened for traffic.

1949 — City Curb Market constructed on what is now Beattie Place.

1950 — United States Census revealed that Greenville County had the largest population of any county in the state.

1950 — Fifth and present County Courthouse opened on East North Street.

1951 — School District of Greenville County formed by the consolidation of the existing eighty-two local districts into a single county-wide district.

1955 — Joanne Woodward came home to Greenville for the world premiere of her first motion picture, *Count Three and Pray,* at the Paris Theater on October 24.

1958 — Furman University moved the Men's College to its new campus. The Woman's College was moved out in 1960.

1962 — Greenville Technical Education Center classes began September 5.

1962 — Donaldson Air Force Base closed.

1962 — Greenville-Spartanburg jetport opened.

1963 — First Greenville Arts Festival held.

1967 — Vice President Hubert H. Humphrey participated in groundbreaking ceremonies September 20 at Marshall I. Pickens Hospital, the first unit of the Greenville Hospital Center.

1970 — Greenville County Library moved into its new College Street building on the one-time site of the Female Academy and the Greenville Woman's College.

1972 — Construction began on the present City Hall.

1974 — Greenville County Museum of Art moved from the Gassaway Mansion to its new building on the one-time site of the academies and the Greenville Woman's College.

1974 — Heritage Green proclaimed by Mayor Max M. Heller as the official name of the College Street cultural complex which provides homes for the Little Theater of Greenville, the Greenville County Library, the Greenville County Museum of Art, and the Greenville Symphony Association.

1979 — Andrew Wyeth paintings from the Magill collection first exhibited at the Greenville County Museum of Art.

1982 — Hyatt Regency of Greenville opened January 15, culminating the Downtown Revitalization project begun in the 1960s.

Founded in 1869 as a private academy for young Greenville blacks, Sterling High School served for years as the only black high school in the county and educated generations of black leaders until it burned in 1968. Courtesy, John Holmes Collection, Greenville County Library

BIBLIOGRAPHY

I. Books

Ashmore, Harry. *"An Experiment in Democracy": The Third Annual Report of The Greenville County Council for Community Development.* Report for year of 1939.

Bagwell, William. *School Desegregation in the Carolinas, Two Case Studies.* Columbia: USC Press, 1972.

Bailey, Louise, and Elizabeth Ivey Cooper. *Biographical Directory of the S.C. House of Representatives vol. III, 1775-1790.* Columbia: USC Press, 1981.

Barnes, Frank. *The Greenville Story.* 1956.

Brunner, Edmund de S. *Community Organization and Adult Education, A Five Year Experiment.* UNC Press, 1942.

Canup, C.R. ("Red"), and W.D. Workman, Jr. *Charles E. Daniel, His Philosophy and Legacy.* Columbia: R.L. Bryan, 1981.

Chicora College for Young Women. *Catalogue 1911-12.* Greenville: Peace Printing Co., 1912.

Confederation of S.C. Local Historical Societies. *Official South Carolina Historical Markers.* Columbia: R.L. Bryan, 1978.

Crain, J. Dean. *A Mountain Boy's Life Story.* Greenville: Baptist Courier Company, 1914.

Crittenden, Stephen Stanley. *The Greenville Century Book.* The Greenville *News,* 1903.

De Forest, John William. *A Union Officer during Reconstruction.* New Haven: Yale University Press, 1948.

Ebaugh, Laura Smith. *Bridging the Gap, A Guide to Early Greenville, South Carolina.* Greater Greenville Chamber of Commerce, 1966, 1970.

Educational Services Department of the Greenville *News* and the Greenville *Piedmont. Rutledge to Riley: Governors of South Carolina, 1776-present.* 1985.

Edwards, Ann D., George D. Terry, Walter B. Edgar, George C. Rogers, Jr., and Augustus T. Graydon. *The Governor's Mansion of the Palmetto State.* 1978.

Flynn, Jean Martin. *A History of North Greenville Junior College.* Tigerville: NGJC, 1953.

Forrester, Penny, Tinie Freeman, Choice McCoin, and Albert Sanders, compilers. *Selected Chronology of History of Greenville.* Greenville County Library Sesquicentennial Commission, 1982.

Gates, Albion A. *Mansion House and its Surroundings.* South Caroliniana Library, n.d., c. 1895.

Gilreath, John H. *P.D. Gilreath, High Sheriff, Biographical Sketch of Perry Duncan Gilreath.* 1968.

Goodlett, Mildred W. *Travelers Rest, at Mountain's Foot.* 1966.

Hilborn, Nat and Sam. *Battleground of Freedom, South Carolina in the Revolution.* Sandlapper Press, Inc., 1970.

Howard, James A. *Dark Corner Heritage.* 1980.

Hoyt, James A. *Confederate Memories.* Address at the unveiling of the Confederate Monument, Greenville, SC. Sept. 27, 1892.

In Memoriam, Elizabeth Frances McCall, beloved wife of Governor B.F. Perry, born October 28, 1818, died September 24, 1891.

Jarrell, Hampton M. *Wade Hampton and the Negro: The Road Not Taken.* Columbia: USC Press, 1949.

Jones, Lewis. *South Carolina, One of the Fifty States.* Orangeburg, S.C.: Sandlapper Press, Inc., 1985.

Kibler, Lillian A. *Benjamin F. Perry, South Carolina Unionist.* Durham: Duke University Press, 1946.

Ladd, Everett Caroll, Jr. *Negro Political Leadership in the South.* Ithaca, N.Y.: Cornell University Press, 1966.

Lander, Ernest M., Jr., and Robert K. Ackerman, eds. *Perspectives in South Carolina History, the First 300 Years.* Columbia: USC Press, 1973.

Loomis, Clarence B. *An Experience in Community Development and the Principles of Community Organization.* Clayton, Ga.: The Rabun Press, 1944.

Lumpkin, Henry. *From Savannah to Yorktown: The American Revolution in the South.* Columbia: USC Press, 1981.

Marsh, Blanche. *Hitch Up The Buggy.* Greenville: A Press, Inc., 1977.

McCoin, Choice. *Greenville County: A Pictorial History.* The Donning Company, 1983.

McKoy, Henry B. *The Story of Reedy River.* Greenville: Keys Printing Company, 1969.

Mills, Robert. *Statistics of South Carolina, Including A View of Its Natural, Civil and Military History.* Charleston: Hurlburt and Lloyd, 1826.

Neuffer, Claude Henry, ed. *Names in South Carolina.* vols. I-XII, 1954-65. Columbia: State Printing Company, 1967.

Northwest Middle School students. *Echoes, Reflections of the Past.* Vol. 1 (Spring 1985). Travelers Rest, SC.

Patton, James Welch, ed. *Minutes of the Proceedings of the Greenville Ladies' Association in Aid of the Volunteers of the Confederate Army, Historical Papers of the Trinity College Historical Society, Series XXI.* Durham: Duke University Press, 1937.

Reid, Alfred S., ed. *The Arts in Greenville, 1880-1960.* Furman University, 1960.

Richardson, James M. *History of Greenville County, South Carolina.* Atlanta: A.H. Cawston, 1930.

Roberts, Nancy. *South Carolina Ghosts, From the Coast to the Mountains.* Columbia: USC Press, 1983.

Robertson, Linda, Bennie Lee Sinclair, and Lori S. Pahlitzsch. *South Carolina's International Greenville, A Guide.* Greenville: Writers Unlimited, 1982.

Shriners' Hospital for Crippled Children Board of Governors and Staff. *"...Unto the Least of These": A Story of the Shriners' Hospital for Crippled Children.* 1948.

South Carolina Writers Project. *South Carolina: A Guide to the Palmetto State.* 1941.

Utsey, Walker S., ed. *Who's Who in South Carolina, 1934-35.* Columbia: Current Historical Association, 1935.

Wallace, David D. *The History of South Carolina.* New York: American Historical Society, Inc., 1934.

Wheless, Roberta, and Warren Mersereau, eds. *A Greenville County Album: A Photographic Retrospective.*

Published jointly by the The Metropolitan Arts Council and the Friends of the Greenville Library, 1977.

Wood, Robert C. *Parish in the Heart of the City.* Greenville: Keys Printing Company, 1976.

Wright, Louis B. *South Carolina: A Bicentennial History.* New York City: W.W. Norton and Company, Inc., 1976.

II. Unpublished Papers

Bainbridge, Judith Gatlin. "Greenville's 'Big Idea.'" Paper on May 1950 report by the Community Council on a survey of Negro conditions.

Bleser, Carol K. "The Perrys of Greenville: A Case Study of a Nineteenth Century Marriage." Address delivered at the University of South Carolina, March 1985.

Dryden, Felicia Furman. "Guidelines for the Preservation of the Reedy River Commercial and Industrial District." Thesis for Master of Science in Historic Preservation, Columbia University, 1979.

Farley, Foster M. "Lives of Certain Eminent Loyalists in South Carolina and Georgia." Newberry College, 1982.

Gettys, James Wylie, Jr. "Mobilization for Secession in Greenville District." M.A. thesis, University of South Carolina, 1967.

Huff, A.V. "Greenville—The Place and The People: How We Got This Way." Furman University, 1985.

Kennerly, Edna. "The Civilian Conservation Corps As a Social Resource in South Carolina." M.A. thesis, University of South Carolina, 1940.

Mathis, Joseph D. "Race Relations in Greenville, South Carolina, From 1865 through 1900, As Seen In A Critical Analysis of the Greenville City Council Proceedings and Other Related Works." M.A. thesis, Atlanta University, 1971.

Minutes of the Commissioners of the Streets and Markets in the Town of Greenville, S.C., March 1825 to May 1831. Copy of original manuscript in the Greenville County Library collection.

III. Journals, Magazines, and Newspapers

Clear water from the Paris Mountain reservoirs began to be piped into Greenville in 1888. This photograph was taken by W.P.A. workers in the Depression years. Courtesy, South Caroliniana Library

Bane, Garnette Helvey. "The Greenville Report." *PACE, Inflight Magazine of Piedmont Airlines,* vol. 12, no. 7 (July 1985).

Oliver, Warner. "Jess Mitchell's Private War." *New Republic,* March 31, 1947.

Reid, Alfred S., "Recent Literary Developments in Greenville: 1959-1963." *Furman Studies,* November 1964.

Sloan, Cliff, and Bob Hall. "'It's Good to Be Home in Greenville'. . . But It's Better if You Hate Unions." *Southern Exposure,* vol. 7, no. 1 (Spring 1979).

Numerous articles in *The Proceedings and Papers of the Greenville County Historical Society,* 1962-83.

Several articles in *Sandlapper* magazine.

Numerous articles in the Greenville *News* and Greenville *Piedmont.*

IV. Miscellaneous

Chamber of Commerce publications, 1925, 1949, 1985.

State Development Board publications.

273

INDEX